THE BLUEPRINT

Jaeson's zeal to raise up campus houses of prayer, contend for the power of God and release students to plant simple churches is a strategy from heaven to impact nations. This heavenly vision is actually happening on campuses all over the world! I pray God will use this book to envision and equip students all over the earth to bring about a reformation by releasing new wine through campus houses of prayer and new wineskins through student-led simple churches that will reap a great end-time harvest!

MIKE BICKLE
Director, International House of Prayer of Kansas City

Our campuses are in crisis. A battle is being fought for the hearts and minds of an entire generation. God help us, then, if we squander these precious years engaged in sectarianism and ecclesiastical politicking when we could and should be uniting in prayer, proclaiming the gospel and courageously planting churches on the campuses of America. Jaeson is galvanizing people all over the world to make their student days count for eternity. In this timely book, you can connect with his message and capture the passion of his heart.

PETE GREIG
Author, *Red Moon Rising*
Director, 24-7 Prayer International

Jaeson Ma is part of the next wave of emerging leaders that I believe will experience the greatest revival and ingathering of harvest throughout Church history. Jaeson writes to share how we can reach and conserve the harvest. This book is a must-read for those who want to serve the purposes of God in their generation.

DR. CHÉ AHN
President, Harvest International Ministry

The Blueprint is a fire starter! It is destined to be one of those books that change a generation. It is a signpost of God's moving! Jaeson releases ⸻ ⸻ ⸻ God that will burn trails for others in the ge⸻ ⸻ ⸻ ⸻ ⸻end it!

Four ⸻ ⸻ nal

D1370624

Jaeson's book is likely to make some people uncomfortable . . . and it should. We cannot stay in our comfort zones and expect God to do great things. We must get out of our small and familiar boxes, where we know and manage everything, and take risks if we want to see the kingdom of God come and transform our campuses, cities and world. My hope, prayer and expectation is that we will soon see that the kingdom of God is expanding rapidly in the United States as it is in other places in the world. This book lays out a blueprint for such a transformation.

C. NEIL COLE
Author, *Organic Church: Growing Faith Where Life Happens* and *Cultivating a Life for God*

It is my passion to see God raise up this next generation to finish the task of the Great Commission. *The Blueprint* has the power to release students all over the world to transform not only their campus but also cities and nations. Jaeson's passion for prayer and missions will challenge you to the core. The Holy Spirit is raising up young leaders like Jaeson and others to lead a new student missionary movement!

DR LUIS BUSH
Founder, Transformworld and AD 2000 Beyond Movement

Jaeson's passion for revival permeates every page of *The Blueprint*. His conviction is that a move of God on our campuses is not just possible but also that the first raindrops are already starting. Read this book if you dare. Take it seriously and your spiritual life will never be the same again.

TONY AND FELICITY DALE
Founders, *House2House* Magazine and Home Church Network

This book needs no endorsement. It already carries the fingerprints of God all over it! It will fuel the hearts and minds of a generation called to take hold of Christ and His unshakable kingdom. May universities all over the world be burning with the fire of ongoing prayer, and may they become vital hubs for a reformation of Church and a transformation of society.

MARC VAN DER WOUDE
Founder, Joel News and Joel Ministries
www.joelnews.org

The Blueprint issues a clarion call to the youth army of this generation to seize its destiny. It is a book with one aim in mind—to release a vision that every university campus across the face of the earth be flooded with true, authentic and apostolic Christianity—and a manual for revival. Read, weep and catch the vision! I highly commend to you the ministry and writings of Jaeson Ma.

DR. JAMES W. GOLL
Cofounder, Encounters Network
Author, *The Seer* and *The Prophetic Intercessor*

I long for revival, like the one I experienced in 1935 in Beijing, China, when I was 11 years old. Both the ancient city and the sleepy churches came alive when Dr. John Sung, the dynamic revivalist God had given to China, preached three times a day in the largest auditorium people could find. *The Blueprint* is a call to arms to the Church in general and to younger Christians and workers in particular that will serve as a workable road map toward the fulfillment of Christ's Great Commission.

DR. THOMAS WANG
President, Great Commission Center International

Only 5 percent of students on most colleges are practicing Christians. If we ever want to reach a larger part of the campus, we must alter how we are structured instead of just increasing the amount of money or people we send to the campus. Jaeson Ma's book lays out the clearest blueprint available of exactly how we must change our structures in campus ministry. It is a unique and vital blueprint to follow for those who yearn for more of Christ's presence and want to reap the plentiful harvest on colleges and beyond.

JEREMY STORY
President, Campus Renewal Ministries
Cofounder, Campus Transformation Network

Revival has begun on campuses across America! God is stirring the hearts of students to believe for the impossible and see their campuses transformed by the power of God. Jaeson Ma is a catalyst for campus revival and is being used by God to train and equip young reformers who know how to move heaven by their prayers and see the unsaved encounter God through signs and wonders. This book will ignite a passion for revival and reformation that will shake campuses.

BANNING LIEBSCHER
Youth Pastor, Bethel Church, Redding, California
Director, Jesus Culture

Jaeson's new book is a blueprint for the coming revival. It represents the heart-cry of a new generation of young people who want to get real in developing a vital relationship with God and who want to actualize a social transformation from within. This is a new Jesus movement of the twenty-first century that will herald in the second coming of our Lord Jesus. I heartily endorse it.

PASTOR ERNEST CHAN
President, Agape Renewal Ministries International

Jaeson is a radical firebrand in the prayer movement that is sweeping our world today. With his passion and determination to go all out for the Lord, he represents the quiet tsunami of youth that God is raising up to pray revival into the Church and transformation into our world. You may not agree with everything he says, but you will be challenged profoundly by his intimate encounters with the Holy Spirit and by the miracles that have attended his risking all to make Jesus known to a largely unchurched generation of youth.

JOHN ROBB
Chairman, The International Prayer Council

The Blueprint is a book that releases a supernatural strategy to the Body of Christ for practically taking the devil's greatest strongholds of our day . . . college campuses.

PASTOR JOEL STOCKSTILL
Youth and Young Adult Pastor, Bethany World Prayer Center

In *The Blueprint* is a rich manual for those set on seeing the Great Commission fulfilled and Jesus glorified and honored through the incoming harvest. College students, fully surrendered to God's purposes in their generation, have always played a huge role in every spiritual revolution, and this will continue to be the trend until Jesus returns. Jaeson's prophetic encounters with God, experiences as a campus revivalist and Scriptural insights highlight the necessity of a paradigm shift in the Church today.

RYAN SHAW
Executive Director, Student Volunteer Movement 2 (SVM2)
www.SVM2.net

JAESON MA

THE BLUEPRINT

:: A REVOLUTIONARY PLAN TO PLANT
MISSIONAL COMMUNITIES
ON CAMPUS

Regal

From Gospel Light
Ventura, California, U.S.A.

Published by Regal Books
From Gospel Light
Ventura, California, U.S.A.
Printed in the U.S.A.

Regal Books is a ministry of Gospel Light, a Christian publisher dedicated to serving the local church. We believe God's vision for Gospel Light is to provide church leaders with biblical, user-friendly materials that will help them evangelize, disciple and minister to children, youth and families.

It is our prayer that this Regal book will help you discover biblical truth for your own life and help you meet the needs of others. May God richly bless you.

For a free catalog of resources from Regal Books/Gospel Light, please call your Christian supplier or contact us at 1-800-4-GOSPEL *or* www.regalbooks.com.

Map on page 266 is used by permission of Dr. Thomas Wang, President, Great Commission Center International, 848 Stewart Drive, Suite 200, Sunnyvale, CA 94085.

Library of Congress Cataloging-in-Publication Data
Ma, Jaeson.
    The blueprint : a revolutionary plan to plant missional communities on campus / Jaeson Ma.
        p. cm.
    ISBN 978-0-8307-4408-4 (trade paper)
    1. Church work with students. 2. College students—Religious life. 3. Universities and colleges—Religion. 4. Missions—Theory. I. Title.
    BV4447.M225 2007
    259'.24—dc22
                                                                            2007000037

1 2 3 4 5 6 7 8 9 10 / 10 09 08 07

Rights for publishing this book in other languages are contracted by Gospel Light Worldwide, the international nonprofit ministry of Gospel Light. Gospel Light Worldwide also provides publishing and technical assistance to international publishers dedicated to producing Sunday School and Vacation Bible School curricula and books in the languages of the world. For additional information, visit www.gospellightworldwide.org; write to Gospel Light Worldwide, P.O. Box 3875, Ventura, CA 93006; or send an e-mail to info@gospellightworldwide.org.

To Dad, Mom, Joyce, Nancy and Grandma—

*Without each of you, I would not be who I am. I love you dearly
and thank God for each of you. God is faithful. Amen.*

*I would also like to thank Dr. Gary Greig at Regal Books for his
commitment to see this book published, Christine Hsu for her help in
editing the initial manuscript and Brian Kim, my covenant brother,
for coming up with the title. Finally, thanks to every student on every
campus who has contended for the power and promises of God to be
released in this generation. May we walk in our identity as beloved
sons and daughters, highly favored and well pleasing to God.
We have nothing to prove and nothing to lose. Keep on, keep
faithful and never surrender. Our God reigns!*

*"O God, You have taught me from my youth; And to this day
I declare Your wondrous works, Now also when I am old and gray
headed, O God, do not forsake me, Until I declare Your strength
to this generation, Your power to everyone who is to come"*
(Psalm 71:17-18).

CONTENTS

FOREWORD 12
Lou Engle

PREFACE 15

INTRODUCTION 20

CHAPTER ZERO 33
Reformation Generation

SECTION ONE:
PASSION FOR PRAYER

CHAPTER ONE 45
Repentance Prayer

CHAPTER TWO 59
Holy Spirit Prayer

CHAPTER THREE 73
Waiting Prayer

CHAPTER FOUR 82
Faith Prayer

CHAPTER FIVE 92
Revival Prayer

CHAPTER SIX 102
24/7 Campus Houses of Prayer

SECTION TWO:
PASSION FOR POWER EVANGELISM

CHAPTER SEVEN 127
Prophetic Worship Power

CHAPTER EIGHT 137
Apostolic Preaching Power

CHAPTER NINE 150
Demonic Deliverance Power

CHAPTER TEN 163
Prophetic Evangelism Power

CHAPTER ELEVEN 173
Divine Healing Power

CHAPTER TWELVE 185
Marketplace Reformation Power

SECTION THREE:
PASSION FOR PLANTING SIMPLE CHURCHES

CHAPTER THIRTEEN 199
Simple Church Planting

CHAPTER FOURTEEN 212
Saturation Church Planting

CHAPTER FIFTEEN 225
Strategic and Student-Led Church Planting

CHAPTER SIXTEEN 239
Start-up Church Planting

CHAPTER SEVENTEEN 264
Every Campus, Every City, Every Nation—Back to Jerusalem

RESOURCES FROM CAMPUS CHURCH NETWORKS (CCN) 272

FOREWORD

As I write this foreword, tears run down my face. I am praying and believing for such a revival to sweep our nation that homosexuals by the thousands could be transformed. My cry is that a bridal love could seal a generation's heart in such a way that sexual sin could be quenched by a love stronger than death—a flame far hotter than the flames of pornography and lust. My prayer is that abortion, the greatest injustice of our day by which God sifts and judges nations, could be exorcised by a great people who could suffer and seize the day—a people much like those great generations in the days of Abraham Lincoln and Martin Luther King, Jr., who let justice roll down like water and righteousness like an ever-flowing stream.

I dream of an awakening in universities in America that will shake humanism and its professors like a terrier shakes a rat in its teeth. I dream that Christian students would become more radical than anarchists, and that the preaching of Christ and the healing power of God would create riots in the public squares . . . that fraternity houses with sons of Greek philosophy would be taken over by the sons of Zion with their 24/7 houses of prayer! But is it merely a dream? No! A thousand times, no! We are in the throes of a great reformation of prayer. In the past two years, spontaneously and almost undirected by human hands, student-run houses of 24/7 prayer have popped up in colleges all across the nation. When God is getting ready to do something atomic, He always sets His people to praying. It seems that our universities are going to be ground zero for the revival balm of God.

Thousands of our churches' sons and daughters have been taken captive by the wisdom of fools. They have rejected revelation for speculation and have spun out of control into the sexual seduction of the antichrist culture produced by the pagan professors and present-day prophets of Baal. God is demanding a new breed—a new leadership with a commanding moral vision that will lead our Christian clubs out of cruise control and into commanding destiny. A new apostolic witness is being demanded in our universities. Through fasting, prayer and dedication to a stand of no compromise, the Daniels of God are being forged into prophets who will be 10 times better than their peers in the hotly contested battleground for truth.

This is the new breed that will not be silent in the face of pressure to be politically correct. They are not the angry right, but neither are they those who cry "Peace, peace" when there is no peace. Their message and life is filled with compassion, but they will disturb the status quo by their unbending allegiance to a culture of life, love and the liberty to speak their faith and be heard.

This new breed is not interested in grades; they are committed to God alone. They are gathering into student communities—churches, if you will—of a righteous resistance to the culture of compromise. They are confessing their sins and confessing their Christ publicly. These little bands of Daniels will proliferate, and with their preaching and with their prayers they will permeate the current stifling atmosphere of the dominating darkness that remains virtually unchallenged in our universities today. A great light dawns! A new student mission movement is getting ready to rumble!

These are not just words! Words are taking on flesh and blood. The survivors of the abortion holocaust have been given the rod of deliverance and destiny. Jaeson Ma, my friend and compatriot in prayer, is one of those survivors who light my inward torch of zeal and generate within me spiritual groans for a Gideon greatness to expel our demons of defeat and despair. Jaeson is not one of those seminary-trained technicians of the Bible, but rather he has been summoned and sent by the Word of the Lord to preach the gospel of the Kingdom in the lions' den of our universities. His book carries an authentic vision of hope that I believe will be the seed of the tree of life that will ultimately cut down the tree of the knowledge of good and evil that has found such fertile soil in our schools. That seed of the tree of life, though small and young, is nevertheless already sprouting with obvious Kingdom power and vitality.

This book is not theory. This spiritual revolution has actually begun; and of those who read this book, many will take up its message and run with it! That which most people would say is impossible could actually become possible. Harvard's halls could be filled with heaven, and Berkeley's rebellion could be betrayed by obedience! The students of this present day could become the professors of our schools tomorrow and disciple the next generation in wisdom and in righteousness.

So go on, Jaeson! May you and your comrades be strong and courageous! Just as Churchill, that great leader of men, declared, "History will speak kindly of me, for I intend to write it," so too, if you become the apostles of this present throbbing moment, history will speak kindly of you. If you win the universities, history will be your prisoner.

Lou Engle
President, Justice House of Prayer and
The Call International

PREFACE

The thief does not come except to steal, and to kill,
and to destroy. I have come that they may have life,
and that they may have it more abundantly.
JOHN 10:10

I love life. I thank God for letting me live, because Satan tried to kill me before I was born. My mother, who was only five minutes away from making the decision to abort me, was lying on a hospital bed when a Christian doctor from her church suddenly walked by her room and recognized her. He stopped and inquired how she was doing. When he looked up at the monitor screen, he exclaimed, "Mrs. Ma, congratulations! You have a baby!" Then he smiled and walked off. He didn't know my mother's real intention for being there. But God knew, and my mom knew that this doctor walking by wasn't just a random accident, but a sign from God. At that moment, she knew in her heart that she couldn't abort me. That day my mother left the hospital and repented to God for trying to take away the life He had created. Soon after I was born, my mother dedicated my life to the Lord.

This story took place in 1980, in Lubbock, Texas. Twenty-two years later, my mother shared with me what happened that day. As she spoke, she wept and asked for forgiveness. She explained that at that time, she was determined to divorce my father. Their marriage was broken, and she didn't have the strength to go on. She knew that if she gave birth to me, she could not divorce my father, because she could not afford to raise another child on her own. My mother was afraid and helpless. She did not speak English, and she already had my two older sisters to take care of. In my mother's mind, I was an accident, so the most logical option was to abort me.

"Jaeson, forgive me for trying to abort you and for believing the lie that you were an accident," she said.

"Mom, it's all right. I forgive you. I love you."

God does not make accidents. He makes destinies.

Bound 4 Life

In October 2005, I, along with hundreds of others, released a cry of justice for the unborn destinies in our generation.

There I was, standing in front of the Supreme Court in Washington, D.C., with red tape over my mouth and the word "LIFE" inscribed in black over the tape. I was pleading and crying out from the depths of my heart to God to end abortion in America. I wasn't alone. There were about 100 other young people with the same red tape and the word "LIFE" stamped over their lips, praying in silence. People walking by thought we were crazy; other onlookers didn't understand what we were doing. But we knew why we were standing in front of the Supreme Court. We were there to change history through our prayers. We were there not to appeal to a human court of law but to a higher court in heaven. It wasn't a protest; it was a cry for justice. It was a silent cry of prayer for the millions of aborted babies in our nation who never had a voice or a choice to live. It was a prayer for mercy, asking God to forgive our generation for the sin of abortion.

Thousands of students have joined this movement to pray for the end of abortion in America.[1] They stand in front of courthouses and abortion clinics wearing red wristbands with the word "LIFE" engraved on them. They worship, they fast and they pray one prayer daily: "Jesus, I plead Your blood over my sins and the sins of my nation. God, end abortion and send revival to America."

I am bound for life. I will not stop praying, night and day, until God releases justice in this generation. I pray for life because my life was almost taken away.

A Destined Generation

In 1973, a landmark court case, *Roe v. Wade*, legalized abortion in the United States. Since that time, more than 47 million babies in our nation have been aborted in the womb.[2] More than one-third of my generation has been murdered, destroyed and stolen before they had a chance to live out their God-given destinies. Why this massive bloodshed? Why at this time in history?

Every generation has a specific calling and purpose in God's ulti-mate plan. The Enemy knows that our particular generation has a unique destiny in God's end-time purposes. He recognizes that this generation is destined not only to change history but also, quite pos-sibly, to finish history, and so he will do all he can to destroy the des-tiny of this generation. Our generation must respond to these attacks. We must understand the times and know what to do.

King David was a man after God's own heart, who served the specific will of God in His generation. "I have found David the son of Jesse, a man after My own heart, who will do all My will . . . for David, after he had served his own generation by the will of God, fell asleep, was buried with his fathers, and saw corruption" (Acts 13:22,36). We must do the same. God's purpose for us is to seek His face as lovesick worshipers and pursue revival in our generation.

"Revival" can be a worn-out or overused word. But when we truly understand what revival is, our hearts will pursue it with passion.

What Is Revival?

Revival is God's arrival. Revival is when the kingdom of heaven invades the kingdom of Earth in power. Revival is a restoration to life and consciousness. It causes the hearts of entire generations to turn back to God in repentance, love and power. Revival occurs when *all* are saved—not just a few on our campuses or in our cities or nations—because it is God's desire that all come to a knowledge of the truth (see 1 Tim. 2:4). Revival radically transforms the masses and causes the kingdoms of men to yield to the kingdom of our God. Revival is justice. It causes wrong things to be made right. It is a radical com-mitment to completely obey God's Word. Revival is heaven on Earth.

I call this generation—the generation of young people in the early twenty-first century—a "revival generation." In my heart, I believe this generation will usher in the fullness of God's kingdom and bring back the return of the King. This is an end-time revival generation destined to finish the task. I know this is the case because Satan has attacked this generation like no other before it. Satan knows his time is short.

If we look at biblical history, there were only two other periods in time that experienced the degree of genocidal attack this generation has faced: the time of Moses and the time of Jesus. Satan attacked both of those generations, attempting to kill off every baby boy in the land. Why did those generations face satanic opposition? It is because the enemy understood the destiny each possessed in bringing revival according to God's timetable.

Right now, the third revival generation is taking place. Two thousand years after the birth of Jesus, another generation has been destined for a great historic revival. The enemy knows that these individuals have the power to finish history. As a result, he is using every possible means, including abortion, to attempt to kill them off. But God will protect those He has called, just as He protected Moses and Jesus. In this end-time, however, God will raise up not only one deliverer but also an entire generation of deliverers.

As I mentioned earlier, God does not create accidents; He creates destinies. You are alive not by mere chance but by God's purpose. You are not only a survivor but also a deliverer called to bring revival to your generation. Your life is not your own; it has been given to you by the grace of God. Therefore, you must live for God and for His purposes.

> I have been crucified with Christ and I no longer live, but Christ lives in me. The life I live in the body, I live by faith in the Son of God, who loved me and gave himself for me (Gal. 2:20, *NIV*).

I often ask myself as well as others the question "What are you living for?" My passion in life is *to know God's presence and to make His presence known to my generation.* I have encountered His life, His manifest presence, and I can't turn back. I can't turn back until every living person experiences this presence too, this eternal life, this love I have tasted. Millions of young people in our generation do not know the love of God and the power of His transforming presence. They do not know that they are His beloved sons and daughters who are well pleasing to Him (see Matt. 3:17). For this my heart breaks. I do not want to die without seeing revival in my generation!

This book is in your hands because you, too, do not accept the status quo. You are not satisfied with religious games, with playing church or with the state of Christianity around you. You are hungry for God to do more in your generation. Deep down there is a passionate cry in your heart for God to show up in power, as He did in the book of Acts. There is something burning inside of you, screaming, "There has got to be more!"

Trust me, there is. But are you willing to do whatever it takes to experience the more? If so, read on.

Notes

1. For more information on the movement to end abortion in America, visit www.bound4life.com.
2. "Abortion in the United States: Statistics and Trends," National Right to Life website. Data based on numbers reported by the Alan Guttmacher Institute 1973-2002, with estimates of 1,293,000 for 2003-2005. http://www.nrlc.org/abortion/facts/abortionstats.html (accessed January 2007).

INTRODUCTION

The Passion

The word "passion" comes from the Latin word *paserre*, which means "to suffer." I once heard a pastor preach, "If you don't have a passion worth dying for, you have nothing worth living for." Really, if you're not willing to suffer for something, you really aren't passionate about it. When I was a freshman in college, God put an all-consuming passion in my heart to see my campus come to Christ. In pursuing this passion, God placed in me a burning vision to see simple new churches planted on colleges and universities to reach the most unchurched demographic group in America—young adults between the ages of 18 and 25.[1]

Passion is born when you are willing to die for something you can't live without. I can't live without God's presence. I have a passion for God because I have experienced His passion for me. If you want a passion for God, you must study and encounter His passion for you. We love Him because He first loved us (see 1 John 4:19). Passion is sustained by intimacy with Christ, and this passion is released by sharing God's love with the world. It is my passion to know His presence and make His presence known. And it is my passion to see the souls of this generation saved and completely transformed. This passion rises up in my heart when I think about the countless millions who don't know about, don't care about or have never experienced God's love, power and presence. I pray that it is your passion as well to see millions in your generation swept into the kingdom of God. May we realize that, ultimately, this is God's passion, too.

> The Lord is not slack concerning His promise, as some count slackness, but is longsuffering toward us, not willing that *any* should perish but that all should come to repentance (2 Pet. 3:9).

My passion for revival was born during my freshmen year at San Jose State University. I was sitting in my Philosophy 101 class when the professor asked, "Who here believes that Jesus Christ is the Son of God?" Being a new Christ follower, I raised my hand without hesitation. As I looked around the room containing 100-plus students, I realized that I was the only one with my hand raised. I was shocked. How could I be the only one in that entire classroom who knew the love of Christ?

After this experience, I began to pray daily for hours in my room, crying out to God to show His love to the students on my campus. My prayers became more desperate when I discovered that the number of Christians on my university campus was fewer than 250 out of a student population of 28,000. This was not okay. I became so burdened for the lost on campus that I began to gather with student leaders from other fellowships early in the morning to pray for revival.

Soon, the Holy Spirit began to show up in power. Our prayers were answered and doors opened for us to share Christ to almost the entire university. We saw hundreds of students commit their lives to Christ through our outreaches and evangelistic Bible studies on campus. Yet it wasn't enough. Something in me was still stirring to see God do more.

The Vision

During that same year in college, in 1999, I became tired of playing church and developed a hunger for the presence of God. Every day I locked myself in my room and waited on God for hours. It was during these daily encounters with the Holy Spirit that I received a recurring cinematic vision for 14 days straight.

> And it shall come to pass afterward
> That I will pour out My Spirit on all flesh;
> Your sons and your daughters shall prophesy,
> Your old men shall dream dreams,
> Your young men shall see visions (Joel 2:28).

In the vision, I saw a field full of young people crying out to God—so many, in fact, that I couldn't see to the end of the field. There were young people, some jumping, some screaming. Others were on their faces weeping and praying, but they were all seeking God's face. I didn't know what to think of what I saw, but something in my heart was stirred and my spirit became excited with hope for my generation. There was a deep sense that soon multitudes of young people were going to radically turn to Christ.

I shared what I had seen in the vision with my friend who was in Bible college, and he responded, "What do you mean . . . like revival?"

I asked him, "What's revival?"

He said, "It's like, when a lot of people get saved!"

I paused for a second, then responded with, "Cool . . . I think I like revival."

When I was introduced to this term "revival" and the concept of "many people turning to Christ," I began to study everything I could about it. To my surprise, I discovered that throughout history, God has shown up time and time again in supernatural power just as He did in the book of Acts. God would touch entire cities and nations with a sweeping move of His Spirit in a short period of time. Hundreds of thousands repented and were saved in the first and second Great Awakenings in America. Millions were swept into the kingdom of God in a few decades through the Welsh and Azusa Street revivals. Millions of young hippies were touched in the Jesus People movement in North America in the 1960s.[2] And the list goes on.

I could only think of one thing as I studied these revival accounts: *God, if You did it before, You will do it again!*

The Call

Revival became the burning passion in my heart day and night. I couldn't eat or sleep without hoping to one day witness thousands on my campus, in my city and all over the world encounter the presence of God.

During my years in college, I sought revival through prayer and seeking the power of the Holy Spirit on a daily basis. I witnessed a measure of revival when we started a series of Bible studies with students. The Bible studies and outreaches touched hundreds on a weekly basis, and within two years we reached more than 2,000 students with the gospel. But it wasn't enough. I knew there had to be more than what I had experienced up to that point. I needed God to show me that the vision of massive revival I received years before was from Him and not just my own imagination. I needed confirmation that the vision was indeed going to come to pass.

In 2002, someone introduced me to a student prayer and fasting movement called "The Call." In 2000, The Call had gathered nearly half a million young people to pray and fast for 12 hours at the Washington, D.C., mall. There they prayed for revival in America. I asked the Holy Spirit, "Is this the sign of revival I have been looking for?" A friend told me this movement would be holding another prayer and fasting event called "The Call NYC" in June 2002. I was determined to go.

On June 28, 2002, I took a flight to New York City. I went by myself and had no clue where I was going to stay. But God provided miraculously through some old friends who helped me find a place. On June 29, 2002, I woke up at 5:00 A.M. to prepare for the day of encounter. At 6:00 A.M., I arrived at Flushing Meadows Park in Queens, where the event was to be held. By 9:00 A.M., the police estimated that more than 85,000 people—mostly young people— had filled the park to pray and fast for revival.

The vision of student revival I received years back was unfolding right before my eyes. I was literally in a field full of young people crying out to God for revival. Just as I had been shown in the vision, some students were jumping, others screaming, some were on their faces weeping, but all were seeking the face of God. The entire park was filled with young people crying out to God to the point that I could not see to the end of the field. For 12 hours I prayed, fasted and wept with thousands in my generation for God to come and save the youth of America. It was heartfelt, it was powerful and I knew that God heard our cries for our generation.

On the airplane ride back to California, I felt the Holy Spirit say to me, "Jaeson, the vision I gave you three years ago has just come to pass. Get ready; revival is beginning to rumble. Prepare yourself, fast and pray!"

I knew that God was confirming to me that the vision I received three years before had not been my imagination—that indeed revival was beginning to rumble and a last great awakening was about to shake the nations of the earth.

The Three Dreams

In the two years following The Call (2002 to 2004), I entered into the school of the Holy Spirit. I lived a lifestyle of radical prayer and fasting to prepare for the coming move of God. I would daily pray and often fast to seek God's specific will and purposes for this generation. In my heart was a burning passion to see revival come to pass, but I did not know how it could happen. Through The Call, I had witnessed masses of students praying and fasting for revival. But I wondered how they would be mobilized to accomplish the vision.

Throughout Scripture, God has spoken to His people through dreams (see Gen. 28:12; 31:10; 37:5; 1 Kings 3:5; 9:2; Dan. 7:1; Matt. 1:20; 2:13; Acts 2:17). In 2004, during this intense time of seeking the Lord's will, the Holy Spirit impressed upon my heart a new revelation through a series of three dreams. The dreams revealed to me and later confirmed how God would mobilize an entire student army for His end-time purposes. The dreams also revealed that this generation needed more than just revival; it needed a complete reformation. If we are going to reach the lost and reclaim the kingdom of God, it will take a total reforming of church as we know it.

Background to the Dreams

Before sharing these three dreams, I need to share the background behind them. By 2004, through a series of divine appointments, I had begun to work for The Call and was commissioned by the leaders of the movement to plant a student-led church at San

Jose State University. I was attending a church-planting workshop when I received a revelation. I was reading the book of Acts, which is about restoring a simple approach to church planting for the next generation. God began to speak to me about planting churches—not building-, program- or personality-based churches, but planting "simple" house churches, similar to those in the book of Acts, on campuses. These simple churches would be led by students and be mobile, meet-anywhere churches. Their focus would be on winning souls, making disciples and multiplying new churches. Through this revelation, God called me to plant simple churches on university campuses. But before I ventured out, I received the following dreams.

Dream #1: The Bob Weiner Dream

In the first dream, I found myself standing in front of Pastor Bob Weiner. (Bob Weiner was known in the 1970s and 1980s for planting student-led churches on university campuses.) In the dream, I was holding in my left hand large white printout sheets of papers. On these papers were thousands of names of students from different college campuses. At the top of the printout sheet, in large letters, was written, "Campus Revival."

Bob came up to me and said, "Young man, put your left hand over your left eye. I am going to pray for you with my left hand and God's anointing will come upon you to finish the task. But before I do that, I have to staple another printout sheet of paper to yours and then I will pray for you!"

I was bewildered at his comment. He then took another printout sheet of papers and stapled them to my Campus Revival printouts. His sheets of paper had another list of student names. At the top, it was titled, "Student Activists in Washington, D.C." He then stapled his "Student Activist" list to my "Campus Revival" list and the dream ended.

I woke up from the dream in the middle of the night with my left hand over my left eye. The presence of God was all over me and I knew God was trying to get my attention. Yet, I was so tired I fell back asleep after 10 minutes.

Once again, Pastor Bob Weiner was standing in front of me in my dream! He told me, "Now put your right hand over your right eye. I am going to pray for you with my right hand, and the anointing of God's power will touch your right side to accomplish the task." He then put his right hand over my right hand and eye. The power of God surged through my body and immediately the dream switched scenes.

Dream #2: The Mike Bickle Dream

In the second dream, I was standing in front of a large Christian conference. I knew for some reason that it was a conference at the International House of Prayer (IHOP). For more than seven years now, there has been 24/7 (24 hours per day, 7 days per week) worship and intercession at the International House of Prayer in Kansas City, Missouri.[3] Hundreds of full-time intercessory missionaries go there with only one purpose: to worship and pray for the nations around the clock, non-stop, in two-hour shifts. The founder, Pastor Mike Bickle, started the IHOP ministry in 1999 with a mandate to raise up a house of prayer for all nations. This ministry would focus on fulfilling the Great Commandment first through a lifestyle of intimate and dedicated prayer, in order to obey the Great Commission. Pastor Bickle and IHOP intercessors believe that non-stop prayer will be the key to bringing in the final great harvest of souls and the return of Christ.

So, in my dream I was standing outside an IHOP conference when Pastor Mike Bickle walked by me and said, "Hey, young man, I would like to talk to you!" I thought to myself, *Why would he want to talk to me? He doesn't even know me!* Yet, I was honored and didn't want to pass up the chance. So I said, "Sure!"

Mike Bickle then said to me, "I'm kind of hungry and want some coffee. Do you know any place we can go get something to eat and drink?"

I told him, "There is a place right around the corner. My car is parked here, so why don't we take my car over?"

Mike then saw a car pulling up and said, "No, it's all right. My driver just pulled up. Let's take his car instead!" Then the dream ended.

When I woke up, I couldn't figure out the meaning or interpretation for either dream. I ended up writing each dream down in my prayer journal and put them away.

Dream #3: The Lou Engle Dream

A month later, I received a third dream that I believe was connected to the first two dreams. In this third dream, I was in a large airport. It looked like Los Angeles International Airport. In the dream I was going down an escalator with many students following behind me. On the opposite side, going up the escalator, was my pastor, Pastor Lou Engle. There were a few students standing behind him going up the escalator.

As we passed each other, going up and down the escalator, he turned, winked at me and said, "It's time!" I then turned, winked back at him and said, "It's time!" Then the dream ended.

Interpretation of the Dreams

In February 2004, I was in Los Angeles and met with Pastor Lou Engle for lunch. I was still confused about my dreams, so I shared the first one with Pastor Lou. He immediately understood the interpretation of the dream. He explained, "Jaeson, it's easy. It's revival and reformation!"

I didn't understand what he meant and asked him to explain further. He said, "Bob Weiner, in the '70s, mobilized and trained thousands of students to plant churches on university campuses for revival, but he also mobilized thousands of students to reform society by being active in the political sphere and every other area of society!" Lou then explained that you can't have revival without reformation. He explained that Bob's praying for my left and right sides meant that you can't have one without the other. It is like the left and right wings of the government. There needs to be a balance. At that time, I didn't have much of a concept of the importance of why we needed to reform society. I was only passionate about planting student-led churches on university campuses for revival, as I had been commissioned to do by my senior pastor, Ché Ahn.

Lou then shared with me that for the past six months the Lord had been strongly laying on his heart to start a new movement called The Cause that would mobilize all of America, specifically young adults from college campuses, to vote and pray for the coming 2004 elections in Washington, D.C. He said that Bob Weiner's stapling the list of student activists in Washington, D.C., to my list of students involved in campus revival was a confirmation that we must mobilize both revivalists and reformers in this generation.

As I was still in awe and trying to grasp what he had just explained, Lou interpreted the next part of my dream. He said, "Now, your dream with Mike Bickle means that God is saying we must first raise up houses of prayer on every campus, in every city, before we launch out to bring revival and reformation. Mike didn't get into your car, which represents your vehicle of ministry for campus revival, but you first got into his car, which represents his vehicle of ministry—raising up the House of Prayer!"

After these two interpretations, Pastor Lou asked me to seriously pray and think about going with him to university campuses for 12 months to mobilize students to vote and pray for the coming elections and to challenge college students all over the United States to revive and reform their campuses. I told Lou that it was my heartbeat to do so but I was working full time. He told me, "I'm not saying this is God speaking, but just pray on it and we'll talk again in 30 days."

In April 2004, when I received the third dream of Lou and myself at the airport, I shared it with Lou and he again interpreted it for me. During those months the Lord had been giving Lou revelations on equipping "fighter pilots," or young radicals, that would war for our nation's future in the heavenly places through fervent 24/7 intercession. He explained, "Jaeson, I was going up the escalator because God has called me to attack the heavenly places to break open the heavens for revival, but God is calling you to go down the escalator to mobilize the ground troops for campus revival and reformation."

By that time, in April 2004, the Lord had also given me a clear conviction to leave my job and step out in faith to start the campus church-planting ministry that He had put in my heart. That very week, God put it on the heart of a Christian businessperson to finance my first 12 months of ministry without me even asking or telling this person about what I was doing.

I knew God was confirming His will for me to join and serve Lou in mobilizing students on every college campus to focus on and accomplish three things: (1) prayer, (2) power evangelism, and (3) planting simple churches.

The Confirmations

As I stepped out in faith, the Holy Spirit confirmed each step through manifestations in the real world of all I had seen in my dreams. In July 2004, I was scheduled to speak to the youth at an International House of Prayer conference among Chinese-speaking Christians, in Fremont, California. It so happened that the main speaker for the adult congregation was Mike Bickle.

That morning, I sensed that the Holy Spirit was telling me to take a chance and call Pastor Mike. At 8:00 A.M., I called the front desk of the hotel and asked only for Mike's room number. Instead, the receptionist put me right through to his room and Mike picked up the phone! I told him who I was and asked if it would be possible to get 15 minutes of his time. He told me to meet him downstairs!

We walked outside and I explained to Mike how God had called me to plant student-led house churches on university campuses and to raise up campus houses of prayer. As we talked, we both began to connect on a heart level. Suddenly he said, "Hey, let's go get some coffee and talk some more." So I asked him, "You want to take my car?"

Mike responded, "No, my driver just pulled up; we'll take his car!" Then déja vu hit me. I knew at that moment that God was confirming to me that I would first have to give priority to pursuing God in intimacy before ministry and that I would have to establish 24/7 campus houses of prayer at every university in order to break open the heavens for campus revival and reformation to take place. During the next two days, Mike and I had deep conversations on how to network together in starting campus houses of prayer and simple churches on university campuses.

During this same conference, the dream I had about Bob Weiner was also confirmed. A few days after meeting with Mike Bickle, I received a random call from Bob Weiner's secretary that Bob was expecting me to join him in a youth crusade in Indonesia. I was surprised because although Bob had invited me to go to Indonesia, we had not yet made definite plans. Something in my spirit told me I needed to make the trip to Indonesia to meet with Bob. Though I had no money to pay for airfare, by God's grace I received an honorarium from my speaking engagement for the exact cost of the plane ticket to Indonesia. So I decided to go.

After the IHOP conference in California, I immediately flew to Indonesia to help minister with Bob at the student crusade and to train college leaders in campus ministry. While at dinner the first night, I explained to Bob what God had been showing me during the previous 24 months regarding mobilizing houses of prayer, student activism and church planting on campuses throughout America. I shared the three dreams that I received in early 2004 and he responded, "Jaeson, it's easy! It's Revival and Reformation!" Not only did he have the exact interpretation Lou had, but he also went on to explain, "Jaeson, do you know what I trained the Indonesian college leaders on last night? I preached on the three Rs: Revival, Reformation of Society and Restoration of the New Testament Church!" I almost fell out of my chair when I heard it. The three things the Holy Spirit had been revealing to me for months were the exact messages Bob had just been preaching in Indonesia and around the world!

The Three Rs

Through these real-life confirmations, I began to understand the significance of the three Rs and the mandate for this generation. As I studied these three Rs, I discovered their meanings.

Revival

Revival begins with a recovery of the Lord's testimony in a given generation. The resulting effect on society (the revived Church with large numbers of people being converted) is termed "a spiritual awakening." In this generation, *revival* represents the full expansion of God's kingdom and it must begin with revival prayer (*campus houses of prayer*).

Reformation

This is defined as the corresponding effect of a spiritual awakening on a particular society. Great social reforms occur due to the sanctifying power of a revived Church acting as a redeemer to its culture. In other words, *reformation of society* has to do with mobilizing God's army to take dominion and preach the gospel through the power of the Holy Spirit (*power evangelism*) in every sphere of society: government, business, education, media, arts, family and religion.

Restoration

This occurs as each successive wave of revival restores great truths that were part of the normal experience for the Early Church of the apostolic age but were neglected since then.[4] In my experience, *restoration of the New Testament Church* has to do with the revelation God had given me to empower students and every believer to be missionaries to all of society by planting relationship-based, student-led house churches—particularly, networks of campus churches (*planting simple churches*) like they did in the book of Acts!

The Blueprint

Through the confirmations, I was convinced that revival, reformation and restoration were the will of God. God was calling me to step out and reclaim every college campus, city and nation for His glory. In the years since 2004, the prophetic fulfillment of each of my dreams has begun to transpire. On college and university campuses all across North America and other nations there has been a sweeping move of 24/7 campus houses of prayer. We have recorded reports of non-Christian students experiencing the presence of God through power evangelism encounters on numerous campuses.

At the same time, a new generation of leaders is being commissioned in the power of the Holy Spirit from the campus into every sphere of society. More and more, Christian students are realizing that they are not on their campuses just to fellowship but also to be campus missionaries. They are invading lost pockets of unreached student groups on campus and planting simple churches or missional communities among the lost. We must have a passion to see these strategies mobilized, but we must first understand the reality of what the Church is up against in this generation. This is the blueprint. This is God's game plan to release an apostolic and prophetic generation to fulfill the Great Commandment and finish the Great Commission. It is time! Let the second reformation begin!

Notes

1. The Barna Research Group, "Most Twentysomethings Put Christianity on the Shelf Following Spiritually Active Teen Years." http://www.barna.org/FlexPage.aspx? Page=BarnaUpdate&BarnaUpdateID=245 (accessed January 2007).
2. Jeff Ziegler and Jay Rogers, "Revival and Spiritual Awakening," *The Forerunner*. http://forerunner.com/forerunner/X0606_Revival_Spiritual_A.html (accessed January 2007).
3. For more information on the International House of Prayer, visit their website at www.ihop.org.
4. Ziegler and Rogers, "Revival and Spiritual Awakening."

REFORMATION GENERATION

Repent, then, and turn to God, so that your sins may be wiped out,
that times of refreshing may come from the Lord, and that he may
send the Christ, who has been appointed for you–even Jesus.
He must remain in heaven until the time comes for God to restore
everything, as he promised long ago through his holy prophets.
ACTS 3:19-21, *NIV*

We owe this generation an encounter with God. Let's look at the facts: 80 percent of all high school students who attend church before college do not return to church after college.[1] Barna Research shows that 18- to 25-year-olds are the least likely age group to attend church.[2] The national average of Christians on university campuses is less than 5 percent.[3] Ultimately, if we don't reach the campus for Christ today, we will not have a Church tomorrow. Something must change drastically if the Church is going to reach this generation. Yes, this generation needs revival, but we have to go one step further. We need more than just revival. We need a reformation.

"Reformation" may be defined in many ways, including (1) improvement (or an intended improvement) in the existing form or condition of institutions or practices that are intended to make a *striking change* for the better in social or political or religious affairs; (2) *a religious movement* of the sixteenth century that began as an attempt to reform the Roman Catholic Church and resulted in the creation of Protestant churches; (3) rescuing from error and returning to a rightful course—the "reclamation of delinquent children."[4]

The Need for Striking Change

We have many churches in America, but we don't have revival. We have church programs, but we don't have God's presence. We need striking change. I grew up in church, attended church, "played" church and, finally, left church before I was born again at age 17. I'm not only speaking for myself; I am also speaking for millions of young people in this generation who have had a similar experience. My heart breaks for those in my generation who, growing up, experienced a form of religion but never experienced the presence of God. They wanted God, but they couldn't find Him, so they left the church institution and looked elsewhere.

If we don't change the way we do church, we won't have a generation to do church with. I'm not talking about improving church. I'm talking about changing church as we know it to reach a lost generation. Statistics show that only 4 percent of this millennial generation (born after 1984) believe in the Bible as infallibly true.[5] If this is the current trend, 10 years from now we will have a completely post-Christian young adult generation. I refuse to take that. God refuses to take that. It is time to strike back and take back what the enemy has stolen.

In the sixteenth century, Martin Luther nailed his 99 theses to the front doorpost of the Roman Catholic Church in an attempt to reform it. Instead, he started a revolution that resulted in the formation of the modern Protestant Church. Thus, revolutions occur because people recognize a need for change. Again, "reformation" means to "re-form, re-do or re-make" because something is inherently wrong with what is current. Today we have many churches with great preaching, wonderful programs and big buildings. We have campus fellowships with good Bible studies and fun social events. We have a Christian culture with more Christian books, Christian TV, Christian music and everything you can think of that is Christian.

Yet if you look around our world, you can see that society is not changed and that our cities are not transformed. Statistics show that in the last 40 years we have had increasingly more divorce, more poverty, more abortions, more violence, more sexual immorality, more materialism, more disdain for God and more people still leaving the Church in our nation.

"Thus also faith by itself, if it does not have works, is dead" (Jas. 2:17). We need a second reformation. The first reformation was about our belief . . . the second reformation will be about our behavior.[6] The first reformation was about faith. The second reformation will be about faith coupled with action.

For too long the Church has separated itself from the world. Instead of influencing it, we have been influenced by it. Jesus said, "They are not of the world" (John 17:16). God has called the Church to be salt and light, to shine in the darkness, but where? I don't see much of it. Something has to change. It is no longer about going to church; it is about being the Church in this generation. Our paradigm of church must shift if a generation is to be saved. We must take church outside the four walls and into society with God's power.

The Challenge to Reclaim Campuses

Dr. Bill Bright, founder of Campus Crusade for Christ, always said, "Win the campus today and change the world tomorrow!" He understood that reaching college students for Christ is the key to transforming society. His vision to change the campus in order to reach the world has impacted countless millions with the gospel. We must establish God's kingdom, His Church, on every college and university campus in this generation because this is where reformation begins.

The campus is the greatest mission field in our world today. Just think, according to the United Nations Population Reference Bureau, more than half the world's population is under the age of 25.[7] Where are these young people? *On the campuses!* If we can transform campuses, we can ultimately transform cities and nations with the gospel.

Why else is it important that we reach the campus?

- Throughout history almost all great revivals and missionary movements started on the campus.

- The campus is where the future leaders of tomorrow are located, trained and most available.

- Statistics show that more than 77 percent of all Christians make a decision for Christ before the age of 21.[8]

- There are more than 550,000 international students who attend American universities and 600,000 more worldwide in foreign universities who will be the future leaders of their nations.[9]

- If we can reach the campus, we can reach our cities and the nations for Christ.

Revolutions Start on Campuses

Almost every revolution started with students on college and university campuses. From Nazism, Communism and Marxism to the great missionary movements such as the Moravian missionaries, the Azusa Street Revival and the Jesus People movement, every revolution—*bad or good*—started with or had a great influence on students who were hungry for change and willing to lay down their lives for a cause.[10]

Is there not a cause? Is there not a cause today to fight for the dying souls of a lost generation?

It is our responsibility to re-dig the wells of revival on every college campus. Almost every college and university that was founded in this country before the Civil War was dedicated at its founding to Jesus Christ and His cause.[11] The students on these campuses do not belong to Satan; they belong to God. They don't belong to the enemy. The campuses belong to you! "The highest heavens belong to the LORD, but the earth he has given to man" (Ps. 115:16, *NIV*).

The Strategy

How will we reclaim our campuses for the glory of God? How will another student revolution for Jesus take place? I asked the Holy

Spirit these questions daily during my college years. It was during my college days and through the series of prophetic dreams I shared earlier that God revealed to me three strategies to transform our nation's campuses. My heart was burning to share these strategies because I had personally experienced the fruit and power of each to bring campus revival, reformation and restoration. If we want to see not only our campuses but also our cities and nations transformed with God's glory, we must have (1) a passion for prayer, (2) a passion for power evangelism, and (3) a passion for planting simple churches.

In the following pages of this book, I will go into depth on how God is transforming campuses in the power of the Holy Spirit through these three specific strategies. Through personal stories about Holy Spirit encounters and with biblical principles, I will explain practical ways that you can release God's glory on every campus and in every city and nation. But you must be willing to do what it takes to see change. You must be willing to do what others on your campus are not willing to do. You must be willing to lay down your life as a pioneer, a forerunner and very possibly a martyr to see your generation saved. Are you willing?

Who will be a part of this reformation generation? It will be those who are willing to deny themselves, take up their cross and follow Christ. These will be the new revivalists and reformers of our day. God is raising up an end-time army that is passionate for His purposes. Those who are willing to do whatever it takes, those who are willing to take the Church out of its four walls and into society to reach the lost, will be a part of this new reformation student force on Earth. Jesus is coming back. The day of the Lord is beckoning and we must be prepared to follow the Lord of Hosts. This generation is the end-time army that will fulfill the Great Commandment and finish the Great Commission. It is the reformation generation that will not only change history but also finish it. Do you believe it?

You may be on your campus looking at the darkness around you, thinking it is impossible to see God's presence break in. I urge you, don't look with your physical eyes but with eyes of faith.

Reclaim your campus for God! It is your inheritance as a son or daughter of God. Prophesy and speak life to that valley of dry bones (see Ezek. 37)!

There is coming a day when the book of Acts will break out on every campus. There is coming a moment when hundreds if not thousands of students will turn to Christ in a brief moment. There is coming a movement of supernatural sons and daughters who will walk in their identity as His beloved, move in God's power and boldly speak God's prophetic message unashamed. It will shake campuses and cities to the core. Signs, wonders and miracles will be performed again like in the days of the early apostles. Heaven will invade Earth. An army of light will outshine the darkness. The Church will no longer be about personalities, programs or buildings, but only one thing: Jesus Christ. The Church will be about a united army of ordinary people who will do extraordinary exploits for God. There is a new reformation arising. It is a return to the supremacy of Scripture as final authority. It is a generation that will hear and obey God's voice by living out radical obedience to God's Word. A day of reckoning is upon us. It is time for us to enter into this end-time battle.

I will not be satisfied until I see the power of God shake campuses and cities the way it shook Jerusalem in the book of Acts. It can happen. It must happen. It will happen. But it starts with us.

If we want to see God's power show up in this generation, it will take drastic change. It will take our first changing our hearts. It will require our humbling ourselves before Almighty God, turning from our wicked ways and releasing a desperate cry for revival (see 2 Chron. 7:14). It will require praying as if it all depends on God and living as if it all depends on us.[12] Prayer brings revival. Action brings about reformation. We need both desperately.

God is calling forth a generation that is passionate for His presence. A generation that knows who they are and Whose they are. He is calling forth sons and daughters who don't find their identity in revival but in Christ. For the Great Commission must flow out of the Great Commandment. Our destinies must flow out of our identities as beloved children of God who know their worth, value and honor before the Father. Out of this place of rest will flow the greatest revival in human history. We are sons and daughters first, revivalists second. We have nothing to prove and nothing to lose. God is raising up a student-led army that is passionate for prayer, power evangelism and planting simple churches in this end-time hour. It is time for change. It is time for revival and reformation in this generation.

I pray this book will set your heart ablaze with a passion and fire to see this generation saved—no matter the cost. *God, give us every campus, every city and every nation in this generation! Revival and reformation—nothing less!*

Notes

1. The Barna Research Group, "Most Twentysomethings Put Christianity on the Shelf Following Spiritually Active Teen Years," *The Barna Update,* September 11, 2006. http://www.barna.org/FlexPage.aspx?Page=BarnaUpdate&BarnaUpdateID=245 (accessed January 2007).
2. Ibid.
3. "College Students: The Powerful Percent," Campus Renewal Ministries. http://campusrenewal.org/about/need.html (accessed January 2007).
4. *Dictionary.com,* s.v. "reformation," *WordNet® 2.0,* Princeton University. http://dictionary.reference.com/browse/reformation (accessed October 2006).
5. Ron Luce, *Revolution YM* (Colorado Springs, CO: Cook Communications Ministries, 2006), p. 15.
6. Ken Camp, "Rick Warren: 'Second Reformation' Will Unify Church, Warren Tells Dallas GDOP." http://www.pastors.com/article.asp?ArtID=8280 (accessed January 2007).
7. "World Population Day 2006 Raises Awareness of Youth Issues," Population Reference Bureau, July 2006. http://www.prb.org/Articles/2006/PRBCoversWorld PopulationDay2006RaisesAwarenessofYouthIssues.aspx (accessed January 2007).
8. The Barna Research Group, "Research Shows That Spiritual Maturity Process Should Start at a Young Age," *The Barna Update,* November 17, 2003. http://www.barna.org/FlexPage.aspx?Page=BarnaUpdate&BarnaUpdateID=153 (accessed January 2007).
9. "U. S. Sees Slowing Decline in International Student Enrollment in 2004/2005," Institute of International Education, November 14, 2005. http://opendoors.iienetwork.org/?p=69689 (accessed January 2007).
10. J. Edwin Orr, "Why Campus Revivals Spark Missionary Advance," Awake and Go! Global Prayer Network. http://www.watchword.org//index.php?option=com_content&task=view&id=62&Itemid=62 (accessed January 2007).
11. George Marsden, *The Soul of the American University: From Protestant Establishment to Established Nonbelief* (Oxford, England: Oxford University Press, 1994).
12. Pete Greig, *Red Moon Rising* (Lake Mary, FL: Relevant Media Group, 2003), p. 150.

And pray in the Spirit on all occasions with all kinds
of prayers and requests. With this in mind, be alet and
always keep on praying for all the saints.
EPHESIANS 6:18, *NIV*

A Student Prayer Awakening

During the spring of 2006, I was on my face praying for college revival with other students at the 24/7 campus house of prayer near the University of California at Los Angeles (UCLA). While praying for God to pour out His spirit on college campuses across our nation, I heard the Lord speak to my spirit two specific words: *"rain, fall."* I then heard the Holy Spirit say, "Revival rain is beginning to fall. I am beginning to pour out a move of My Spirit that will bring many students into My kingdom across America." I felt sure that a new season was upon us in which the Lord was beginning to move powerfully on the campuses of America. I knew this was a direct answer to the many prayers going up from different 24/7 houses of prayer on college and university campuses in our nation.

After checking the Campus Transformation Network e-mails, I discovered that other prayer leaders who were mobilizing 24/7 prayer on more than 40 campuses were hearing the same thing from the Lord: *that the Lord was pouring out His Spirit and was going to be moving and bringing many students into His kingdom over the ensuing weeks and months.* It was clear that the Lord was hearing our prayers and that heaven was beginning to move in power to answer our cries for revival.

Later that same day, I received an e-mail from a prayer leader in our network with the message, "Revival has broken out at Asbury College." Hundreds of students had begun to repent, confess their sins and testify of God's transforming power in the Asbury College chapel that very morning while we were praying near UCLA. The revival report was astounding. The Asbury chapel was packed with students praying for days on end. Students would not leave because the presence of God was so powerful. Students, teachers, faculty and people from the surrounding community were continually seeking the face of God and testifying of His love.

It was like a dream, but in the weeks and months following the breakout at Asbury College, we counted more than 70 colleges and universities across America that signed up on our www.campus transformation.com site to join in 24/7 prayer for college revival. We were able to cover an entire semester with non-stop prayer.

Indeed, the Holy Spirit was birthing a new college revival awakening through prayer. It was not led by any man, but by the Spirit of God. Prayer was once again at the forefront, making college-revival history and changing a new generation.

Why Be Passionate for Prayer?

I have a passion for prayer. I am nothing without it. I am everything with it. It is my greatest blessing and my greatest challenge. It is all I've got. This passion for prayer did not come easy. It came with a price of sacrifice. God began to stir in my heart years ago that I should give my life to prayer. I didn't know how to do it; I didn't know how to pray. But I simply obeyed and, as a result, I encountered God's manifest presence.

My life mission statement is "to know His presence and to make His presence known in my generation." This can't happen without prayer and this can happen only through prayer. Do you want to know His intimate presence? Do you want more of God? Is there a divine dissatisfaction crying out in your heart? Then give yourself to a life of passionate prayer.

My prayer for you is simply that prayer would become your passion. Why? It is only through prayer that heaven can touch Earth. It is only through prayer that God can intervene into the affairs of humankind. Without prayer nothing can happen; with prayer anything can happen. Prayer is the substance behind all miracles. It is the key to fellowship with the Holy Spirit. Prayer is what births intimacy with Him and sustains our identity in Christ. Prayer is what the devil hates and what he is most afraid of. Prayer changes history. Prayer changes you. Prayer changes everything. Prayer is the key to revival. Prayer is God's secret weapon to transform your generation. Prayer is the instrument to release the sound of revival on your campus. How badly do you want it? What are you willing to sacrifice in order to have it operating in your life?

According to *Webster's Dictionary*, the word "passion" means "suffering or agony," "the sufferings of Jesus," "or agony . . . of a martyr."[1] This definition blows me away. *Jesus is passion.* His suffering, torture and death on the cross gave meaning to the whole concept of passion. To me, passion is when the heart is set free to pursue that which is truly worthy. It springs from desiring something so badly that you are willing to suffer and even die for it; you are willing to give up everything and anything to have that for which you are passionate. No matter the cost, you are willing to do whatever it takes to obtain the object desired.

You will never find passion unless you find something worth dying for. If you don't have a passion worth dying for, you have nothing worth living for! What are you living for? What was Jesus living for?

Jesus' Passion for Us

What was Jesus so passionate about that He was willing to suffer and even die for it? What was His passion? Simply put, we are His passion. We are the objects of His burning desire that motivated

His suffering and torture on the cross. If you want a passion for Jesus, study His passion for you. Jesus' passion was for you and me to have intimate relationship with Him.

Jesus' passion was for one thing and one thing only: that we would know Him. His death and resurrection on the cross paid the ultimate price for our sins to be forgiven in order that we may know eternal life (see John 17:3). The price He paid on the cross enabled us to come into the presence of God. His blood sacrifice—His victory over death—caused the temple veil that separated sinful man from God's holy presence to be torn in two. Now anyone and everyone who calls on the name of the Lord can experience this glorious presence of God. How do we experience this glorious presence of God? It is only through the righteousness of Jesus Christ and through prayer.

> Let us then approach the throne of grace with confidence,
> so that we may receive mercy and find grace to help us in
> our time of need (Heb. 4:16, *NIV*).

We approach the throne and enter into the presence of God when we pray. We have confidence in His grace that He will not turn us away but will embrace us with mercy. Jesus began His ministry in prayer and fasting (see Luke 3:21). Jesus prayed often through the day, through the night and early in the morning (see Mark 1:35; Luke 5:16; 6:12). Jesus prayed in the garden of Gethsemane before His death on the cross (see Mark 14:32). Jesus prayed while He was on the cross (see Luke 23:34). Jesus is still praying right now at the mercy seat of God for the souls of mankind (see Heb. 7:25). Jesus prayed and He continues to pray. His passion was a passion for prayer. Why? Because prayer was the channel that brought Jesus into intimacy with the Father. Jesus knows it is only prayer that will bring *us* into intimacy with the Father as well.

What is your passion? I have already told you that my passion is to know God's presence and to make His presence known, and that this can only happen through prayer. Oh God, give me one pure and holy passion! Give me a passion for prayer so that I may know You and follow hard after You!

In the first section of this book, I will share my personal journey about how I encountered God and saw Him move on campuses, in cities and in nations through the different dimensions of prayer. The different kinds of prayer shared in this book are not an exhaustive list of every way to pray; they will explain the dimensions of prayer that I have experienced personally, that have impacted my life and that form the essential foundation to planting missional communities on campus.

Many students tell me, "Jaeson, I have a passion for prayer, but I don't know how to pray." May these following chapters give you the practical understanding of how to pray, how prayer can change you and how prayer can change your campus, city and nation with God's power! *Simply put—pray.*

Note

1. *Webster's New World College Dictionary,* third ed., s.v. "passion."

CHAPTER ONE

REPENTANCE PRAYER

*Truly, these times of ignorance God overlooked, but now
commands all men everywhere to repent.*
ACTS 17:30

I grew up in church but did not like it. Personally, I thought church
was lame and nothing but a bunch of rules and regulations. Every
Sunday morning, my mom would drag me down the driveway and
force me to get into the car to go to our conservative Chinese Baptist
church in East San Jose. She would say, "Jaeson, as long as you are
my son, you go to church!" So I did. I went as long as I *had* to go. I
would always tell my mom, "You just wait till I turn 18! I'll never
come back to church again!" You see, I did not have a problem with
Jesus. I had a problem with religion. To me, church was a system of
dos and don'ts.

When I was 13, I left church and planned to never come back.
I told God, my mother and the old Chinese Baptist church, "Peace
out." I decided that I would party hard, get drunk, get high, get
rich or die trying, and when I was 85 years old on my death bed,
I would repent and give my life back to Jesus. That was my plan.
But God had another plan.

"For I know the plans I have for you," declares the LORD,
"plans to prosper you and not to harm you, plans to give
you hope and a future" (Jer. 29:11, *NIV*).

I grew up to be an Asian mother's nightmare. I wanted to live
my own life and did not care what my parents thought of me. There

was not much love in my home. Instead, there was constant fighting, yelling and screaming between my parents and siblings. By the age of 13, I could no longer handle the chaos in my house and chose to run wild in the streets and hang out with Asian gangsters.

I became heavily involved with drinking, growing and selling marijuana, getting into gang fights, and living the hard-knock street life. In high school I tried to find my identity in the people I knew, what I had and what I did. I became popular in school, had a lot of money, had a lot of nice clothes and gained a reputation as an Asian thug who could rap. I thought these superficial things could satisfy me, but they didn't. The more I had, the emptier I felt inside.

God Can Use Me? Yeah, Right!

When I was 15 years old, I received a prophetic word from my older sister. I still remember the night it happened. I was lying down on our living room couch, coming off of a marijuana high. Suddenly, my sister came rushing through the living room door and woke me up.

She exclaimed, "Jaeson, oh my gosh! Oh my gosh! I saw your book of life!"

I responded, "What do you mean, you saw my book of life?"

She said, "God took me to heaven and, Jaeson, I saw your book of life and it was huge. You are going to do so much for God. Oh my gosh, Jaeson, you are going to be a youth pastor. You are going to help thousands of young people find Jesus Christ!"

I snapped back, "Shut up! I'm not gonna be no youth pastor! How could God use a person like me? I don't wanna be no youth pastor anyway!"

While this was happening my mother was in the kitchen washing dishes, listening to my sister share the prophecy with me. As she listened, she became excited and started jumping up and down, shouting out loud in a Chinese Cantonese accent, "Yea! Jaeson going to be youth pastor! Yea, Jaeson going to be youth pastor!"

I couldn't listen anymore. I knew my mother and my older sisters had been praying for me daily, but I didn't care. I couldn't believe that God could use a sinner like me and I didn't want to live for Him anyway.

180-Degree Turnaround

I continued to live a life of rebellion against God and kept pursuing the things of this world. I was looking for love in all the wrong places. I tried to satisfy the emptiness in my heart with worldly possessions and false love, not knowing that Jesus was the satisfaction I was ultimately seeking. I finally came to the end of my rope when I was caught by the police for grand theft.

You see, I had one chronic problem that seemed to satisfy me more than any other "satisfaction" in my life at the time: I was addicted to stealing. From a young age, I would steal for no apparent reason. I stole anything, from stereo systems to bubble gum—it didn't matter what it was—and I loved the rush.

I had been caught for theft more than three times, and for some crazy reason the policemen would let me go without throwing me in jail. Each time my mom found out, she would cry and say the same thing, "Jaeson, don't you understand that God is giving you a chance? Stop stealing and give your life back to God!" I never listened to her until one fateful day when I could no longer ignore her words.

My mother called me after school and said, "Jaeson, the police called and said they have you on video stealing from your suit store, and they are looking to arrest you. Is this true?"

Although I denied it, deep down, I knew it was true. I had been laundering and stealing Giorgio Armani and Valentino suits worth a few thousand dollars a piece for the last year as an employee at a fine Italian suit store in the mall. I knew the police were lying about having caught me on videotape; they wanted to trick me into confessing. I could have denied the charges and fought the case in court. But for some reason, I finally woke up. I knew something wasn't right. I realized later that all of this was God moving in my life.

It dawned on me, *Jaeson, what are you doing? You're almost 17 years old; you have police with a warrant out for your arrest. You have everything you could ever want, but at the same time, in your heart, you feel you have nothing. Where is your life going? What are you living for?*

At that moment, I fled back to my house, went into my room, emptied out my closet of every remaining suit I had stolen and threw them into two big garbage bags. I had no knowledge of why or what I was doing. All I knew was that something in my life wasn't right and that I needed to change it.

I called my friend to take me to the police station and he said, "You're crazy! Just give them back a couple of shirts. Tell them that's all you stole and it won't be considered grand theft!" Nevertheless, I ignored my friend's suggestion and went to the police station with the two big bags of stolen suits.

Outside the station, I paced back and forth for two hours, contemplating my options. Finally, I called my mom on a pay phone. I told her the truth and the options set before me. If I turned myself in, I was going to jail for sure because I was already on probation. If I lied about the amount I stole, I could get away with minor charges. Suddenly, I asked her, "Mom, what do you think Jesus would do in this situation?"

She was quiet and then responded, "He would probably turn in everything and get rid of His sin so that He could start all over again." Hearing those words cut my heart like a sword. I knew it was the right thing to do. I knew I had to repent. I had to repent to God for the wrongs I had done against Him. I realized I also had to repent to my mother for the dishonor I had brought against her. Standing there at the payphone, I asked my mother for forgiveness for putting her through hell for seven years. My vow and prayer was to give my life back to God, even if it meant going to jail. I didn't feel any tingly sensations; there were no visions of angels or God speaking to me in an audible voice. I simply made a decision in my mind and in my heart to give my life back to God, no matter what the cost.

My mother told me, "Jaeson, all you can do now is pray that the policeman will have mercy on you." I prayed that God would give me a miracle. As I was entering the front door of the police station, one of my accomplices came out crying and handcuffed, with a policeman behind him; he had no prior record.

I thought, *If he's in trouble with no record, then I'm screwed!*

I walked in and the officer looked up and said sternly, "So you're Jaeson Ma?" He took out his handcuffs and was about to arrest me, but when he saw my two big bags filled with thousand-dollar suits, he was shocked. He pulled me to the side and asked me to explain.

I told him the truth and said, "You might think I'm weird, but I'm giving my life back to God."

The officer looked at me bewildered and said, "I don't know why, but when I saw you with those two big bags in your hands, something told me that there's something different about you. I've never done this before. I should be taking you to jail, but I'm not going to." Whoa. God had answered my prayer right then, faster than I thought He would.

Then the officer continued, "I'm sorry to say this, Jaeson, but because you're already on probation, there's a 99 percent chance that you'll still serve time in jail when this case gets to court." I didn't care at that point; I simply gave my future to God. This is where the miracle really begins.

My Day in Court

God had a plan for me that included divine intervention. They lost my court case for six months. During those six months I quit drugs, gangs and partying. I threw away my marijuana plant, quit drinking and began to share the love of Christ with every one of my friends. I went from having a 2.0 GPA to earning nearly straight As. It truly was the power of God at work in my life. I could not have changed without Him empowering me to do so.

I went back to church and invited all my gangster, hip-hop and drugged-out friends to the Billy Graham Crusade in San Jose. Many of my friends committed their lives to Christ there. At the crusade I rededicated my life in service to God. I ended up starting Bible studies with my lost friends, and nearly 100 of my classmates came to Christ during my senior year in high school. When I finally got a letter by mail in January 1998 for my court date, there was proven evidence that I was not the same Jaeson that I was six months before.

After my court date was miraculously postponed by the judge twice, I finally went back to court for the third time, in May 1998. My accomplice, who didn't have a record and had only confessed to stealing a few shirts, had already been sentenced to six months house arrest. I didn't know what would happen to me.

The judge told me to stand up. He looked me straight in the eye and said, "Jaeson, after reviewing your case, the court has come to a decision: We find you not guilty." I couldn't believe my ears. I had pleaded guilty! How was this possible?

I asked the judge, "I don't have to go to jail?"

"No."

"I don't have to pay the company back any money?"

"No."

"Tell me I have community service hours."

"No community service hours."

"Wait a second, what about my probation officer?"

"Starting now, you no longer have a probation officer."

I began to realize the judge was not joking. I made one last comment, "So I can just get up out of here and leave like nothing ever happened?"

The judge smiled back and said, "Yes, get out of here!"

Therefore if anyone is in Christ, he is a new creation; old things have passed away; behold, all things have become new (2 Cor. 5:17).

I had walked into the courtroom a criminal; now I walked out a free man. It was as if my sin had never happened. On that day I finally understood the meaning of the cross, the very meaning of grace. I should have gone to jail, but God's grace allowed me to go free. I should have gone to hell, but Jesus suffered, died and was resurrected to forgive my sins and to save me from eternal punishment. Who am I that He would die for me and set me free?

As I walked into the parking lot outside of the juvenile hall, I looked up at the clouds and the bright, shining sun. I couldn't express in words my gratitude toward the God who had given me a second chance. I simply smiled, lifted up a prayer and said, "God, you are the nicest person I have ever met." Then I declared, "God, I repent and turn from my old life of sin. Today I am getting out of the driver's seat of my life and into the passenger seat. You take the driver's seat—take this life where You will." I was on my way to an adventure with God that I would never have imagined possible. And it all began with a prayer of repentance.

Repentance Prayer

From that time Jesus began to preach and to say,
"Repent, for the kingdom of heaven is at hand."

MATTHEW 4:17

The prayer of repentance is the most powerful act on Earth. It releases heaven on Earth. It establishes God's rule and Lordship in your life. It establishes God's kingdom and dominion into all of society. The prayer of repentance is what opened the heavens over my life for miracles to happen. The prayer of repentance is the foundation for releasing revival in you and your generation. Without true repentance prayer, you cannot know God and you cannot fully enter into His kingdom or into the power of His presence.

Many people believe the prayer of repentance is simply saying you're sorry to Jesus or attending a church service and feeling remorseful for sinning. Others think repentance is saying a prayer of casual faith in God's grace, or think it is only necessary for those who have sinned big-time.

A prayer of repentance is none of the above. A true prayer of repentance is not a feeling; it is a decision. It is the beginning of true freedom. It is where life starts. Repentance is the moment you make the conscious decision to completely surrender your will and selfish ambition to God. It is the ultimate act of humility. It is when you begin to turn from your way of thinking and back to God's way of thinking:

That if you confess with your mouth the Lord Jesus and
believe in your heart that God has raised him from the
dead, you will be saved. For with the heart one believes unto
righteousness, and with the mouth confession is made
unto salvation (Rom. 10:9-10).

Repentance is when you make Jesus the Lord of your life and
tell Him, "Lord, not my will, but Your will be done. What do You
want to do with my life?" And when He answers, you obey.

If Christ followers truly lived a life of repentance prayer, we
would see revival. We would see God's rule established on Earth as
it is in heaven. Many in our generation have prayed a prayer of salvation, but they have not cried out a prayer of true repentance.

What Is Repentance?

The New Testament Greek word for "repentance" is *metanoeo*.[1] It
means "to repent" or "to change one's mind." We must understand
that repentance is not an emotion. It is a conscious, inward decision to change your mind. It is turning from your sin and turning
to God.

The Old Testament Hebrew word for "repentance" is *shuv*, "to
turn back, to return."[2] It is the outward expression of turning back
or turning around. If we want to see revival in our own lives and in
the lives of others, then we must "turn back" toward God in humble repentance:

If My people who are called by My name will humble themselves, and pray and seek My face and turn from their
wicked ways, then I will hear from heaven, and will forgive
their sin and heal their land (2 Chron. 7:14).

We must turn back to God both individually and corporately.
If we want to see heaven descend on Earth, then we must be a people who pray a prayer of repentance for our own sin and the sins
of our land. Revival begins first in our own hearts. Send revival,
Lord, *and start with me!*

Combining the two definitions of "repentance" used in the Old and New Testaments, the prayer of repentance can be described as an *inner* change of mind that results in an *outward* change of action that moves us toward a completely new direction in God.[3] When I decided to recommit my life to God near the police station that fateful day, I prayed a prayer of repentance. I didn't pray a casual sinner's prayer. Instead, I made an internal decision to turn my life fully back to God. I was convicted of my sin. I acknowledged that I had sinned against God, my mother and others I had wronged. I was willing to face the consequence of my sin, own up to it and do what was right.

True repentance will cost you sacrifice—your will and your very life. But it is a sacrifice motivated from love. I prayed the prayer of repentance because I realized how much God loved me and how much I had hurt Him, others and myself. I didn't want to live that way anymore. On that day I made a firm decision to deny myself, take up my cross and follow Christ—no matter the cost. That is repentance prayer.

What True Repentance Looks Like

The story of Zacchaeus in Luke 19:1-10 is a perfect example of the prayer of repentance in action. Jesus' purpose was to come to seek and save that which was lost—and Zacchaeus was a very lost man. Being a sinful tax collector, Zacchaeus knew he was not worthy to welcome such a holy man as Jesus into his home, yet the love of Jesus overwhelmed him. In the end, the love of Christ convicted Zacchaeus of his need for God and made him aware of his wrongdoing ("God's kindness leads you toward repentance" [Rom. 2:4, *NIV*]). Thus, he publicly confessed Jesus as Lord and was converted to Christianity:

> Then Zacchaeus stood and said to the Lord, "Look, Lord, I give half of my goods to the poor; and if I have taken anything from anyone by false accusation, I restore fourfold" (Luke 19:8).

Zacchaeus made an inward decision to change his mind by repenting of the sins he had committed. This resulted in an outward change of action by restoring fourfold to all those from whom he had stolen. He was willing to give up all the riches he possessed, receive Christ and reconcile with those he had wronged. Zacchaeus not only received Christ as Savior, but he also obeyed Him as Lord. Zacchaeus made Jesus Lord of his life and so must we.

Repentance Prayer Is Making Jesus Lord

"Therefore let all the house of Israel know assuredly that God has made this Jesus, whom you crucified, both Lord and Christ.*"* *Now when they heard this, they were cut to the heart, and said to Peter and the rest of the apostles, "Men and brethren, what shall we do?" Then Peter said to them, "Repent, and let every one of you be baptized in the name of Jesus Christ for the remission of sins; and you shall receive the gift of the Holy Spirit."*

ACTS 2:36-38, EMPHASIS ADDED

My prayer is that you would recognize your need to make Jesus not only Savior but also Lord of your life. Making Jesus Lord is an attitude of complete surrender and obedience to Christ. "Why do you call me 'Lord, Lord' and do not do the things which I say?" (Luke 6:46). Making Jesus Lord begins with a prayer of repentance unto God and ends by living out the fruit of repentance.

We cannot truly repent unless we have first been cut to our hearts and convicted of our sins. We must cry out to God in repentance for our selfishness and self-living. We must take necessary action to do what is right. Faith without works is dead. If we want to see revival and reformation in this generation, we cannot settle for half-hearted devotion to Jesus. We are to love God with all our heart, soul, strength and mind (see Matt. 22:37). This is the first and greatest commandment we are to obey. We must be a generation after God's own heart.

We do this by being (1) radically committed to obeying God's Word and making Jesus Lord, and (2) understanding that God enjoys us even in our weakness, like King David (see Acts 13:22). For we are not sinners who struggle to love God, but our primary identity is that we are lovers of God who sometimes struggle with sin. Yet we live a lifestyle of true repentance by being fiercely committed to a hundredfold obedience in God's grace. Revival is nothing more than a total commitment to obey God's commands.

We cannot fulfill the Great Commission unless we first fulfill the Great Commandment. Like King David, we must daily be quick to repent of any and every sin, knowing His mercies are new every morning (see Lam. 3:23; Ps. 51). We are to be dead to self but alive in Christ (see Rom. 6:4-8; Gal. 2:20). The believers who are most dead to self will be those who are most on fire for Christ. History will prove that the heroes of the faith will be those who have no self-will, but only God's will in their lives.

Repentance Prayer Bears Worthy Fruit

Therefore bear fruits worthy of repentance.
MATTHEW 3:8

True repentance bears fruit. When you have truly repented, others around you will see the change and notice the attitude of humility and submission to God's purposes in your words and actions. You will be completely sold out and wholly given to God. There will be no hypocrisy in your faith. You will be the same person on Monday as you are on Sunday. You will do what you say and say what you do. Repentance prayer is not cheap grace. If you have truly repented, you cannot go on sinning and using Jesus' blood as a license to sin (see Rom. 6:1). We must repent of sin and turn from it, period.

Repentance prayer is daily making Jesus Christ Lord of every area in your life. He must be Lord over your personal holiness, your relationships, your family, your finances, your possessions, your future, your ministry, your spirit, soul, body—everything. It is making Jesus master over your time, talent and treasure. You must be held accountable to others in the Body of Christ to walk out this repentance. It requires being transparent inside and out and allowing the Lord to guide and decide your every action and decision. Repentance prayer means making Jesus Lord of all or none at all. *Jesus, You are all I want, You are all I need, You are everything, everything that I am.*

Four Evidences of Repentance Prayer

To bear fruits worthy of repentance (see Matt. 3:7-8) means there is evidence that proves our repentance is genuine and true. What are these evidences?

1. *Conviction.* Unless someone is convicted of sin, they cannot truly repent from sin. May your conscience (see John 8:9), the Word of God (see Titus 1:9) and the Holy Spirit (see John 16:8) convict your heart of the sin in your life.

2. *Contrition.* To have contrition is to have deep, godly sorrow and humility of heart because of the sin you have committed. King David had a broken and contrite heart before God over his sin of adultery. He owned his sin, grieved his sin and thoroughly repented of it (see Ps. 51:17). We must do the same.

3. *Confession.* To confess means to agree with God that your sin is unacceptable. I once heard someone say, "Holding on to un-confessed sins in the soul is like keeping a bullet in the body." We must be held accountable to confess our sins to God (see Ps. 51:4), confess our sins to one another (see Jas. 5:16) and confess our sins publicly (see Acts 19:18-19) according to the degree of confession needed in each situation.

4. *Commitment.* To be committed in the biblical sense is to wholeheartedly obey God's commands. There is no

use in saying we are sorry if we do not actually turn from our wicked ways and do what is right. We walk out our repentance by forsaking sin and, like Zacchaeus, paying restitution and reconciling with those we have wronged (see Matt. 5:23-24). Restitution, reconciliation and walking in truth will demonstrate our repentance with works (see Eph. 4:28-29).

When I lead someone to Christ or even a believer into a true prayer of repentance, I share with them that they can't turn to Christ unless they first understand that Christ has turned to them. We love Him because He first loved us by suffering and dying for our sins on the cross. Here are what I call the four passions of Christ:

1. Jesus suffered because you are His passion (see Rom. 5:8).

2. Jesus suffered because He loves you and has a plan for you (see John 3:16).

3. Jesus suffered, died and rose from the dead to forgive your sins (see Rom. 3:23; 6:23).

4. Jesus suffered to give you eternal life and asks you to give your life completely to Him (see Mark 8:34-35; John 14:6).

When we turn to God in repentance, we surrender our strength, will and ability to turn from sin. We can't do it, but He can. It is not about what we can do for Jesus; it is about what He has done for us. We can't be holy; only He is holy. We can't be perfect, but Jesus became perfection for us. By faith, we put on the cross and receive His righteousness by letting go of our own. When I gave my life to Jesus, I gave Him all my *F*s and He gave me all His

As. The moment we put our faith in Christ and truly repent, the grace of God is given to us at that instant to live a holy life. Pray with me the prayer of repentance below.

Prayer of Repentance

Father, thank You for loving and accepting me as Your child, just as I am. Today I choose to deny myself, take up my cross and make a firm decision to follow You. I know I have hurt You and I confess my sin to You. I confess that I am helpless to defeat the sin in my life and that only You can change me. I repent of my sin and I surrender my strength and will to You. I make a conscious inner decision to turn from my wicked ways and commit my life to follow only Your commands. Help me to turn from my sin, to make restitution and to reconcile with those I have wronged. Jesus, today I not only make You Savior, but I also make You Lord of my life. Jesus, I make You Lord of my body, soul and spirit. Let not my will but Your will be done each day. I will give my life to obey the Great Commandment and fulfill the Great Commission. Jesus, You are my Lord, King, Master, Savior and Friend. Jesus, I thank You that You are with me always. From this day forward, I wholeheartedly follow You. In Jesus' mighty name, Amen.

Notes

1. Bauer, Arndt, Gingrich and Danker, *A Greek-English Lexicon of the New Testament and Other Early Christian Literature* (Chicago: University of Chicago Press, 1979), pp. 511-512.
2. James Strong, *The New Strong's Exhaustive Concordance of the Bible* (Nashville, TN: Thomas Nelson Publishers, 1984), Hebrew #7725.
3. Reverend H. Kong, *Laying Foundations* (Singapore: City Harvest Church, 1998), p. 22.

CHAPTER TWO

HOLY SPIRIT PRAYER

I indeed baptize you with water unto repentance, but He who is coming after me is mightier than I, whose sandals I am not worthy to carry. He will baptize you with the Holy Spirit and fire.
MATTHEW 3:11

The first Christian book I read after I was born again was a book my mother gave me one night while I was sitting in my room, bored—doing nothing, as usual. The book was titled *Power in Praise* by Merlin Carothers. As I read, I became absorbed in testimony after testimony of how God worked miracles in the lives of the author and others around him through the power of praising God in every circumstance. I felt like I was reading straight out of the book of Acts. I couldn't stop reading. What happened next was a supernatural experience that opened the door to my lifelong encounters with the person, power and presence of the Holy Spirit.

As I read the third chapter, "Power Unlimited," something in my heart began to get excited with expectation. The author wrote about the baptism of the Holy Spirit and how God has unlimited power for us to live a victorious Christian life. He wrote:

The very first gift God wants His new children to ask for is the baptism in the Holy Spirit. That's right. The baptism in the Holy Spirit is provided as a "first feeding" for new-born believers. They need it to grow. The Holy Spirit comes to dwell in the new believer the moment He accepts Jesus Christ as His Savior. He is born of the Spirit. But Jesus also told His disciples that they would have to wait until they were baptized with the Holy Spirit before they could be His witnesses and spread the Good News with power and authority. Acts 1:5,8.[1]

While reading this, I was reminded that the disciples waited in Jerusalem, just as Jesus had told them, and that on the day of Pentecost all the believers were filled with the Holy Spirit and began to speak with other tongues (see Acts 2:2-4). But I still didn't understand what the author was trying to explain.

You see, although I grew up in church, I had never heard any teaching on the baptism of the Holy Spirit. This was all new to me. But something inside of me wanted this power of God that the author was talking about. He went on to share Scriptures supporting the biblical understanding of the baptism in the Holy Spirit, while also sharing stories of how he and others had been radically changed by praying for the fullness of the Holy Spirit in their lives.

I now understand that though we initially receive the Holy Spirit when we put our faith in Christ (see John 3:3,5-8; Rom. 8:9; 1 Cor. 12:13; Gal. 3:26; 4:6; Eph. 1:13-14; Titus 3:5), like the believers in Acts, we must also ask the Lord to fill and empower us with His Spirit repeatedly after conversion (see Eph. 5:18; after initially being filled and baptized in the Spirit in Acts 2, the believers in the Early Church were also filled and empowered by the Spirit on numerous other occasions, such as in Acts 4:8,31; 7:55; 13:9,52).

Near the end of the chapter, Merlin Carothers described one way to pray to be baptized or filled with the Holy Spirit. I began to understand that we were to pray for Jesus to fill us with the Spirit and receive it by faith and not feeling. We were to thank Him for it, because being filled with the Spirit is a free gift and it isn't something we can earn. Furthermore, Carothers explained that throughout the book of Acts one evidence that someone was baptized or filled with the Holy Spirit (though there are clearly other evidences as well) was that they started "speaking in tongues." This was just one initial sign that someone had been filled or baptized with the Spirit, but the book of Acts shows that there were also other evidences, such as in Acts 2:4; 8:14-25; 9:17-20; 10:44-48; 19:1-7.

I do not mean to say here that in order to be filled with the Holy Spirit a person must speak in tongues. I believe that when a believer is filled with the Holy Spirit there is an evidence of a transformed life—there are many evidences in the book of Acts, and the gift of tongues is only one evidence of many gifts given by the Holy Spirit. I also know many great men and women of God who do not have the gift of tongues but who are filled with the Holy Spirit and whose lives are a powerful testimony to Christ.

Finally, Carothers shared that if you pray for Jesus to fill you with the Holy Spirit and start to see or sense words and sounds forming in your mind, then you should just open your mouth and speak them out by faith. If you don't feel anything at all, don't worry; just thank Jesus by faith that you have been filled and baptized with the Holy Spirit and continually, daily, seek to be filled with the Holy Spirit. As the apostle Paul commands us in Ephesians 5:18, "Be filled with the Spirit."

As I read the accounts in the book of Acts of different disciples being filled with the Holy Spirit and after seeing the power of God fill them and transform them, I was willing to do whatever it took to have what they had. Before reading Carothers's book, I had never even heard of the gift of speaking in tongues. I wasn't sure what Carothers was talking about, but I was hungry for more of God. I was hungry for the power of God.

After reading the chapter I decided to step out in faith and pray for Jesus to fill me with the Holy Spirit. I was hungry to be filled with more of the Holy Spirit's manifest presence.[2] I desired more. I had nothing to lose. I wasn't sure what to expect, but alone in my room, I knelt next to my bed and prayed, "Jesus, I am hungry for more of Your power in my life. I need You to transform me. I want all that You have for me, so I surrender myself to You and ask You, Jesus, to fill me with the Holy Spirit and fill me to overflowing right now. I receive this by faith and thank You, Jesus, for filling me with the Holy Spirit. Amen."

All of a sudden my room began to shake! . . . Just kidding; nothing happened at all. I didn't feel anything; I didn't see anything. I simply prayed the prayer and received the filling and baptism of the Holy Spirit by faith. Honestly, I thought to myself, *This prayer for the baptism of the Holy Spirit doesn't really work; I don't feel different at all,* and I was a bit discouraged. After praying the prayer, I got ready for bed. I brushed my teeth, washed my face as I normally would, and went back to my room. Before I would go to sleep, I was in the habit of saying a bedtime prayer.

As I knelt down beside my bed to pray, something interesting started happening. I started praying, "Jesus, thank You for this day. Thank You for my family. Please bless my schoolwork, and please *bleh . . . bleh . . . bleh.*"

The more I tried to pray, the more I couldn't get the proper words out of my mouth. Suddenly, my body started to feel burning hot, my heart began to beat faster and it felt like a surge of warm fire began to fill my body. Inside my belly I felt an overwhelming presence that wanted to burst out of my body. It felt like an oasis or a fountain of water springing up from within me. It's hard to explain the feeling and experience. Trust me, at that moment even I had no idea what was going on. All I knew was that it was God. I had only experienced the presence of God a few other times, but I had come to recognize the supernatural feeling that came along with it. The next thing I knew, I was praying out loud—almost screaming out loud—with gibberish coming out of my mouth. For the next hour or so I was caught up in a vision while speaking in some language I had never learned.

The vision I saw was simple but profoundly powerful. In this vision I saw a vast black space, and in the middle was Jesus hanging on the cross. He was suffering, barely able to breathe, but the cross itself was shining increasingly brighter and brighter. The more I looked at it, the brighter it became until I could no longer control my emotions. I began to break down and cry, weeping like a little baby. I knew at that moment—not in my mind, but in my spirit—how much, just how much Jesus loved me. It felt like I was right there with Him 2,000 years ago as He hung on the cross for my sin. Tears began to roll down my face like running water. At that moment I felt the love of God hold me and pour over me with rivers of liquid love. The love of God and the presence of Jesus were so real, so tangible and so powerful; I could only attribute it to being a work of the Holy Spirit. I knew I was filled and baptized with the Holy Spirit and power.

This encounter transformed my life forever. God had completely consumed me with His Holy Spirit and I would live to be on holy fire for Him. I would live to know and make known the person, power and presence of the Holy Spirit.

After being filled with the Holy Spirit, there was a new boldness in my spirit. I began to courageously share my testimony daily with my lost friends and I started evangelistic Bible studies on my campus. That school year, I saw nearly 100 of my lost friends commit their lives to Christ. It was a supernatural work. It was a work of revival and completely a work of the Holy Spirit.

The Holy Spirit and Prayer

It is only through prayer that we are filled with the Holy Spirit and can intimately know Him. Who is the Holy Spirit? The Holy Spirit is our best friend. The Holy Spirit is our Counselor (see John 14:16). The Holy Spirit is our Helper (see John 14:26). The Holy Spirit is the Spirit of truth (see John 14:17). The Holy Spirit is the Spirit of peace, righteousness and joy (see Rom. 14:17). The Holy Spirit is the person, power and presence of God. The Holy Spirit is the most beautiful person in the world. If I had to choose between spending five minutes in the presence of the Holy Spirit, seeing revival or seeing the dead raised, I would choose spending five minutes with the Holy Spirit. If I do not have intimacy with the Holy Spirit, I have nothing. He is the most precious person in my life and I pray that He will be that precious to you.

We are in the age of the Holy Spirit. Jesus told the disciples it was imperative for Him to leave in order for the Holy Spirit to come (see John 16:7-8). The Holy Spirit would come to convict the world of righteousness, sin and judgment. The Holy Spirit would also come to fill every believer with the Spirit of Christ so that the work of Jesus would be multiplied in power all over the earth.

Most assuredly, I say to you, he who believes in Me, the works that I do he will do also; and greater works than these he will do, because I go to My Father . . . And I will pray the Father, and He will give you another Helper, that He may abide with you forever—the Spirit of Truth, whom the world cannot receive, because it neither sees Him nor knows Him; but you know Him, for He dwells with you and will be in you (John 14:12-14,16-17).

The desire of Jesus is that we would pray—just as He prays for us—to be filled and to have an intimate friendship with the Holy Spirit. Why is prayer essential? Because prayer is the path that leads you to encounter the person, power and presence of the Holy Spirit.

Prayer Encounters the Person of the Holy Spirit

Please listen: The Holy Spirit is not a thing; He is a person. He is not only a force and not only a power, but He is also a person with a personality. He has a mind (see Rom. 8:27), He has a will (see 1 Cor. 12:11) and He has emotions. He can be grieved (see Eph. 4:30) and He can be made happy. He can be lied to (see Acts 5:3). He can be blasphemed (see Matt. 12:31-32). The Holy Spirit brings the presence of Jesus (see John 14:16-23). The Holy Spirit glorifies Jesus (see John 16:14). He is the Spirit of Christ (see Rom. 8:9). He is the Spirit of Grace, Life, Holiness and Adoption (see Rom. 8:15). Yes, He is the Holy Spirit. He is my friend.

If we want to know the Holy Spirit intimately as our friend, we must learn to pray. Prayer opens the door for the Holy Spirit to come into our lives. Through prayer we get to know the mind, heart and emotions of the Holy Spirit (see Rom. 8:26). It is also through prayer that we talk with the Holy Spirit, listen to the Holy Spirit and have relationship with the Holy Spirit. Prayer, then, is how we communicate and fellowship with the Holy Spirit (see 2 Cor. 13:14). When we pray, we acknowledge the Holy Spirit's person-hood in our lives. We can do nothing apart from the Holy Spirit and we can partner with Him only through prayer.

When I wake up every morning, the first thing I say is, "Good morning, Holy Spirit, what shall we do today?" After I was first filled with the Holy Spirit, His presence was so prominent in my daily life that I could not help but talk to Him all the time. I realized after that encounter that He was truly with me at all times (see Matt. 28:20). So throughout the day I would talk to the Holy Spirit as I would talk to my best friend. In every conversation, at every meeting, in the car, walking to class, in the classroom, washing dishes, talking with friends, wherever I went, the Holy Spirit went with me and He still does today. I would speak to the Holy Spirit out loud at times; others times I would speak to Him in my heart. Sometimes I would not speak, but my heart would be listening and I would hear Him speak to me. Many times I would just wait in silence and let my heart be present to His heart in love. These were the sweetest of moments.

Today, I still speak continuously with the Holy Spirit. Holy Spirit prayer is about a constant and continuous relationship with Him. Invite the Holy Spirit to be a part of everything you do, all throughout the day, every waking moment, because He is your best friend, and best friends do everything together. Honor Him and count it a privilege that the Holy Spirit, the very Spirit of Christ, the very person of God, wants to be with you and have friendship with you. Simply say out loud right now, "Holy Spirit, I love You and I want to know You more!"

Prayer Encounters the Power of the Holy Spirit

Through prayer we also encounter the *power* of the Holy Spirit. The Holy Spirit is a person, but He is also the power of God. Before Jesus ascended into heaven, He told the 120 disciples:

> For John truly baptized with water, but you shall be baptized with the Holy Spirit not many days from now . . . But you shall receive *power* when the Holy Spirit has come upon you; and you shall be witnesses to Me in Jerusalem, and in all Judea and Samaria, and to the end of the earth (Acts 1:5,8, emphasis added).

This power that the Holy Spirit desires to fill us with is a supernatural miracle-working power. It is the same power that anointed Christ to heal the sick, cast out demons, raise the dead and preach the gospel (see Luke 4:14,18). It is the power with which Jesus said we would do even greater works than He did (see John 14:12). The early disciples were so filled with the power of the Holy Spirit that even the shadow of the apostle Peter would heal the sick as he passed by them (see Acts 5:15). There was so much Holy Spirit power in the ministry of the apostle Paul that hand-kerchiefs he touched that were passed on to the sick would instantly heal them (see Acts 19:12). Both Peter and Paul were men of constant prayer who knew the Holy Spirit intimately.

Jesus' desire is that we would also be filled with the power of the Holy Spirit to be His witnesses to the ends of the earth in power and authority. Through a lifestyle of prayer, we encounter the power of the Holy Spirit daily. The more we pray, the more we know His unlimited power and the glory He desires to release through us. As we come to be present to the Holy Spirit's power in prayer, He releases His power through us. We become conduits, empty vessels, for the Holy Spirit to fill with overflowing power to touch others (see Phil. 2:5,7 and 2 Cor. 4:7). How is this Holy Spirit power demonstrated?

The power of the Holy Spirit is manifested through the gifts of the Holy Spirit (see Rom. 12:6; 1 Cor. 12:7). It is only through prayer and godly character that we can exercise our spiritual gifts. I always tell the students I minister to the comment Peter Parker's uncle shared with him in the movie *Spiderman*: "With great power comes great responsibility!" The gifts will take us there, but it is character that will keep us there.

In order to exercise the gifts of the Holy Spirit, we must simul-taneously produce the fruit of the Holy Spirit (see Gal. 5:22-23) by living a life of Christlikeness. At the same time, we are not to be ignorant of the spiritual gifts given to us by the Holy Spirit, for by exercising them we glorify God and strengthen the Church. If we don't exercise our spiritual gifts, we are not appreciating the gift of the Holy Spirit that has been given to us.

But the manifestation of the Spirit is given to each one for the profit of all: for to one is given the word of wisdom through the Spirit, to another the word of knowledge through the same Spirit, to another faith by the same Spirit, to another gifts of healings by the same Spirit, to another the working of miracles, to another prophecy, to another discerning of spirits, to another different kinds of tongues, to another the interpretation of tongues. But one and the same Spirit works all these things, distributing to each one individually as He wills (1 Cor. 12:7-11).

Paul lists a multitude of gifts of the Spirit, but how do we know which ones have been given to us? We must pray to the Holy Spirit and ask. We do not have because we do not ask the Holy Spirit (see Jas. 4:2).

A short while after I was first filled with the Holy Spirit, I came across 1 Corinthians 14:1: "Pursue love, and desire spiritual gifts." I was not familiar with the gifts of the Holy Spirit, but I knew after reading this verse that I was to chase after two things: love and spiritual gifts. From that point on, I daily sought the person of the Holy Spirit, seeking to know Him more and to know His love and the truth of His love as found in the Scriptures (see 1 Cor. 13). I learned that love is the litmus test. Without love and compassion for people, the gifts of the Holy Spirit are good for nothing (see 1 Cor. 13:1-3).

At the same time, I understood by studying the Scriptures that we are to pursue both love and spiritual gifts with eagerness, with love being the priority, or most excellent way. As for spiritual gifts, Paul uses the Greek present active imperative form (command form) when he says to "eagerly desire" spiritual gifts (1 Cor. 14:1). The word in Greek is *zeloo,* meaning, "to burn with desire, to pursue ardently, to desire eagerly or intensely."[3] Some people have told me, "You are to seek the Giver and not the gifts," but I believe that we are to seek both, as Paul exhorted the Church to do.

Even as a new believer, I desired to pursue the spiritual gifts, but I didn't know where to start. I thought, *If I am to desire spiritual gifts, I should probably ask the Holy Spirit for them.* So I took a piece of paper and wrote down the entire list of spiritual gifts found in 1 Corinthians 12. Then I taped the list to the lampstand next to my bed. Every morning when I woke up, I would pray for the Holy Spirit to give me each of the spiritual gifts on that list, because I didn't know which ones He wanted to give me and I didn't want to miss out on any spiritual gift that was available to me. Slowly but surely, through consistent prayer, the Holy Spirit opened doors for the spiritual gifts to operate in my life.

As I look back now, I can honestly say that because of consistent prayer, pursuing love *and* desiring the Holy Spirit gifts, I have operated in all nine gifts that are manifestations of the Holy Spirit listed in 1 Corinthians 12:7-11. The Holy Spirit has used the gifts operating in my life to strengthen, encourage and bless many students and many people in different nations. I say this not to boast but to understand what happens when we pray in partnership with the Holy Spirit, and to realize what can happen when we pursue the unlimited power that is available through prayer in the Holy Spirit.

The apostle Paul taught Timothy that meditating in prayer would help develop the gifts of the Holy Spirit in him:

> Let no one despise your youth, but be an example to the believers in word, in conduct, in love, in spirit, in faith, in purity . . . Do not neglect the gift that is in you, which was given to you by prophecy with the laying on of the hands of the eldership. *Meditate* on these things; give yourself entirely to them, that your progress may be evident to all (1 Tim. 4:12,14-15, emphasis added).

No matter how young you are, like Timothy, be an example in your generation by *pursuing* love, faith and purity, and by developing the gifts of the Holy Spirit in your life through the practice of prayer.

Prayer Encounters the Presence of the Holy Spirit

There is one thing I love more than anything else and that is the *presence of the Holy Spirit.* Throughout the years, I have experienced how prayer brings me closer to the presence of the Holy Spirit. This presence is real. It is tangible. It can be felt and experienced every day, every moment of your life. The presence of the Holy Spirit is the manifest glory of God. Do you believe you can feel the presence of the Holy Spirit with you always? I can almost sense His very intimate presence with me at all times.

There are seasons in life when you may feel that His presence is not with you, but no matter what, we need to cling to the promise that nothing shall be able to separate us from the love of God (see Rom. 8:39) and the promise that the Holy Spirit dwells in us always (see Rom. 8:11). Spending time in prayer, and simply loving and letting the Holy Spirit "love on you," is the most refreshing and satisfying experience one could ever have. I love to spend my waking moments simply lingering and soaking in the presence and love of the Holy Spirit, whether it is for five minutes or five hours. It is my daily joy to fellowship and have communion with the Holy Spirit.

May we pray as the apostle Paul, "The grace of the Lord Jesus Christ, and the love of God, and the 'fellowship of the Holy Spirit' be with you all" (2 Cor. 13:14, *NIV*). This is what we were created for—to dwell in the very presence of God. When you are caught up in the presence of the Holy Spirit, nothing else matters. Time stops, and your heart is filled with joy, just as it says in Acts: "You will make me full of joy in your presence" (2:28).

The presence of the Holy Spirit comes to us in three ways:

1. The Holy Spirit is in us (see John 14:17).
2. The Holy Spirit is upon us (see Isa. 61:1; Acts 1:8).
3. The Holy Spirit is with us (see Matt. 28:20).

The Holy Spirit is in us so that we may know the person of the Holy Spirit. The Holy Spirit is upon us so that we may operate in the power of the Holy Spirit to preach the gospel boldly with signs, wonders and miracles. The Holy Spirit is with us so that we may spend time in the presence of the Holy Spirit to be refreshed, renewed and restored daily. My spiritual big brother Pastor Philip

Mantofa in Indonesia told me that his definition for ministry is simply this: *"Me and the Holy Spirit."* May we each know the Person and the work of the Holy Spirit in this intimate and powerful way.

Receiving the Filling of the Holy Spirit

In summary, the Holy Spirit first enters us when we are born again in Christ (see John 3:3,5-8; Rom. 8:9; 1 Cor. 12:13; Gal. 3:26; 4:6; Eph. 1:13-14; Titus 3:5). Simultaneous with this, or after this, we are to come into the fullness of the Holy Spirit by asking Jesus to fill and baptize us with the Holy Spirit (see Acts 9:17); and we are to ask the Holy Spirit to fill us every day thereafter (see Acts 4:8,31; 7:55; 13:9,52; Eph. 5:18). Once we receive this free gift of blessing, we are able to walk intimately with the person, power and presence of the Holy Spirit.

If you have put your faith in Christ and do not know if you have been filled with or baptized by the Holy Spirit, it is imperative that you pray for His filling immediately. When Scripture talks about being baptized with the Holy Spirit, it means being filled, saturated or immersed with the person, power and presence of the Holy Spirit. We must also understand that Jesus is the one who sends and baptizes us with the Holy Spirit (see John 1:33). The word "baptize"—in Greek, *baptizo*—is the word used to describe being "waterlogged."[4] So when we ask Jesus to baptize us in the Holy Spirit, we are surrendering ourselves to be filled, saturated, immersed—waterlogged—with His Holy Spirit. It is crucial to be filled with the power of the Holy Spirit so that His very presence lives within us and empowers us to know Him intimately and to be powerful witnesses of the gospel.

Why Be Filled with the Holy Spirit?

There are many reasons why we are to be filled or immersed with the Holy Spirit. The following are biblical reasons to do so:

1. It is a command (see Eph. 5:18).
2. It is needed power (see Acts 1:8).

3. It is a promise (see Acts 2:38-39).
4. It is biblical (see Acts 2:4; 8:14-25; 9:17-20; 10:44-48; 19:1-7).
5. It is for spiritual gifting (see 1 Cor. 12:7-11).

What are the benefits of being filled with the Holy Spirit?

- A life encountered—In every biblical incident of the Holy Spirit filling believers, there was a strong encounter and breaking in of God's powerful and intimate presence.
- A life transformed—The disciples who were filled with the Holy Spirit in the New Testament had radically transformed lives.
- A life empowered—It was after being filled with the Holy Spirit that the New Testament disciples had a "bold" gospel witness.

How do we receive the filling or baptism of the Holy Spirit?

- We must be born again (see Rom. 8:9).
- We must ask (see Luke 11:8).
- We must surrender (see Rom. 12:1).
- We must be willing to obey the Holy Spirit (see Acts 5:32).
- We must believe (see Gal. 3:2).
- We must exercise what God has given us (see Acts 2:4).

Holy Spirit Prayer

Dear Jesus, I thank You that You send the Holy Spirit and that You are the one who baptizes me and fills me with the Holy Spirit. Right now, I surrender my body as a living sacrifice to You and Your purposes. I am willing and desirous to obey the Holy Spirit and I ask You, Jesus, to baptize and fill me with the Holy Spirit in power in this very moment. I receive the filling and baptism of the Holy Spirit by faith and not by my feelings. I praise You and thank You, Jesus, that You have filled me with Your Holy Spirit right now. I also ask that You give me every spiritual gift You have in store

for me, that I may pursue a life of love and that I may desire the spiritual gifts to be used for Your glory. Holy Spirit, please teach me and guide me to pray in the Holy Spirit daily. Release this gift and all Your gifts in me now, I pray. I commit to pray in partnership with the Holy Spirit at all times in order that I may know the person, power and presence of the Holy Spirit more and more, and that through Him I may know Jesus more and more in my life. Come, Holy Spirit, fill me to overflowing!
In Jesus' mighty name,
Amen.

Notes

1. Merlin R. Carothers, *Power in Praise* (Escondido, CA: Merlin R. Carothers, 1972), n.p.
2. That the Holy Spirit can be more manifestly present or present in greater measure in a person's life is clearly a biblical concept, according to 2 Kings 2:9, where Elisha asks for a double portion of the Holy Spirit's anointing on Elijah and later receives it from God.
3. James Strong, *The New Strong's Exhaustive Concordance* (Nashville, TN: Thomas Nelson, 1984), Greek #2206; Bauer, Arndt, Gingrich and Danker, *A Greek-English Lexicon of the New Testament and Other Early Christian Literature* (Chicago: University of Chicago Press, 1979), p. 338.
4. Compare the term "waterlogged" to the meaning of "drench" in Bauer, Arndt, Gingrich and Danker, *A Greek-English Lexicon of the New Testament and Other Early Christian Literature*, p. 131, column b.

CHAPTER THREE

WAITING PRAYER

But those who wait on the Lord shall renew their strength;
they shall mount up with wings like eagles, they shall run and
not be weary, they shall walk and not faint.
ISAIAH 40:31

"God, I don't care what it takes; I want to be on fire for You 24/7!" This was my daily prayer as a freshman in college. Be careful what you pray. After I received the baptism of the Holy Spirit, the Spirit of God birthed inside me a supernatural hunger to know Him better. The more I read about the life of the apostle Paul, the more I thought about how awesome it would be to be as intimate with the Holy Spirit as Paul was. Paul had only one desire in life:

That I may *know* Him and the power of His resurrection, and the fellowship of His sufferings, being conformed to His death, if, by any means, I may attain to the resurrection from the dead (Phil. 3:10-11, emphasis added).

The word "know" in the Greek is *ginosko,* which means to "intimately experience."[1] It wasn't enough for me to be filled with the fullness of the Holy Spirit once; I wanted to intimately know the Holy Spirit on a daily basis, just as the apostle Paul did. I kept praying, "God, make me on fire for You 24/7!" My prayers were answered.

One day after school, I received a package of cassette tapes from my mother. She told me, "Jaeson, you must listen to these tapes. They are the power of God!"

I thought to myself, *Yeah, right. What are these tapes?* The tape album was called *Waiting upon the Lord* and it was a seven-tape teaching series by my mother's senior pastor on how to wait upon the presence of God in solitude and silence. I didn't want to listen to the tapes, but my mom kept bugging me to listen to them, so I gave in.

One afternoon I popped the first teaching tape into my stereo system. There was a Chinese man, speaking English with a Chinese accent, interpreting the pastor's teaching. He said, "Waiting upon the Lord, are you hungry for more of God? Do you want to be on fire for God 24/7? Then you must learn to wait upon the Lord." I couldn't believe my ears! This was the answer to my prayers! However, the more I listened, the more I couldn't stand the teaching. The guy kept saying the same thing over and over again. Basically, the teaching tapes kept repeating the need to wait on God by being still, silent and by daily gazing at God's beauty for long periods of time. By the second tape, I got the picture and decided to go for it.

For two weeks straight I locked myself in my room, knelt on the floor and waited on God. I waited and waited and waited, and nothing happened. For at least two hours daily I waited, with no results. Sometimes while waiting I fell asleep, felt stupid or got totally distracted. But I remembered Isaiah 40:31 and held on to the promise: "But those who wait on the Lord *shall* renew their strength" (emphasis added). I wouldn't give up. I kept pressing in and, finally, the presence of God broke in.

After two weeks of daily waiting upon the Lord, I began to sense the presence of the Holy Spirit more strongly in and around me. It would usually take at least one or two hours of quieting my soul from any distractions before I began to experience the tangible presence of the Holy Spirit. The presence of the Holy Spirit would come so strongly in my room that I could not contain it. The presence and love of God were so immense that I would begin to weep. My heart would begin to flutter, my body would at times shake uncontrollably and I would begin to sing out loud in tongues. During those moments, the Holy Spirit would shine His judgment light upon me. I felt as if I was completely naked before Him. As I knelt before the light of the Holy Spirit, all my sin and pride was exposed, but then His loving presence would flood over me and wash my sins away. My spirit-man was being transformed in the fire of God's presence. There was an unspoken cry deep in my spirit to know the Holy Spirit more intimately and I became addicted to the presence of God.

For weeks on end I waited on the presence of the Holy Spirit. Every day, after quieting and silencing my mind, will and emotions from inner distractions, the presence of the Holy Spirit would fill my being again and again. The experience was powerful and transforming, but I knew something was still missing.

One day, while waiting on God, I heard the Holy Spirit speak to me: "Jaeson, you must know My Word or you will not recognize My voice, for My voice will always confirm My written Word." I responded to the Holy Spirit in prayer: "Holy Spirit, You know I love Your presence, but I have a hard time reading Your Word. I don't understand it as I should; but if You open a door, I will obey." Then a random idea came into my mind and I brought it to the Holy Spirit in prayer. I told the Holy Spirit I would commit to reading the entire Bible if He would open a door for me to find an empty house in the mountains during the winter break. If so, I would go there and take the whole week to read the Bible from beginning to end. A week later, the Holy Spirit answered my prayer.

I was at church that Sunday when an elder walked up to me and said, "Jaeson, I felt led to give you these keys while I was praying for you this week." Not knowing what the keys were for, I asked him why he was giving them to me. He told me, "I don't know why, but while I was praying for you, I felt the Holy Spirit tell me that you needed to spend some time alone in solitude, praying and reading the Word of God. These keys are to an empty two-story house I have for sale in the Santa Cruz Mountains. You can stay there for a whole week if you want to." I was stunned but not stunned. I knew that the Holy Spirit was opening a door for me to obey His command.

But the anointing which you have received from Him abides in you, and you do not need that anyone teach you;

but as the same anointing teaches you concerning all
things, and is true, and is not a lie, and just as it has taught
you, you will abide in Him (1 John 2:27).

I knew the Holy Spirit wanted to teach me that my waiting on
God was not complete without having my foundation built upon
the Word. A few weeks later, I packed up a few gallons of water and
some bread, and headed for the Santa Cruz Mountains. What happened in that mountain house was supernatural.

Through the grace and power of the Holy Spirit, I finished
reading the Bible from Genesis to Revelation in four and a half
days. For the last three days I didn't have any desire to eat or even
drink water; in fact, I didn't eat or drink at all. My food was the
very Spirit and the Word of God.

But the hour is coming, and now is, when the true worshipers will worship the Father in spirit and truth; for the
Father is seeking such to worship Him. God is Spirit, and
those who worship Him must worship in spirit and truth
(John 4:23-24).

I am not allowed to fully explain what happened on that
mountain. However, daily, as I waited on the presence of the Holy
Spirit and read the Scriptures, God's power invaded my body, soul
and spirit to the point where I thought I was going to explode. At
times, after reading the Word for hours on end, the Spirit of God
would strike me to the ground for hours and my body would feel
like it was being filled with supernatural fire and electricity. My
hands felt like they were struck with lightning, but I realized it was
the very presence of God. This same experience would happen
each day as I waited on God and read the Bible. It was as if I had
met God face to face. All I can say is this: God is real.

On that mountain, I learned a powerful spiritual secret. I
learned to wait on the Holy Spirit and to meditate upon the Word
of God together with Him. Daily, as I read through the Holy
Scriptures, the very words in my Bible came alive out of the pages

and were emblazoned upon my heart with fire. The Word of God became a love letter and every word became precious. But this would not have been possible unless I had learned to wait on God's presence. It was by waiting on God that my spirit was sensitized and the Holy Spirit was able to teach me God's Word in a new and greater dimension.

> But the natural man does not receive the things of the Spirit of God, for they are foolishness to him; nor can he know them, because they are spiritually discerned (1 Cor. 2:14).

After this mountain encounter with God, my spirit was completely set ablaze. I knew that for the rest of my life I would give myself to a life of waiting on God, waiting on the presence of the Holy Spirit. I would dedicate my life to waiting prayer, because waiting prayer is the fire that sets ablaze the Word of God in my life. The Holy Spirit had answered my prayer to be on fire for Him 24 hours a day, 7 days a week, 365 days a year—but first, I had to learn to wait upon Him.

What Is Waiting Prayer?

My soul waits for the Lord more than those who watch for the morning.

PSALM 130:6

Waiting prayer, or waiting on the Lord, is the silent surrendering of the soul to God. It is wordless worship. It is seeking God not from without but from within. It is to seek God in your heart. By frequently waiting silently in the presence of the Holy Spirit, you become more and more sensitive to His manifest presence in your life. After all is said and done, you wait on God because it is what your spirit hungers and longs for most. It longs for intimacy with Christ. Waiting prayer is what you do when you have prayed all your prayers and you can't pray anymore. Waiting prayer is what you do after you have read the Word over and over and want to meet with the Author of the Word. Waiting prayer is what you do after you sing a praise song to God in the privacy of your room—it's when, after singing your heart out, you can sing no more. It is then, when you can do no more, that you sit silently in the presence of the Holy Spirit and let Him love on you. This is when you have entered into waiting prayer.

Ultimately, waiting prayer is setting apart regular time, specifically and exclusively, to be with our Lord. We cannot wait on the Lord without practicing the spiritual disciplines of silence and solitude with God. Thus, in order to wait on the Lord, you must be alone. Waiting upon the Lord is practicing intimacy with God, because the ultimate goal of prayer is not to ask; the ultimate goal of prayer is a relationship. Waiting on the Lord is being still in order to know God's presence. It is love on fire, combined with intimate devotion. It renews our strength like the eagles (see Isa. 40:31), because it is through waiting that our spirit becomes one with the Holy Spirit. Remember, we are not waiting for God. Rather, He is waiting for us to be present to His presence.

Waiting upon the Lord has been the secret to my spiritual life. It is what keeps my heart burning with passion for Jesus 24/7. But how do we practice waiting prayer? There are three key Hebrew words that are used for "waiting" upon the Lord. Each of these words carries practical insight on how to spend time waiting in God's presence.

Waiting Prayer Is Silent Trust in God

The first key Hebrew word for "waiting" is *damam*, which means "to become silent and still"[2] and which is used as in "silently waiting with a quiet trust or of quieting oneself, resting, being silent or being still."[3] The thought conveyed by the word is a strong, calm, quiet trust in the Lord. King David wrote, "Truly my soul silently waits for God; from Him comes my salvation. He only is my rock and my salvation; He is my defense; I shall not be greatly moved" (Ps. 62:1-2).

In order to wait upon the Lord, we must be silent, we must be still and we must trust God. Without stillness we cannot know God. We are exhorted in Psalm 46:10, "Be still, and know that I am

God." The word "to know" in Hebrew is *yada;* it means "to know intimately"[4] or as a close friend.[5] The Hebrew word in Psalm 46:10 meaning "be still" also means "to cease, refrain, relax, let go."[6] We are to cease from striving, cease from activity, cease from our worldly desires and cease from distractions.

In practical terms, find a place of solitude each day and take at least 10 minutes to be silent in God's presence. From there, let your time spent in silent waiting grow.

Waiting Prayer Is Desiring God

The second key Hebrew word for "waiting" is *chakah;* it means to "adhere for" or "long for."[7] This word is used in Psalm 33:20: "Our soul waits for the Lord; He is our help and shield." And, "I will wait on the LORD . . . I will hope in Him" (Isa. 8:17). *Chakah* expresses a burning desire, a longing for something you want desperately. This is what King David felt when he said, "My soul thirsts for God, for the living God. When shall I come and appear before God?" (Ps. 42:2). David was doing what the word *chakah* denotes—longing for God's presence. How thirsty are you for God's presence?

Waiting prayer desires God as your sole satisfaction. You have tasted the presence of the Holy Spirit, and you are addicted. There is nothing better in life and it is the one thing you desire: "One thing I have desired of the LORD, that will I seek; that I may dwell in the house of the LORD all the days of my life" (Ps. 27:4). *God, make me a man after Your own heart, one who longs day and night for Your intimate presence!*

Waiting Prayer Is Union with God

The third key Hebrew word for "waiting" is *qavah*. It means to "wait, look eagerly for,"[8] and it is used for waiting with eager expectation, to look and to patiently tarry.[9] The root meaning of the word may have been "to bind something together by twisting or braiding."[10] The main usages of the word *qavah* involve the idea of "eager expectation and oneness; a joining, a braiding together."[11] "Wait on the LORD; be of good courage, and He shall strengthen your heart; Wait, I say, on the LORD!" (Ps. 27:14).

Waiting on the Lord brings us into union with God. We spend time waiting in God's presence so that we can become one with His Spirit. Whenever I wait on God, I always pray, "Holy Spirit, shine Your judgment light on me." As I wait in silence, the Holy Spirit reveals my sins to me so that His loving presence can wash them away. Waiting on God is the practice of saying no to the flesh and yes to the Spirit. The fire of His presence burns away all our impurities for one purpose: to leave us fit for divine union. Study the lives of saints like Madame Jeanne Guyon, St. John of the Cross, Teresa of Avila and Brother Lawrence and you will understand what it means to be one with God's Spirit. Ultimately, we wait on God to become transformed into His image from glory to glory (see 2 Cor. 3:17-18).

Waiting Prayer Made Practical

In his book *Intercessory Prayer*, Dutch Sheets sums up the uses of the three Hebrew words for "waiting" as "silently waiting with a strong, calm trust, longing for His presence and eagerly expecting Him—for you know He'll show up—anticipating and then experiencing the oneness that results as your hearts become entwined."[12] Please take heart: Waiting prayer will not always be a mystical spiritual encounter. You will have times in which you wait on God and feel nothing. But it's not about feeling; it's about faith. Remember, waiting on God is never time wasted. It is always time gained, for He rewards those who diligently seek Him (see Heb. 11:6). The Holy Spirit spoke to me in prayer saying, "Jaeson, if you will teach this generation to wait upon the Lord, the enemy will not be able to touch them—they will be invincible."

Now, how do you practice waiting prayer?

• Spend time in praise, prayer and reading the Word daily. After this time, bring your mind and heart into complete silence to the world, and welcome the presence of the Holy Spirit. (Start with at least 10 minutes; aim for 1 hour.)

- Come into God's presence with no agenda but to love God and let Him love you. Your identity is not found in your doing but in your being with God. It is not about feeling; it is about coming to God in faith (see Heb. 11:6).

- Focus your thoughts on the love of the Father, the Son and the Holy Spirit.

- If your mind wanders, whisper a prayer like, "I love You, Holy Spirit," or "I long for You, Jesus" to re-center your mind on His presence.

- Listen and be open to the voice of the Holy Spirit. Write down what He says to you (see Hab. 2:2) and keep a prayer journal.

- Close your time with a prayer of thanksgiving.

Notes

1. Bauer, Arndt, Gingrich and Danker, *A Greek-English Lexicon of the New Testament and Other Early Christian Literature* (Chicago: University of Chicago Press, 1979), p. 161, no. 5.
2. Francis Brown, S. R. Driver and C. A. Briggs, eds., *A Hebrew and English Lexicon of the Old Testament* (Oxford: The Clarendon Press, 1951), p. 198.
3. James Strong, *The New Strong's Exhaustive Concordance* (Nashville, TN: Thomas Nelson, 1984), Hebrew # 1826.
4. Brown, Driver and Briggs, eds., *A Hebrew and English Lexicon of the Old Testament*, p. 394.
5. Strong, *The New Strong's Exhaustive Concordance,* Hebrew #3045.
6. Brown, Driver and Briggs, eds., *A Hebrew and English Lexicon of the Old Testament*, pp. 951-952.
7. Ibid., p. 314.
8. Ibid., p. 875.
9. Strong, *The New Strong's Exhaustive Concordance,* Hebrew #6960.
10. Ibid.; Brown, Driver and Briggs, eds., *A Hebrew and English Lexicon of the Old Testament,* p. 875, which mentions cognate words in other Semitic languages meaning "cord" or "thread."
11. Dutch Sheets, *Intercessory Prayer* (Ventura, CA: Regal Books, 1996), p. 144.
12. Ibid.

CHAPTER FOUR

FAITH PRAYER

The effective, fervent prayer of a righteous man avails much.
JAMES 5:16

During my college years, I spent hours daily meditating on God's Word, waiting on the Lord and soaking in the presence of the Holy Spirit. It was during this season of encountering God's presence that I learned faith prayer, or the prayer of faith: "And the prayer of faith will save the sick, and the Lord will raise him up" (Jas. 5:15).

As I went deeper into the presence of the Holy Spirit, I knew He was preparing me to make a deep impact on my university: "But the people who know their God shall be strong, and carry out great exploits" (Dan. 11:32).

I had encountered God's presence, but now it was time to take that presence to the lost souls on my campus. It would not be easy. It would take great faith, for there were many giants in the land. Like young David, I had to leave the safety at the back of the field and face the Goliath on campus.

While in college, I had begun to pray weekly with a group of students for revival on our campus. During these revival prayer meetings, God put in my heart faith to produce a massive hip-hop outreach festival to reach lost students at San Jose State University. This vision had been burning in my heart for more than two years, because I had almost lost my closest friend to drug poisoning at a massive rave party in San Francisco. She was a student in a sorority at San Jose State, was drugged at a party, went into a coma for two days and nearly lost her life. After this incident, I told God I would not let this happen again to one of my friends. I asked God to give me a platform to show this college party-subculture that the drug *e*, or ecstasy, was not their answer to happiness, but that the true *E*—eternal life in Jesus Christ—was the solution to their emptiness.

In December 2002, many miracles began to happen. We had the idea of holding an evangelistic outreach event on campus, and God began to open doors with the sponsorship of the associated student body government of San Jose State University. As I began to cast the vision to different leaders in my local church, people everywhere responded. Within a few weeks I formed a committee of young adults and students who were passionate about making a change in the college hip-hop/party culture for Christ. We agreed to name the event "UNIVERSOUL," a catchy, cool name to bring unity among the Body of Christ and students, with the ultimate goal of saving souls. The estimated cost to produce the event was going to be $40,000. As a young college student with no experience, this was a huge mountain of money to raise, but I took the step of faith and trusted God.

There were three main hurdles our team needed to overcome. The first was to secure a major hip-hop celebrity who was Christ-centered to headline the event. The second was to get permission from the president and faculty of San Jose State University for us to do an evangelistic outdoor event on campus. The third was to raise the insurmountable $40,000 to produce the event. It all happened by God's grace through faith and dedicated prayer.

Faith and the First Miracle

The first miracle happened when God put it on my heart to invite KRSONE to headline the event. KRS is a legendary rap artist who promotes true hip-hop culture to be positive, safe and transforming. He is the antithesis of the hip-hop rappers you hear on the radio who talk about drugs, sex and violence. Word on the street was that he had recently become a Christ follower and had produced a Christ-centered rap album. I knew he was the right artist, but I wondered how we would afford a rap legend of his caliber.

I started the process by contacting his management agency by e-mail. They responded to me, saying that he would not be able to make the event because he would be touring on the east coast and because we could not offer him his normal performance fee. I was bummed. With this news, I told my pastor that I didn't think the event would be possible because I felt so strongly that KRSONE had to be the headline performer. But I continued to pray in faith.

The next day my friend called me and said, "Jaeson, you know KRSONE is performing in downtown San Jose tonight, right?" I couldn't believe my ears; I knew if I could only talk to him personally and tell him the purpose of this event, he would agree to do it. By God's grace I got into the club, snuck past the security guards and got into the V.I.P. guest room. When I got into the room, KRSONE was not there, but his personal bodyguard met me and told me to get lost! Right before he threw me out of the room, KRSONE's manager, who was with the bodyguard, said, "Wait, did you say your name is Jaeson Ma, the guy I've been e-mailing?" The rest is history.

I met with KRSONE, and when I told him that the purpose of the event was to combat drugs and violence and to glorify Christ, he was in! He even cut his performance fee in half and changed his entire tour schedule in order to do our event. He said, "This is what I call a good event, something with a purpose." Through faith, prayer and obedience, God came through.

The Second Miracle

The second miracle happened when we finally got the okay from the president and faculty of San Jose State University to do the event. There was a battle in the heavenly places from December to the end of March between our prayers and the spirit of the antichrist. The associated student body fought to convince the governing faculty of the university to let us put on this evangelistic festival, but the faculty raised objections because we were a Christian organization. We almost gave up on the event because without having the location secured we had to delay promotions, performers, fund-raising, vendors and everything else involved in planning the event.

After four months of persistent prayer and waiting, the day came for the faculty board to make their decision. That morning I prayed with our team and cried out to God for a miracle. During our time of prayer, I knew God had heard our cries. I told my team, "It's done. We don't need to pray anymore; the faculty will approve the event." We found out later that during the faculty meeting, the student body vice president, who was helping us throw UNIVER-SOUL, stood up and told the governing board of the university, "Look, we can't keep letting the decision to okay this event drag on. I don't care if the ones throwing this event are Christian, KKK or Muslim; they have a right to believe in what they believe in and we should let them throw this positive event—our school needs it!" With this statement, the whole boardroom became quiet and the event was unanimously approved.

From the time the event was approved to the date of the actual event was 45 days. We had a little more than a month and a half to raise the remaining $25,000, promote the event, secure the performers and organize more than 100 volunteers. But through persistent prayer, God had already won two major battles of faith. Through faith prayer, we knew that God would come through again.

The Third Miracle

We witnessed the third miracle after San Jose State's associated student government told us we had to give them a certain amount of money up front in order to hold the event. They said, "We're sorry, but if you guys don't raise $15,000 by this coming Monday at 10:00 A.M., we are going to have to cancel the event to protect our liabilities. You will really have to pray for your God to provide!" They told us this on Friday. We had 72 hours to raise $15,000. As I left the room, I told God by faith, "Look, if this is Your vision, then You are going to provide the $15,000 from somewhere. This is *Your* problem!"

On Saturday I had no idea where the money would come from, so I just prayed in my living room and remembered Jesus telling

His disciples, "Whatever things you ask when you pray, believe that you receive them, and you will have them" (Mark 11:24). I prayed for the $15,000, received it by faith, and knew in my spirit that it would come some way, somehow. I started shouting out loud in my living room, "The $15,000 is coming. The $15,000 is coming!" Moments later I got a call from a lady I had met at a church conference. She told me that it was her fiftieth birthday that night and that she wanted me to share my testimony with all her non-Christian friends at her birthday party. I thought it was odd, but I went anyway. After I shared my dramatic street testimony to the room full of affluent adults, the lady pulled me aside and asked me if she could bless me in some way. I told her about the financial need for our event but did not disclose to her the amount needed. She said, "I'll see what I can do; let me pray about it."

The next morning after church I received a phone call from a man I didn't know. He told me that a lady had left a check at his house in the Hills for me to pick up for our outreach event. I went with no idea of what to expect. I arrived at a gated community and walked up to a huge mansion where a Chinese man opened the door and handed me a check for $10,000 dollars! It was a miracle! That wasn't all. Fifteen minutes later I got a call from a pastor at my home church telling me they had talked to their missions committee and could only help my financial need for the event with a $5,000 credit. It was too perfect! God provided exactly $15,000 within 72 hours.

On Monday morning I walked into the office of the associated student body and told the head of staff, "Before you say anything, here are two checks for $15,000. Now don't tell me my God doesn't provide! Booyah! What now?" They couldn't say a word; they stood there astonished. In the next few weeks, God poured in the rest of the $10,000, and the outreach event was well on its way. Again, the prayer of faith prevailed and another victory for God was won.

The Event Day!

On the day of the event, May 11, 2003, it was estimated that a few thousand students attended the outdoor hip-hop rave festival.

A good majority of those who attended were non-Christians. They not only experienced a mind-blowing event featuring four stages, a break dance competition, a DJ competition, two outdoor dance arenas, an urban art exhibit and 50-plus performers, but they also heard testimonies from more than 20 students whose lives had been changed by Christ.

We almost ran into a problem when KRSONE almost didn't make it because he got lost on the freeway, but it was all in God's plan. In order to stall for time, I gave my full testimony, unplanned, and preached the full gospel. When I challenged the students to commit their lives to Christ, all across the field hands shot up and students shouted the sinner's prayer! Students everywhere asked to receive the infilling of the Holy Spirit, and the glory of God filled the very middle of the secular university with power. It was a beautiful sight.

In addition, KRSONE finally did make the show and rocked it hard! God was glorified, revival was rumbling and a movement started. After the event, we started a series of evangelistic Bible studies to reach those who committed their lives to Christ, which, in turn, gave birth to our passion to plant simple churches on universities everywhere. As I look back, although I wanted to give up time and again during the process, it was through persevering prayer and unwavering faith in God that we overcame every obstacle. Faith prayer is the key to releasing God's glory on our campuses and to bringing revival and reformation to our generation. In the next section, we will look at how to operate in faith prayer.

The Foundation of Faith

Now faith is the substance of things hoped for,
the evidence of things not seen.
HEBREWS 11:1

Faith is a substance. Faith is supernatural. Faith is a spirit. It is an attitude. It is a confidence of heart that stands on God's unwavering Word. Faith is what God responds to. Faith pleases

God. The absence of faith displeases God. Without faith, nothing can happen; with faith, anything can happen. Faith moves God to action. Faith moves mountains and makes the impossible possible.[1]

In Hebrews 11, the heroes of the Bible were called the "heroes of faith." They were heroes not because of their abilities and not because of their accomplishments, but because of their faith. We must be people of faith—a generation that walks by faith and not by sight. Faith believes God at His Word to do what He says He will do. Faith knows that God will do what He has spoken. What has He spoken to you?

"So then faith comes by hearing, and hearing by the word of God" (Rom. 10:17). The foundation of faith is the Word of God. Without hearing the Word of God, we cannot have faith in God. The Word of God is eternal, unchanging truth. It is firm, it is sure, it can be trusted and it is powerful (see Heb. 4:12). In Greek, there are two words for "word": One is *logos*; the other is *rhema*. In order to have faith, we must understand both of these meanings. *Logos* often refers to the expression of a thought, a message or a discourse; whereas, *rhema* often refers to that which is said or spoken—an utterance.

Although the meanings of these two words overlap in the Greek New Testament, we can contrast them this way: *Logos* is the message; *rhema* is the communication of the message. *Logos* is the *said* Word of God; *rhema* is the *saying* Word of God. In reference to the Bible, *logos* is the Bible in its entirety;[2] *rhema* is a verse from the Bible. The distinction can be seen in Ephesians 6:17 ("the sword of the Spirit, which is the word [*rhema*] of God") where the reference is not to the Scriptures as a whole, but to that portion that the Holy Spirit quickens personally to a believer, like wielding a sword in the time of need.[3] *Logos* is the general Word of God written from Genesis to Revelation; you can read it and get knowledge about God. However, just by reading it, you will not receive faith.

In order to receive faith, we read in Romans 10:17 that the substance of faith is not reading the Word (*logos*) but hearing (*rhema*) the Word of God. The expression used for "word" in Romans 10:17 is not *logos*, but *rhema*. Therefore, faith comes by hearing the *rhema* word—the word of God that is immediately spoken by God's Spirit to be used as His sword (see Eph. 6:17). Dr. David Yonggi Cho, pastor of the world's largest church, defines *rhema* as "a specific word, given to a specific person in a specific situation."[4]

As I prayed for the Lord to provide the $15,000 for the hip-hop outreach at San Jose State, the Holy Spirit quickened to me Mark 11:24: "Whatever things you ask when you pray, believe that you have received them, and you will have them." I had received a *rhema* word from God that the $15,000 would be provided in 72 hours for the outreach. I then had the *faith* to believe it would happen. We must pray and receive the *rhema* Word of God daily in our lives to live out victorious faith. Below are four steps of faith prayer that I learned from reading (many times over) one of my favorite books, *The Fourth Dimension* by Dr. Cho.[5]

Envision a Clear-Cut Objective

"Faith is the substance of things hoped for" (Heb. 11:1). What are you hoping for? What is the vision the Holy Spirit has put in your heart? Faith is the substance of things, clear-cut things, hoped for. Faith is specific. Prayer is specific. When you pray, you must be able to envision a clear-cut objective or faith goal. For more than two years, I envisioned a massive outdoor outreach festival on my campus. I pictured it, I saw it and I knew exactly what I wanted in it. And through prayer, the vision came to pass. Write down clearly and with detail the vision the Holy Spirit has put in your heart for your campus and pray over it daily.

Have a Burning Desire

"What things soever ye desire, when you pray" (Mark 11:24, *KJV*). Desire can be born out of need or out of passion. What are you passionate about? I was passionate to reach lost souls on my campus because I couldn't bear the thought of one more of my friends almost dying at another rave party. This gave birth to my vision and burning desire to hold a massive hip-hop festival to reach the college party sub-culture. Psalm 37:4 says, "Delight yourself in the Lord and He will give you the desires of your heart" (*NIV*). As we delight ourselves in intimacy with the Holy Spirit, His desires will become our desires. Once you have a faith goal, you must pray with a burning, red-hot desire to see that goal accomplished in order to see results. Burning desire will give you persevering faith.

Pray for Assurance

"Whatever things you ask when you pray, believe that you receive them, and you will have them" (Mark 11:24). Once you have a clear-cut objective and you have this desire burning in your heart to a boiling point, you must pray for assurance. Faith is the substance, the assurance or the realization of things hoped for. You pray until you realize that you have to pray no more. In your spirit you have a confidence or evidence that what you are praying for is already yours. You've got it, you've received it and it's final before it even happens. No one could tell me UNIVERSOUL wouldn't happen. No matter the challenge, I knew that it would come to pass because I prayed for the assurance.

Speak the Word of Faith

"Whoever says to this mountain, 'Be removed and be cast into the sea,' and does not doubt in his heart, but believes that those things he says will be done, he will have whatever he says" (Mark 11:23). God spoke the world into being. He called those things that are not as though they were (see Rom. 4:17). For example, God told Abraham He would have a son at 100 years old. Abraham had a clear-cut objective, a burning desire and prayed for more than 25 years, when God finally spoke and gave him the assurance that Isaac would be born to him. Abraham received the *rhema* word and God immediately changed his name from Abram to Abraham, which means "father of many nations." People must have thought he was crazy, calling himself Abraham when he had no children. But Abraham learned a secret of faith: We show the evidence of our faith when we call those things that are not as though they are.

As I've just illustrated, there are times to pray, but then there are also times to command. Once we receive by faith what we ask for, we must give the command. We must pray it through and then speak it out. I didn't know if the San Jose State faculty officials would approve our outreach event, but once I received the assurance in prayer that it would be approved, I spoke out loud the word of faith that the Holy Spirit gave me: "It is done; we don't need to pray anymore. The event will be approved!"

Without faith prayer it is impossible to please God (see Heb. 11:6). We must pray with a clear-cut objective and a burning desire. We must pray for assurance and speak the word of faith. If we do, we will see God move with signs, wonders and miracles in our generation.

Notes
1. Dr. Phil Pringle, *Faith* (New South Wales, Australia: PAX Ministries, 2003), p. 14.
2. Bauer, Arndt, Gingrich and Danker, *A Greek-English Lexicon of the New Testament and Other Early Christian Literature* (Chicago: University of Chicago Press, 1979), p. 478.
3. Jack Hayford, *Spirit Filled Life Bible* (Nashville, TN: Thomas Nelson, 1991), p. 1408.
4. David Yonggi Cho, *Prayer that Brings Revival* (Lake Mary, FL: Charisma House, 1998), p. 73.
5. David Yonggi Cho, *The Fourth Dimension* (Gainesville, FL: Bridge-Logos Publishers, 1999), n.p.

CHAPTER FIVE

REVIVAL PRAYER

Therefore I exhort first of all that supplications, prayers,
intercessions, and giving of thanks be made for all men, for kings
and all who are in authority, that we may lead a quiet and
peaceable life in all godliness and reverence. For this is good and
acceptable in the sight of God our Savior, who desires all men to
be saved and to come to the knowledge of the truth.
1 TIMOTHY 2:1-4

In college I always dreamed of revival, but I never thought I would see it happen. While still a student, the Holy Spirit took me on an adventure halfway across the world to Hong Kong. There I witnessed the birth of a student revival movement that would sweep across nearly every campus in the city and throughout all of East Asia.

I used to study revivals as a hobby, dreaming of the day when it would happen in my own life. I studied the principles, the factors and the causes of revival. During my last year in college, it actually happened. I was going to go with my spiritual father, Ché Ahn, to Hong Kong during the winter break to help him mobilize for "The Call Hong Kong," a student prayer and fasting event. Two days before we were to fly out together, he called me, saying, "Jaeson, I have an emergency and can't make the trip to Hong Kong. You will have to go and represent me to all the churches."

I responded with, "Are you kidding? No one knows who I am in Hong Kong, and I'm only 22 years old!"

He said, "Don't worry; you'll do fine. Have fun and eat some *dim sum*."

I started praying desperately and fasting. For some reason, four hours before my flight, I felt led to do some research on the Internet on the churches in Hong Kong. I typed in four words in Google: "Hong Kong + Revival + Churches." The first link that popped up was a ministry focused on city transformation. I clicked the link and read how the ministry's mission was to unite the Body of Christ in Hong Kong for revival and transformation. The leader of the ministry was a woman named "Mrs. Ma." I thought nothing of her last name and sent her a random e-mail to see if she would meet with me to network. Then I was on my way.

A Divine Appointment

When I got to Hong Kong, the Holy Spirit began to open doors for ministry. Students in every meeting were spiritually hungry in a way I had never seen before. I spent hours prophesying over student leaders one by one in the meetings. The power of God broke out in each gathering and word began to get out to other church leaders.

After a week in Hong Kong, I still had not received a reply from Mrs. Ma. Two days before I was to leave, I received a phone call from the pastor of a fellowship in which I had been ministering. She said, "A lady named Mrs. Ma would like to meet with you tomorrow night before you leave. I had breakfast with her this morning and told her to meet you; she said she received your e-mail but didn't know who you were, so she deleted it. She now believes it is not a coincidence that I mentioned your name, and would like to meet with you." I ended up meeting with Mrs. Ma and her team the night before I left, prayed for them and headed back to the States.

A week later I received an e-mail message from Mrs. Ma. She said that God had put it in her heart to hold a citywide youth crusade in the middle of Hong Kong and felt that I should be the one to give the evangelistic message. I prayed about it and decided to go back to Hong Kong during Easter break of 2004, at her invitation. This is when revival broke out.

The night before the citywide youth crusade, we held a revival meeting. I was supposed to preach to a few hundred student leaders, but that night, as I grabbed the microphone to preach, I couldn't speak. The Holy Spirit gripped my heart. I felt the overwhelming burden of God's Spirit to repent and intercede on behalf of the sins of the young people in Hong Kong. I began to pray and repent, interceding for different sins as the Spirit of God led me. The presence of God broke in—students everywhere began to weep, repent and fall on their knees. This lasted hour after hour into the night. Students kept crying out for their sins and for God to save their generation. We knew that God was doing an extraordinary work.

The next night at the youth outreach, hundreds of students committed and recommitted their lives to the Lordship of Christ. In the end, the meeting turned from an evangelistic outreach into a repentance prayer gathering. In the middle of the city, students got on their faces and continued to cry out to God for the sins of their generation, praying for revival to come. The heavens were opening over the students of Hong Kong. We knew something special was stirring in the spirit realm.

The day after the crusade, I was sitting in Mrs. Ma's home. We were both talking about the mighty move of God's Spirit among the students and were contemplating the next steps and whether or not we were called to work together. Then a confirmation like none other occurred. As we talked, I asked her what her Chinese background was. She told me her family was from Shanghai and I told her mine was from Chiu Chou. She said, "Chiu Chou? My husband is from Chiu Chou, China."

I said jokingly, "Really? So is my father, and they both have the surname Ma. It would be funny if they were actually related." Then I asked her by chance if her husband was related to a famous actor in Hong Kong. When I said his name she was shocked and told me that the actor I mentioned was her husband's cousin! I told her it was impossible because he was also my father's cousin. What transpired after that you would probably not believe even if I told you it was true. It turned out that her husband was my father's half-brother by birth. They had the same father but different mothers. During the Cultural Revolution in China, my grandfather fled from Chiu Chou, China, to Hong Kong and started another family. The families never met, but 30-plus years later, God sent me to Hong Kong to reconcile the two families who were both now born-again Christians. It was a divine moment. Mrs. Ma and I looked at each other stunned and knew that we were called by God to work together.

Spreading Revival

In the months following my college graduation, I traveled back and forth from the United States to Hong Kong every few months, because the student revival movement in Hong Kong had broken out like wildfire. By partnering with my new aunt, we held campus revival conferences with students all over Hong Kong, uniting churches and parachurch campus ministries to win every campus and every student to Christ through united prayer and united action.

Everywhere, students began to start prayer cells on their campuses, praying daily for revival. Campus revival reports started rolling in. Students were praying early in the morning, day after day, sometimes three times a day, crying out for revival. Many students would fast from their lunches to pray for God's presence to invade their campus.

At University of Hong Kong, for the first time, we were able to unite nearly all the campus ministry and local church leaders on campus to humble themselves, resolve their differences, repent and pray for God to send revival and save the lost on their university campuses. This gave birth to a university prayer movement that spread to nearly every other university in Hong Kong, mobilizing other Christian students and staff workers to do the same. Hundreds were praying daily and monthly in campus-wide revival prayer rallies.

We then started a citywide campus revival prayer meeting called "The Furnace." Every month hundreds of student leaders would gather from different campuses to pray, share campus revival reports and intercede on behalf of every college and high school in Hong Kong. This citywide prayer meeting began to grow and multiply. Today there are Furnace-type prayer meetings occurring on a monthly or quarterly basis in nearly every region in Hong Kong, uniting the entire Body of Christ to pray for revival on campuses.

After months of non-stop prayer, reports came in telling of more than 100, 200, even 300 or more students getting saved *en masse* on various campuses in one day. We began to train student leaders all over the city to start evangelistic cell groups and student-led house churches to disciple the harvest of the revival on the campuses. I couldn't believe my ears. The book of Acts was breaking out, and God was releasing a genuine work of the Holy Spirit among students in Hong Kong for His glory.

The campus revival movement continued to spread into Taiwan and other parts of East Asia, reviving and touching the lives of thousands of students far and wide. This student prayer movement helped partner local church and marketplace Christian leaders to begin a 24/7 prayer altar in Hong Kong, uniting churches all over the city to lift up non-stop prayer, night and day, over the entire city. It also inspired the Global Day of Prayer movement in Hong Kong and East Asia.

It was during this time in 2004, as I continued to work with Mrs. Ma, that I brought her with me to South Africa, where I was invited to speak at the Global Day of Prayer. On that day in 2004, more than 25 million Africans united in revival prayer throughout the continent. As a result, Mrs. Ma brought the vision of the Global Day of Prayer back to Hong Kong. In 2005, she united more than 300 churches and 40,000 Christians to pray in the two largest stadiums for the blessings, revival and transformation of Hong Kong and China, while an estimated 200 million Christians were praying in more than 150 countries the same day.[1]

Today, reports keep pouring in of masses of students praying on campuses and of souls daily being saved. The movement has slowed down on some campuses and increased in others. We must remember that intimacy with God and radical obedience to His Word are the foundation to birth and also sustain revival. All in all, the Church in Hong Kong and East Asia is arising and uniting as one body in prayer with a vision to spread the Good News to all of Asia, and from there, to the ends of the earth and back to Jerusalem. Revival prayer was the key that started it all with a handful of students in Hong Kong. Revival prayer will be the key to unlocking the gates of heaven on your campus and in your city, and it will also be the key to releasing God's glory. How badly do you want it?

The Role of Prayer in Campus Revival History

In order to understand revival, we must understand the role of prayer in campus revival history. J Edwin Orr, the famous revival historian said, "Young people in student led prayer cells have been at the forefront in almost every awakening."[2] Almost every great revival or missionary movement in history started with students praying on college campuses and then being led out by God. The Moravian 24/7 prayer and missionary movement, for example, was started in 1727 by Ludwig Von Zinzendorf. At the age of 16, Zinzendorf graduated from Halle School after having started no fewer than 7 different prayer groups, and he continued his prayer disciplines while he was a student at the University of Wittenberg from 1716 to 1719.[3]

The First Great Awakenings that swept hundreds of thousands into the Kingdom in Europe and North America were ignited by a Yale University graduate named Jonathan Edwards, and by Oxford students John Wesley and George Whitefield at Oxford University in 1729.[4] The Second Great Awakening was sparked by Timothy Dwight, the grandson of Jonathan Edwards, at Yale University in his 1797 message to Yale students.[5] Nearly half of Yale's student body came to Christ in a few short months![6]

The Student Volunteer Missionary movement, which sent more than 20,000 college students overseas on foreign missions during the span of a few decades, was started by Samuel Mills and the Haystack 5 at Williams College, Massachusetts, in 1806.[7] It was five students, praying under a haystack on a rainy day for revival and world missions, saying, "If we will, we can!" The rest is history and the list of student revivalists goes on.

Will you be the next one to change campus revival history? If so, the key is extraordinary revival prayer. There are four essential kinds of extraordinary prayer found in history that will release revival.

United Prayer

The first kind of revival prayer is united prayer. No revival in history was born or blessed without unity in the Body of Christ: "Behold, how good and how pleasant it is for brethren to dwell together in unity . . . for there the LORD commanded the blessing" (Ps. 133:1,3). In his famous article "Prayer Brought Revival," J. Edwin Orr quoted Dr. A. T. Pierson, who once said, "There has never been a spiritual awakening in any country or locality that did not begin in concerted, united, sustained prayer."[8]

The Early Church was a united church. They were not divided by denominations or doctrines, but they were united by a common denominator: Jesus Christ. Their unity released God's revival fire that swept what Church historians believe to be more than 20,000 to 25,000 new believers into the Kingdom at Jerusalem in only the first few weeks after the day of Pentecost (see Acts 2:41: 4:4: 5:14-16).[9]

Still today, Jesus is contending for His Church to be fully united, that we may be made perfect, a spotless Bride of Christ (see Eph. 4:13: 5:27). If we want to bring revival to our campuses and cities, the first prerequisite is that we lay aside our differences as Christians, humble ourselves and unite in concerted, sustained prayer for revival. At the University of Hong Kong, they did just that. Different staff and student leaders from different campus fellowships and local churches repented of their division and gathered together to pray daily, weekly and in revival prayer rallies monthly.

Revival Prayer Is Intercessory Prayer

We have both a divine task and a divine purpose in life. Our supreme purpose is to glorify God, and our divine task is to evangelize the lost.[10] We love God by obeying His commands. In 1 Timothy 2:1, we are commanded, "Therefore I exhort first of all that supplications, prayers, *intercessions*, and giving of thanks be made for all men" (emphasis added). Therefore, our first priority as the Body of Christ is to intercede on behalf of all people so that they would be saved.

To intercede is to pray for others. It is the heart of prayer and the very heart of God. Night and day, God's heart beats one thing over and over again: "souls, souls, souls!" Intercession is God's method to involve His followers more completely in the totality of His plan for world evangelization. God wants revival and He uses our intercession to get it!

As we offer intercession on behalf of others, we act as a mediator between the lost students on our campuses and Almighty God, praying that each person will come to encounter His presence and salvation. History belongs to the intercessor.[11] In our campus revival prayer meetings, our focus must not be on ourselves, but our focus must be on praying for the lost souls of the harvest (see Luke 10:2)!

Strategic Prayer

Prayer that brings revival is also strategic. In 1 Timothy 2:1, the Bible exhorts us to pray for "all men." So when we pray, we must pray for the "all." It is not enough to pray for a few; God wants all people. Therefore, we must pray for every person on our campus, starting with those in authority, down to each and every student. When we pray for every person, it is impossible for the enemy to veil their eyes from the gospel. The walls will be pulled down and God's glory will be manifested (see 2 Cor. 4:3-4; 10:4-5). Our battle is not physical; it is spiritual first, as Ephesians 6:10-18 teaches. We war against heavenly principalities over our campuses and cities, and it is through prayer and prayer alone that these strongholds are pulled down.

I learned the concept of praying for the all through a prayer movement in Hawaii.[12] A student there mobilized every Christian on his campus and in his city to pray daily for 10 students on his campus by name by writing the students' names on index cards. In a short while, the entire campus experienced revival, and the movement spread to all of Hawaii, touching every sphere of society. We did the same on Hong Kong campuses by training students and local churches to pray for faculty and students by name. It was after this that reports came in that masses of students on different campuses were being radically saved!

Mobilized Prayer

"Men always ought to pray and not lose heart" (Luke 18:1). John Wesley, the great revivalist, once said, "Give me one hundred men who love Jesus with all their hearts and who do not fear men or devils and I care not one whit whether they are clergy or laity, with these men I will change the world and usher in the kingdom of God in one generation!"[13] The Holy Spirit is looking for a few good men and women who are willing to sacrifice and participate in united, fervent and sustained revival prayer for their campuses. Remember, nearly every great awakening started with young people in student-led prayer cells. Revival begins in prayer, and so, whether it is you and only one other student or many others, gather together to pray for revival on your campus. Where two or three gather in His name, Jesus is with them, and all the authority and power that comes with His name is backing them up (see Matt. 18:20)!

As you pray in unity, in intercession and with strategy, mobilize other believers on your campus and the surrounding area to pray with you for revival. Whether through prayer walking or establishing prayer cells all over campus, the vision is to pray a lot. Pray. Fast. Every day. Every week. Don't give up, no matter the outcome. God hears and your prayers will be answered.

Here are some key prayer strategies to get you started:

- Bring together staff, faculty, local church leaders and student leaders on your campus and in your city to pray regularly for campus revival.

- Repent on behalf of known personal and corporate sins and *intercede* for the lost continually.

• Pray strategically for the all to be saved by praying for faculty and students by name.

• Mobilize others to start prayer cells in every area on campus. Coordinate corporate prayer rallies (monthly or quarterly) and prayer walks to cry out for revival, and spread the vision of campus revival and transformation as often as possible, to as many people as possible.

Notes

1. For more information on the Global Day of Prayer, visit the Global Day of Prayer website at www.globaldayofprayer.com.
2. J. Edwin Orr, "Prayer and Revival." http://www.jedwinorr.com/prayer_revival.htm (accessed January 2007).
3. "Zinzendorf's Chronology," *Christian History Magazine*, vol. 1, no. 1, Worcester, 1982; Pete Greig, *Red Moon Rising* (Orlando, FL: Relevant Books, 2003), p. 340; John R. Weinlick, *Count Zinzendorf: The Moravian Church in America* (Nashville, TN: Abingdon Press, 1956), n.p.
4. Sydney E. Ahlstrom, *A Religious History of the American People* (New York: Doubleday, 1975), n.p.
5. W. B. Sprague, *The Life of Timothy Dwight, President of Yale College* (New York: C.C. Little and J. Brown, 1845), n.p.
6. Erwin Lutzer, "Will God Send Revival to America Once Again?" http://www.ser monindex.net/modules/newbb/viewtopic.php?topic_id=12679&forum=40 (accessed January 2007).
7. Sarah Johnson and Eileen Moffett, "Lord, Send Us," *Christian History & Biography*, Spring 2006, p. 35.
8. Orr, "Prayer and Revival." http://www.jedwinorr.com/prayer_revival.htm (accessed January 2007).
9. R. C. H. Lenski, *The Interpretation of the Acts of the Apostles* (Minneapolis, MN: Augsburg, 1934), p. 239.
10. Dick Eastman, *The Hour That Changes the World* (Grand Rapids, MI: Chosen Books, 2002), p. 72.
11. A statement first made by Professor Walter Wink in *Engaging the Powers* (Minneapolis, MN: Augsburg, 1992), p. 297.
12. For more information about the prayer movement in Hawaii, see www.uipha waii.com.
13. Wayne Dean, Sr., "Reminiscence of a Methodist Circuit Rider." http://jacksonsny der.com/arc/slac/sermons/Circuit%20Rider.htm (accessed January 2007).

CHAPTER SIX

24/7 CAMPUS HOUSES OF PRAYER

*I have set watchmen on your walls, O Jerusalem; They shall never
hold their peace day or night. You who make mention of the Lord,
do not keep silent, and give Him no rest till He establishes and
till He makes Jerusalem a praise in the earth.*
ISAIAH 62:6-7

This story is from my personal blog entry dated February 10, 2006:

It *broke out* last night from 11 P.M. to 3 A.M. at UCLA.
Students started showing up and a spirit of revival fell out
of nowhere. Students all over the room started *crying out* to
God for the UCLA campus, and their prayers kept going on
for a few hours. There were student leaders from different
campus fellowships in the room. It was powerful. I thought
I was on Prayer Mountain in Korea or at an underground
Chinese house church prayer meeting.

The fire is burning. Can you believe that we had a map
of UCLA on the wall so we could pray for the campus?
It had the word "REVIVAL" on the top, and candles were
lit under it. All of a sudden, the 2 Chronicles 7:14 banner
that was under the map caught on fire and *smoke* filled
the entire room. Later we looked at the map of UCLA and
noticed that it was shaped like a *heart*. Becky Tirabassi [a
Christian author, speaker and prayer warrior—check out
www.theburningheartcontract.com] took it as a sign from
God that this was the *burning heart* of UCLA. Yes, the very
burning heart contract Bill Bright made 50 years ago before

he started Campus Crusade for Christ at UCLA. The well is being re-dug; the fire is being re-lit . . . IT'S TIME!!!

Pressing in,
Jaeson Ma

Here are a couple of student comments from my blog post:

When I prepare to decorate the room, I have totally no idea where I can find a huge UCLA map . . . but God did it. God is good. When I was there to decorate the room, for safety reasons, I thought about the possibility of the paper catching fire . . . since we have candle holders, it is quite impossible that it will catch fire. I would definitely say it's [catching fire was] a miracle. God is cool~~
Ada (2/10/2006, 09:55:27 P.M.)

Hey Jaeson, I had a chance to meet you right before I left last night and I just wanted to affirm the awesome night of prayer. I definitely felt God's presence in that room last night. I stepped in there at about 11:05 P.M. with a few Bruin Navs [other UCLA students] not knowing what to expect, except that I knew that God's Spirit was going to be pouring down and I wanted to be there. I only had intentions of staying for my allotted hour, but before I knew it, it was close to 2 A.M. I never felt time pass by so quickly. Within those hours I found myself shouting out to God for revival and praying for the souls of thousands. Like *never* before, words of prayer fell from my lips. Words that I knew that I didn't conjure up from my own mind. Promises and verses rose out of my mouth, and I felt completely outside of myself. I've never felt that way in prayer, as far as I can remember. I didn't want to leave the presence of God. I would've stayed there all night if my body didn't need sleep.

I found myself before God asking, could this campus be claimed by its rightful King? Could this be the time that these halls would echo the name of their Savior? Could it

be that a shout of praise to the Lamb of God would rise
up from these hills? Could it be that the sons and daughters of God would be gathered from the lost at UCLA? Get
your glory back, God . . . forgive us of our sins and trespasses . . . and get your glory back. We want to see you
high and lifted up. Amen.
Stephen (2/11/2006, 02:47:26 A.M.)

These blog posts came in after the 24/7 UCLA prayer room
experience. No one would have thought the Holy Spirit would
encounter us the way He did that night. No one would have
thought God would give us a flaming sign on the wall that He
was renewing a covenant He made with Bill Bright (founder of
Campus Crusade for Christ) when he started the first 24/7 prayer
chain at Hollywood Presbyterian Church with a handful of students from UCLA almost 50 years ago.[1]

The covenant Bill made with a few other young leaders was
called the "Burning Heart Contract." In this contract, they committed to the following: (1) not less than one hour in prayer and Bible
reading daily; (2) to offer themselves in sobriety and complete
chastity/fidelity; and (3) to lead at least one person to Christ each
year.[2] It was a radical call, as my friend and author Becky Tirabassi
would say, to be *sold out in prayer, set apart in purity* and to be *sent out
with purpose.* After that contract was signed, it spurred forth a
nationwide awakening on college campuses. Something similar
happened that night at UCLA, but this time it wasn't just a commitment to a contract; it was a commitment to pray non-stop,
24/7, until Jesus returns to every college and university in America!

What has been happening on campuses through 24/7 prayer
rooms has been a confirmation to the dream I received in 2004,
where I got into Mike Bickle's vehicle of ministry (House of Prayer)
before he got into my vehicle of ministry (Campus Revival and
Church Planting). It was a divine download of revelation that in
order for us to see revival and reformation break out on our campuses and cities, we would first have to establish 24/7 Campus
Houses of Prayer.

Since those dreams, I had been prophesying for more than two years to Christian leaders in different schools that the key to unlocking heaven and releasing revival over the campuses of our nation would be through raising up 24/7 Campus Houses of Prayer. No one would believe me. They thought it was too radical, too out there, and they gave me excuses like, "Where would you find a place to pray 24/7 on a campus?" and "College students don't have time to pray." But I didn't care what they said. I kept sharing the vision for CHOP (Campus Houses of Prayer) to be established to break open the heavens for revival.

In the spring of 2006, the prophetic fulfillment of this word began to take place. In one semester our website[3] had signed up more than 70 major colleges and universities across the nation to pray 24/7 for one day, one week, one month or longer, to do their part in establishing a semester of unbroken prayer over the campuses of our nation. It was happening right before our eyes. It was not contrived. It was not planned. It was a move of God completely orchestrated by the Holy Spirit.

We found out later that even more campuses were praying in 24/7 prayer tents and rooms at their schools but had not signed up on the nationwide website. Reports kept pouring in of students encountering God in the prayer rooms, atheists converting, divine healings and Holy Spirit "break outs" in the middle of campus. Something marvelous was unfolding; revival was beginning to rumble, and God was raising up a house of prayer for all nations in our generation!

The Irrefutable Law of Night and Day Prayer

Will not God bring about justice for His elect who cry out to Him day and night . . . ? I tell you that He will bring about justice for them quickly.

LUKE 18:7-8, *NASB*, EMPHASIS ADDED

Shall God not avenge His own elect who cry out day and night to Him . . . ? I tell you that He will avenge them speedily.

LUKE 18:7-9, EMPHASIS ADDED

Night and day 24/7 intercession releases justice, vengeance and God's judgment upon the kingdom of darkness. This kind of prayer makes the wrong things right. It corrects error and restores God's intended purpose. It punishes the rebellious and redeems the responsive. In other words, it brings revival in the Church. For example, God's judgment on sickness is *healing*. God's judgment on the kingdom of darkness is when thousands of nonbelievers get saved on a campus or in a city; it is a judgment on unbelief. It is *revival*. God's judgment on division is *unity* in the Church. God's judgment on sin is deliverance from sinful bondage into a lifestyle of *holiness*.[4] We need God's justice in the earth and on our campuses, and it can only happen through 24/7 prayer.

Throughout history, whenever God's people chose to dedicate themselves to night and day praise, worship and intercession, the kingdom of God expanded in power and speedy justice unlike any other time. As God's people pour forth an onslaught of non-stop prayer, God releases heaven on Earth, and it can't be stopped! Here are just a few examples of this happening throughout the ages.

- The Tabernacle of David in Jerusalem, 1000 B.C., under the leadership of King David: Night and day prayer and worship continued for 33 years into King Solomon's reign (see 1 Chron. 15-16; 2 Chron. 5-7).

- Bangor, Ireland, A.D. 555, under the leadership of Comgall and Columbanus: Night and day worship continued for more than 300 years with a missionary zeal that touched all of Europe.[5]

- Hernhut, Germany, A.D. 1727, under the leadership of Count Zinzendorf: Night and day intercession continued for more than 120 years; in time, the movement sent out more missionaries than the Protestant Church.[6]

- Seoul, Korea, during the last 40 years, under the leadership of David Yonggi Cho: Night and day prayer has continued for more than 30 years with a missionary passion touching many parts of Asia.

- International House of Prayer (IHOP), Kansas City, Missouri, (Mike Bickle) and 24-7prayer.com, England (Pete Greig): Two separate prayer movements, both started in 1999, with continued night and day prayer continuing for more than seven years and passionately reaching the next generation for Christ.[7]

Why Pray 24/7 Today?

In this generation, God is restoring night and day prayer because He is committed to His purpose to release justice on the earth. The goal is not merely to pray 24/7, but rather to seek God's face and to cry out for speedy justice to invade your campus and city. Establishing Campus Houses of Prayer is a move of the Holy Spirit, not a fad, a method or a cool thing to do. It is the holy work of God, a divine strategy released to your generation to reclaim campuses and, ultimately, your generation for the glory of God.

Your campus may start with only one day, one week or one month of 24/7 prayer before establishing a permanent 24/7 house of prayer. Be faithful with a little and He will make you faithful over much. Already, a few college and university campuses in North America (such as the University of Texas and Ohio State University) have established nearly permanent 24/7 prayer rooms. It can be done! Wherever you are in the journey, let me share with you a few good reasons why the Holy Spirit may put a vision in your heart to raise up a permanent campus house of prayer on your college or university campus.

24/7 Prayer Is Done in the Heavens

In Matthew 6:10, Jesus commands us to pray for His kingdom to come and His will to be done, on Earth as it is in heaven. What are they doing in heaven? They are eternally praising, worshiping and praying to the King of kings and Lord of lords. It is not our goal to get to heaven; our goal is to get heaven down to Earth and onto our campuses.

24/7 Prayer Releases God's Speedy Justice on Earth

In Luke 18:7, we learn that God releases speedy justice and makes the wrong things immediately right when we cry out to Him night and day. There are many wrong things that need to be made right in our generation: abortion, homosexuality, poverty, racism, sickness and disease, drunkenness, human sex trafficking and sexual immorality, to name a few. Sound like your college campus? We must pray night and day on our campuses to release God's justice: revival.

I have been part of a movement called Bound4life.com that has mobilized students in Washington, D.C., to pray 24/7 for the end of abortion. God is answering our prayers and placing righteous judges into the Supreme Court because we are crying out night and day for justice for the unborn.

24/7 Prayer Fuels the Great Commission

In Matthew 22:37, we are commanded to love the Lord with all our heart, soul, strength and mind. It is through praise, worship and non-stop intercession that God is glorified. The Westminster Shorter Catechism says, "The chief end of man is to glorify God, and to enjoy him forever." Yes, we enjoy God through our devotion first and our works second. Lovers always outwork workers. By spending time in a prayer room, we encounter God's presence, and He fuels our passion to preach the gospel on our campuses. We are sons and daughters of God, not slaves and servants.

As we give ourselves to one thing—loving and enjoying God—we will do greater works for Him (see John 14:12). And we will be able to do greater works for Him because permanent 24/7 prayer rooms on campus will act as apostolic mission centers that fuel evangelism, simple church planting and missions. They will serve as equipping centers for campus missionaries to encounter God in prayer and be trained and sent out to win the lost. We know some student leaders who have rented out homes and apartment complexes to live in community and also turned them into 24/7 prayer houses and equipping centers. Others, like at the University of Texas, have rented out an office space and turned it into a permanent campus house of prayer.

24/7 Prayer Thwarts the Plans of the Devil

In Daniel 10:12-13, we learn that Daniel had to pray night and day for 21 days straight to receive an important prophetic message from an archangel. This is a clear picture of how demonic armies oppose God's purposes on Earth. There is a divine struggle over our nation's campuses. The false ideologies, philosophies and demonic attacks can only be demolished through our continual prayer, fasting and crying out to God. It is only through our fervent intercession that the enemy's plans can be dismantled. Satan doesn't stop attacking, and neither should we.

24/7 Prayer Releases Revival Breakthrough

Study the historic periods of David, 1010 B.C. (1 Chron. 15–16); Solomon, 970 B.C. (2 Chron. 5–7); Jehoshaphat, 872 B.C. (2 Chron. 20); Joash, 835 B.C. (2 Chron. 23–24); Hezekiah, 729 B.C. (2 Chron. 29–30); Josiah, 622 B.C. (2 Chron. 35); Ezra, 458 B.C. (Ezra 3:10-13; 8:23; 9:4); and Nehemiah, 445 B.C. (Neh. 4:9; 9:1; 12:28-47). In their day, each of these biblical heroes committed to raise up 24/7 prayer and worship to God. These passages show that their dedication released an "open heaven" (a condition where God freely pours out His power and blessings) and a revival that was evident in each of their ministries.

Many of us wonder why it's so hard to evangelize on our campuses. The reason is that winning souls is a spiritual battle that can only be won through non-stop prayer. The enemy has blinded the eyes of the unbelievers, and it is only through our weapon of prayer that we can pull down these blinders and spiritual strongholds that the lost may see the truth of Jesus Christ (see 2 Cor. 3:14; 4:4; 10:14). As we contend in prayer, night and day, through campus houses of prayer, the darkness will have to flee and the heavens will open for us to have powerfully effective evangelism, missions and simple church planting on campus.

24/7 Prayer Prepares the Way for Christ's Second Coming
In Isaiah 62:6-7, we read that the Lord has set each of us as watchmen on the walls to "never hold [our] peace day or night," to "not
keep silent" and to "give God no rest" through continual intercession until He makes Jerusalem a praise in the earth. It is our mandate and calling to pray for the peace of Israel, to pray for the
return of Christ and to pray for the gospel to be preached to all
nations so that the end may come (see Matt. 24:14). To establish a
24/7 campus house of prayer is to start a student-led prayer-, jus-
tice- and missions-movement to usher in the return of King Jesus
in our generation. It can be done!

Raising Up a Campus House of Prayer

If you sense the leading to start a campus house of prayer at your
college or university, now is the time! Spend time in prayer, share
the vision with your friends, listen to the Holy Spirit and follow
His lead. God is doing a new work in our generation. He is releasing a divine strategy to strike back at the enemy in order to release
His justice upon the earth and our campuses. It begins with Him
and ends with Him.

24/7 prayer is displayed through a passionate 24/7 praying
army of God on every campus, and in every city and nation, to fulfill the Great commandment and finish the Great Commission in
this hour. This is it. What are you going to do about it?

Here are a few ideas on how to mobilize a campus house of prayer:

1. Go to www.campustransformation.com and sign up
   your campus for 24/7 prayer in order to be networked
   with other campuses for support.

2. Start praying with others regularly who have a heart
   for a 24/7 campus house of prayer.

3. Call a vision-casting meeting, inviting other student
   leaders and campus staff workers to hear about the
   24/7 campus house of prayer vision and purpose.

4. Challenge other students to mobilize their friends to take a one- to two-hour shift in the prayer room.

5. Meet with all the campus staff workers and student leaders of different fellowships/local churches to share the idea with them and to ask for their help and support of the 24/7 campus prayer room initiative.

6. Ask different campus fellowships and/or local churches if you can share the 24/7 campus house of prayer vision at their large or small student group meetings to challenge students to sign up and take prayer shifts in their fellowships. Be creative on how to promote 24/7 prayer (using www.facebook.com is a great way to spread the vision).

7. Secure a location and prepare and design the prayer room or prayer tent.

8. Go to: www.campustransformation.com and www.campusamerica.org to get more practical resources on how to start a 24/7 campus house of prayer.

Notes
1. Michael Richardson, *Amazing Faith* (Colorado Springs, CO: Waterbrook Press, 2000), p. 63.
2. Earl O. Roe, ed., *Dream Big: The Henrietta Mears Story* (Ventura, CA: Regal Books, 1990), pp. 282-283.
3. To view the website, go to www.campustransformation.com.
4. Mike Bickle, *Harp and Bowl Spiritual Warfare Syllabus* (Kansas City, MO: Forerunner Publishing), pp. 3-4.
5. Gildas the Wise, *Penitential*, online version available at http://www.tertullian.org/fathers/gildas_05_intro.htm (accessed January 2007).
6. See *Christian History Magazine*, vol. 1, no. 1 (Worcester, PA: 1982).
7. For more information on Mike Bickle and the International House of Prayer, see www.ihop.org. For more information on Pete Greig at the 24-7 Prayer Rooms, see www.24-7prayer.com.

PASSION FOR POWER EVANGELISM

*But you shall receive power when the Holy Spirit has
come upon you; and you shall be witnesses to Me in Jerusalem,
and in all Judea and Samaria, and to the end of the earth.*
ACTS 1:8

UCLA Is Shaking

It was just before Easter 2006, at UCLA in Southern California.
I thought I was hearing things, but through a series of confirmations I sensed the Holy Spirit telling me to bring a seven-foot cross
into the middle of Bruin Walk on the campus of UCLA and to
preach to student groups there. So for several days I joined a group
of student leaders from our simple church and from other campus
fellowships and brought the wooden cross out onto Bruin Walk.
For a week, we prophetically worshiped the Lord and prayed for
revival in the open air. We preached to students about Jesus, His
cross and resurrection. Then the power of God broke out. The
entry below was posted on my blog in April 2006. What a small
band of students and I encountered was a foretaste of what is to
come. God is using power evangelism to once again shake college
and university campuses for His glory!

Blog Entry:
A Shift in the Spiritual Atmosphere

"Let us know, Let us pursue the knowledge of the LORD. His going forth is established as the morning; He will come to us like the rain, Like the latter and former rain to the earth" (Hos. 6:3).

A few months back, UCLA established a day of 24/7 prayer for campus revival. Ever since this happened, nothing has been the same. God has been pouring out His Spirit on this campus like never before. At the same time, our ministry (www.campustransformation.com, www.campuschurch.net) has tracked more than 70 24/7 prayer rooms on different major university campuses all across the nation. Something is stirring; the power of God is falling, and the Holy Spirit is preparing a generation for a last great awakening that will shake the nations and finish the Great Commission in our generation.

We recognize that without prayer nothing is possible; with prayer all things can be done. Prayer is the fuel behind our evangelism. Below is a report of what the Holy Spirit has been doing in great grace and power on the UCLA campus. We are not just satisfied with good prayer rooms. We want to see the power of God encounter a generation, and we are seeing it happen right before our eyes here in Los Angeles. Yes, 100 years after the Azusa Street Revival in L.A., an expectancy of God's visitation upon Los Angeles is pregnant in the hearts of many once again. Yes, 50 years since the beginning of the greatest student spiritual revolution on the UCLA campus, led by Bill Bright of Campus Crusade, we are at the threshold of another great student revival awakening. Do not relent; press in with prayer, fasting and a bold gospel witness.

Below is my own story of the powerful things God has been doing through a small band of students in our house church network who are united with other like-minded Christ followers on the UCLA campus.

Completely Satisfied, Yet Utterly Dissatisfied

When I came to you, brothers, I did not come with eloquence or superior wisdom as I proclaimed to you the testimony

about God. For I resolved to know nothing while I was with
you except Jesus Christ and Him crucified. I came to you in
weakness and fear, and with much trembling. My message
and my preaching were not with wise and persuasive words,
but with a demonstration of the Spirit's power, so that your
faith might not rest on men's wisdom, but on God's power
(1 Cor. 2:1-5, *NIV*).

What has been happening at UCLA during the past 10 days is un-
precedented. The Spirit of God is stirring, and we are experiencing
a new outbreak of revival like we have never seen. In the last week
we have witnessed scores of salvations in the middle of campus,
divine healings and the power of God breaking in. This is just the
beginning of something great.

I thought I was losing my mind last week. I had become dissatisfied with the state of American Christianity and the lack of power
in the preached gospel. Why do we preach the gospel and yet have
no response? Why do we see the power of God operating in the book
of Acts but don't see the power of God operating today? Where is
the power and presence of God in my generation? I had lost it . . .

I couldn't do my regular ministry duties. I could no longer settle for church meetings, Bible studies and casual prayer meetings.
I wanted something more. There had to be more. I kept reading
1 Corinthians 2 and Acts 4. Paul never preached with human wisdom and human knowledge; he preached with the power of God.
Today, though, all we have is human knowledge from our pulpits
and no Holy Spirit power.

A Chinese house church leader once visited some major megachurches in Los Angeles, California, and when asked, "What do
you think?" he responded with, "It's amazing what your American
Churches can do without the Holy Spirit." Lord, I pray for mercy
on Your lukewarm Church here in the United States.

Last week I read Acts 4 over and over again:

Now, Lord, consider their threats and enable your servants
to speak your word with great boldness. Stretch out your

hand to heal and perform miraculous signs and wonders through the name of your holy Servant Jesus. After they prayed, the place where they were meeting was shaken. And they were all filled with the Holy Spirit and spoke the word of God boldly. All the believers were in one heart and mind. No one claimed that any of his possessions was his own, but they shared everything they had. With great power the apostles continued to testify to the resurrection of the Lord Jesus, and much grace was upon them all (vv. 29-33).

The apostles preached the resurrection of the Lord Jesus with great power. I am desperate to see that great power at work in my generation. If not, I don't know what to live on for. I did not sign up for a program, an organization or a religious institution. I found Christ at the age of 17 and was radically changed. He transformed me, encountered me, saved me from going to jail, and I have never looked back. But here I am again, as desperate as the day I met Him. God, where is Your power in my generation?

I became so desperate last week that I simply prayed the prayer of Jeremiah 6:16, which says, "Stand at the crossroads and look; ask for the ancient paths, ask where the good way is and walk in it, and you will find rest for your souls." I lost it. I dropped everything and went back to the place of prayer. For days on end I sought only God's presence in the morning and through the night. I found rest for my soul. I found His presence, and He had become everything once again. The only way I could describe how it felt and how I feel at this moment is, "completely satisfied and utterly dissatisfied."

I am completely satisfied in His presence, but I am utterly dissatisfied with the state of Christianity in my generation. Oh God, oh God, oh God . . . if You don't do something, I don't know what else to do! Where is the God of Abraham, Isaac and Jacob in this generation? There are 40,000 students at UCLA, and the majority of them do not know this glorious presence I know. Millions in my generation are leaving the Church because they have encountered a dead religion instead of the manifest presence of God. I am distraught, and, God, You must do something. I only live for one thing—

to see Your name lifted high, to see revival come, to experience heaven on Earth; if not, take me home. Revival or death! I don't mean to sound extreme, but this is how I feel.

This past week at UCLA, I sensed a stirring and experienced a Holy Spirit power I have not seen in a long while. God is here; He is moving and hell is shaking. This is just the beginning. I feel like we have struck water. The well of revival is stirring, but we have to keep pressing in. May God do again what He did with Bill Bright 50 years ago on this campus! May God start a spiritual revolution among students on campuses all across the United States of America, but this time even greater.

The Seven-Foot Cross

I thought I was hearing things. But through a series of confirmations I sensed the Holy Spirit telling me to bring a seven-foot cross into the middle of Bruin Walk and to preach. A sister in our house church on campus had found this seven-foot cross and borrowed it for our 24/7 UCLA prayer room. When I saw it, something in me stirred. I knew that it was meant to be carried and preached with. I asked her if she could ask the owners to let us use it for outdoor preaching on campus. She asked, and they graciously gave it to us.

This seven-foot cross had been sitting in my room for over 2 months because I had not yet felt led to carry it on campus. But this past week, on Thursday, April 13, I was compelled to bring it out. I had told no one that God had purposed in my heart to take this seven-foot cross to campus. But on Wednesday night, a student leader asked me if I would go to worship and preach on campus on Friday, because it was Good Friday. When I heard this brother tell me it was Good Friday, I thought to myself, *If there is any time to bring out a seven-foot cross on campus, it would be Easter.* I was encouraged, yet scared. What would people think? I would be labeled a freak, a fool and a fundamentalist. I didn't care. I just had to take the chance to be obedient.

Thursday morning I got out to campus. The night before I had e-mailed my house church to pray for me because I would be at

Bruin Walk from 12:00 to 2:00 P.M. to pray and seek the Lord's direction. As I began to walk down Bruin Walk holding this large cross, students everywhere started looking at me funny. Some laughed, others jeered, but I kept on walking.

I got into the middle of campus and met up with a few of our student leaders, who began to worship with me on the Bruin Walk steps. It was difficult to worship; it was hard to stay focused. We could feel the spiritual warfare, but we did our best to keep worshiping and praying. A few of us got up to preach, but there was no effect. Students walked right by us. Others laughed as they saw us holding this large cross and preaching.

After about two and a half hours of no response, I became disillusioned. I thought to myself, *Why does this cross have no power? Why do I not see what happened in the book of Acts happen here and now the way Paul and the early apostles experienced it? Is it just because we are in a different generation and we are to resort to seeker-sensitive, relational evangelism? I'm all for personal evangelism, but no, no, no, no, there has got to be more than this!* I had lost it . . .

At about 3:30 P.M., I was standing still on the Bruin Walk grass hill with the large cross on my shoulder. I then made my way down to the Bruin walkway, where all the organizations were tabling [had set up tables advertising their organization] and began to walk up and down the walkway singing to myself my favorite Lifehouse song. "You are all I want, You are all I need, You are everything, everything!" Over and over again, I sang to myself for a good half hour. I wasn't singing to get attention; I was singing to God. I had lost my sense of reality. I didn't know anymore what was real and what was not real. I just knew that God had to be God and that He had to do something.

All of a sudden, I began to talk about God out loud. I began to share about the cross. I shared about the power of the cross and how it is not just a piece of wood, not just a religious symbol or something you hang around your neck for coolness' sake. No, I shared how the cross is the power of God unto salvation! I preached passionately for a half hour to no one. I just preached to the air, because I was so frustrated that the cross, in the eyes of UCLA students, was just another religious ornament. Then something of heaven broke open.

People began to listen. Maybe 60 to 80 students started gathering to listen. One girl was sitting on the steps by herself. I preached to her. She was listening intently as I explained the power of the cross. She began to understand that the cross came with a price; it cost the Son of God His very life and blood. Then others started gathering to listen.

In particular, a fraternity member I had been praying for was gripped by the message. He almost converted on the spot. When I challenged him, he said he wanted to accept Christ but still needed time to seek. I prayed for him. Next thing I knew, the UCLA TV station was filming the whole scene and asking to interview me. After preaching for an hour or so, a crowd of 100 had gathered. The presence of God was thick, and the Bruin walkway was silent once again, like it was earlier in the year when we had preached outdoors. I didn't feel the need to challenge people to respond; I just needed to share my heart on how I felt about the cross. Many did respond, though, including a Muslim student, a whole Philippino dance group and a Latin sorority.

When I finally told the crowd I was done preaching, I walked down the Bruin Walk and the whole crowd began to clap for me. I thought it was interesting. I didn't know what to make of it; I just knew I had needed to share the message of the cross. I had to get out my frustration to let UCLA know that the cross has power and that it cost blood—it cost the blood of God's Son.

Later, the UCLA TV station interviewed me, asking me what made my message different from those other street preachers who condemn others to hell. I simply shared that I had no strategy but was compelled by the love of God in my heart for all to hear His message of salvation. I preached the gospel when they interviewed me, and who knows if maybe some students watched the program and got saved. Whatever the case, in my spirit, I knew something had shifted. The heavens were opened over Bruin Walk in a different way.

This leads me to the next part of the story where the real miracles begin . . .

Divine Healing and Prophetic Evangelism

"For Christ did not send me to baptize, but to preach the gospel—not with words of human wisdom, lest the cross of Christ be emptied of is power" (1 Cor. 1:17).

"My message and my preaching were not with wise and persuasive words, but with a demonstration of the Spirit's power, so that your faith might not rest on men's wisdom, but on God's power" (1 Cor. 2:4-5).

"But if all prophesy, and an unbeliever or an uninformed person comes in, he is convinced by all, he is convicted by all. And thus the secrets of his heart are revealed; and so, falling down on his face, he will worship God and report that God is truly among you" (1 Cor. 14:24-25).

The gospel was meant to be preached with power, not with persuasive words. This past week, God broke out in divine healing and prophetic power in the middle of UCLA. What happened was like it came straight out of the book of Acts. This is only the beginning.

On Monday I was compelled again to bring out a seven-foot wooden cross to the middle of the UCLA campus. I didn't feel like bringing it, but when does your flesh ever feel like bringing out a seven-foot cross to preach with? When I got to the middle of Bruin Walk, students everywhere were again staring, laughing and giving me weird looks. I didn't care. I was at a place in my Christianity where if I didn't see God show up in power like He did in the book of Acts, I wasn't willing to go on.

I met up with a few of our house church student leaders and some of them began to preach. There was not much response from the onlookers. Once again, I became disgruntled in my spirit, so I took the cross and began to pace around Bruin Walk praying silently to myself. For over an hour I stood in the middle of Bruin Walk, holding the cross and staring at the hundreds of student organizations tabling. I felt Jesus' heart of compassion for them, for they were like lost sheep without a shepherd.

One student organization in particular was one of the largest Asian fraternities. I had been praying for the salvation of this fraternity for more than a few months. As I stood there praying for them, I felt the Holy Spirit say to me, "Today I give you this fraternity!" I thought to myself, *Could this be?* I began to envision myself preaching the gospel in front of their table and seeing members call out to God for their salvation. Then it happened . . .

As I was standing there praying to myself in the middle of Bruin Walk, I began to pray out loud. Pretty soon, my prayer turned into preaching, and then into a rap. I had never done this before, but I began to rap out loud the gospel message. It sounded like slam poetry, but the message of the gospel was communicated clearly through each rhyme and sentence. Students around the Bruin Walk began to stop and listen. In a moment, it looked like a crowd of 100 had gathered to listen. Next thing I knew, I found myself in front of this Asian fraternity table, preaching the gospel directly to them.

There were maybe a dozen or more frat members, and they were all listening to me preach for at least one and a half hours. I shared about the meaning of passion and the suffering Jesus went through to save our souls. I explained that the cross is not just a religious symbol but the power of God unto salvation. I shared my life story and called the entire crowd to Lordship in Christ and repentance toward God. By then, Bruin Walk had been dead silent for more than one hour while people listened to me preach the gospel. As I gave the challenge to commit to Christ, students everywhere began to raise their hands to give their lives to Jesus. There must have been at least 18 people committing their lives to Christ. More important, many of the members of the Asian fraternity raised their hands to give their lives to Jesus, just as I saw beforehand in my spirit. It was a holy moment. They prayed out loud with me, and when they had done so, I shouted for joy! I explained that angels were there with us and in heaven rejoicing at the students' decisions.

No one wanted to leave, so I continued to preach the Kingdom. In my heart I felt led to teach on how to pray. I was amazed as all around me, the 100 or more students continued to listen to me teach in the middle of Bruin Walk. I then went on to teach about the power of the Holy Spirit, the gift of tongues and the power to cast out demons and to heal the sick.

It was at this point that a divine outbreak of miracles happened.

Therefore let him who speaks in a tongue pray that he may interpret. For if I pray in a tongue, my spirit prays, but my understanding is unfruitful. What is the conclusion then? I will pray with the spirit, and I will also pray with the understanding. I will sing with the spirit, and I will also sing with the understanding (1 Cor. 14:13-15).

As I preached about the power of the Holy Spirit, I felt inspired to speak a message in tongues. I began to speak aloud a divine message in tongues from my spirit. I asked God to give me the interpretation once the tongue was released. I spoke with my understanding and the interpretation spoke of God's hand being sovereign over creation, His power to do all things and the need to forgive others. At that point, many all around the Bruin Walk were coming under the power of God and were beginning to tear up. I knew in that moment that the Holy Spirit wanted me to pray for the brothers in the large Asian fraternity. Looking at them, I asked if I could pray for them, and they all nodded. I walked up and stretched out my hands to pray a prayer of blessing over each fraternity brother.

Once I began to pray, I immediately received a word of knowledge about one of the fraternity members there whose mother was sick and needed prayer. I asked, "Which one of you in this fraternity has a mother who is sick?" There were a little more than a dozen frat brothers there and one raised his hand. He told me his name, his mother's name and then I said, "The sickness is cancer, isn't it?" He said, "Yes!" The moment this word of knowledge went forth, the entire crowd was astonished. One fraternity member who was not a Christian began to cry uncontrollably. I looked at all of them and told them to immediately pray and believe that their frat brother's mother would be miraculously healed.

I began to explain that it is God who knows all, is sovereign over all and who has the power to heal. They were all bewildered. Then I looked to my left and saw one of the frat brothers, who had listened intently the whole time, sitting on a table with crutches. I knew in my spirit that God wanted to heal him. I asked him, "Why do you have crutches?" He said, "I think I broke my foot yesterday playing basketball; I can't walk or move my foot at all, and it hurts a lot!" I told him, "Jesus has the power to heal the sick, and I'm going to lay my hands on your foot right now so that you will be healed."

The moment I laid my hands on his broken foot, I felt the power of the Holy Spirit shoot through my body. I knew God had healed his foot. I told him to immediately take off his crutches, stand on his two feet and walk. He looked at me as if to say, "Are you for real?" I told him, "Yes, get up right now and walk in Jesus' name!" He got off the table without his crutches and was hesitant to take a step, but I encouraged him to step out in faith.

As he took his first step, I asked him what was happening. I said, "The pain in your foot is leaving, isn't it?" In shock, he responded, "The pain is leaving!" I said, "Keep on walking and the pain will completely go away!" A miracle happened. He began to walk all around the Bruin Walk in front of more than 100 onlookers. The entire crowd was in awe. As he took each step, his eyes began to well up with tears. He kept saying, "The pain is leaving; it's almost completely gone!" The power of God was healing him, and it was a witness for all to see the miracle-working power of Jesus:

> And truly Jesus did many other signs in the presence of His disciples, which are not written in this book; but these are written that you may believe that Jesus is the Christ, the Son of God, and that believing you may have life in His name (John 20:30-31).

Many of the fraternity members were locked in, watching, amazed and in the presence of the Holy Spirit. The one frat brother who was crying uncontrollably began to explain to me, "Many people have shared the gospel with me, but I could never believe in a God I couldn't see. But when you told my friend that his mom had cancer, I knew it was impossible for you to know that, because we don't even know!" As Paul said in 1 Corinthians 2:5, "your faith should not be in the wisdom of men but in the power of God."

We owe this generation an encounter with the power of God. If we think it is only seeker-sensitive evangelism strategies that will win the lost, then we are going to lose a generation. I am convinced that God's Word is true, that if we preach the gospel He will confirm it with signs, wonders and miracles (see Mark 16:20). What happened at UCLA Bruin Walk this Monday was proof. More than six of the fraternity members gave us their contact information and have committed to meeting regularly to learn obedience to Christ. We will now plant a house church among their community.

That same day, an Indian student was listening to me preach the gospel at Bruin Walk. While I shared the need to repent, be baptized in water and receive the gift of the Holy Spirit (see Acts 2), he immediately raised his hands in the air and said, "Baptize me!" We took a large water bottle and immediately poured water over his head and baptized him in the name of the Father, Son and Holy Spirit. He began to give praise to God and was a public testimony for all to see. It was a beautiful moment.

Many more God encounters happened on Monday—too many to count. The Holy Spirit has been pouring out His presence at UCLA like we have never seen. The power of God is in the air. This generation is hungry for a real encounter with the Holy Spirit—not a dead religion or social program. We must contend for heaven to encounter Earth. This cannot just be talk; it must be put into action.

God's power, though, does not come without spiritual violence: "And from the days of John the Baptist until now the kingdom of heaven suffers violence, and the violent take it by force" (Matt. 11:12). If we want to see God's power show up on our campuses, there is a price to pay. We have to press in, pray, fast, do spiritual violence and soak in the presence of the Holy Spirit until we are so filled with Him that nothing but His presence and authority flows out of us. When that presence flows out of us, it manifests itself in a bold gospel witness where we see the cross preached with power, where we see sicknesses healed, demons cast out and souls saved soundly.

Now is not the time to hide in our prayer meetings. If we truly believe for God's power and revival to show up when we pray, then we must step out in faith to see it happen. Faith without actions is dead (see Jas. 2:26). A revival prayer meeting on our campus that does not result in taking the gospel to the lost . . . is just a prayer meeting. We must be moved from prayer to action. By sustaining both, in the power of the Holy Spirit, we will see our campuses flipped upside down for the glory of God!

I challenge every student who reads this book to go out two by two on their campuses and to preach the gospel. Whether in the middle of campus, in a dorm, a classroom or anywhere else, believe God to encounter the lost! Step out in faith, preach, prophesy and let the Holy Spirit lead you to pray for the sick and downtrodden! Change your campus in the power of the Holy Spirit!

Oh God, would You raise up a generation who will be fools for the gospel, those who would care not so much about their reputation, but would only care about advancing the kingdom of God in their generation—no matter what the cost! This is the hope we have, what are we doing with it? Are we going to settle for good church meetings, campus fellowship gatherings, social events and outreach activities week after week, school year after school year? I didn't sign up for a gospel without power. God is God; let Him be God. Stop putting God in a box with your theologies, and believe Him to be the God of the Bible, the God of Acts and the God of now! Jesus Christ is the same yesterday, today and forever, and I refuse to believe anything less than to see Him walk the streets of our campuses in divine power:

I tell you the truth, anyone who has faith in me will do what I have been doing. He will do even greater things than these, because I am going to the Father. And I will do whatever you ask in my name, so that the Son may bring glory to the Father. You may ask me for anything in my name, and I will do it (John 14:12-13).

Jesus, may You send revival to my generation. Send revival to the college campuses of America. Send revival to this nation and bring glory to Your Father.

This is just the beginning . . . God continues to move daily at UCLA. There is more to come.[1]

Power Failure

There is a power failure in today's Church. We need the power of the book of Acts once again. We need to contend for the power of God to show up in this generation in order to effectively evangelize the lost. Why do I have a passion for power evangelism? Why do I believe God desires to release His power in this generation the same way He did in the book of Acts? In Acts 5:12-16, it says:

> And through the hands of the apostles many signs and wonders were done among the people. And they were all with one accord in Solomon's Porch. Yet none of the rest dared join them, but the people esteemed them highly. And believers were increasingly added to the Lord, multitudes of both men and women, so that they brought the sick out into the streets and laid them on beds and couches, that at least the shadow of Peter passing by might fall on some of them. Also a multitude gathered from the surrounding cities to Jerusalem, bringing sick people and those who were tormented by unclean spirits, and they were all healed.

The New Testament Church rapidly grew mainly through signs, wonders and miracles. Multitudes gathered in Jerusalem and from the surrounding cities so that the sick and those tormented by demons would be healed. Unbelievers did not dare join the disciples of Jesus, but they held them in high regard. Do you know one church in North America where unbelievers are afraid to join yet hold the believers in the church in high regard? I know there will be a day in our university courtyards when the sick and demon-possessed will be daily set free to make known the power and works of the Holy Spirit. I am passionate to see New Testament Christianity released in this hour!

Let me tell you more in the following pages about how I was ruined at UCLA to see the power of God break out to confirm the message of Jesus and His cross. I will share with you a few personal blog entries of real power-evangelism encounters with students on campuses, and the ways in which God is restoring the power of the Holy Spirit in this generation. Additionally, I will explain how to biblically understand and practically move out in power evangelism through prophetic worship, apostolic preaching, demonic deliverance, prophetic evangelism and divine healing.

Remember, evangelism is an "overflow." It is not by our power, but by the Holy Spirit's power. As we are daily filled with Him, through prayer and obedience, we will release His power wherever we go!

Note

1. If you want to read about the rest of what happened at UCLA that week, go to www.jaesonma.blogspot.com, click on "April 2006 archives," and then read the post "UCLA IS SHAKING!"

CHAPTER SEVEN

PROPHETIC WORSHIP POWER

But you are holy, enthroned in the **praises** *of Israel.*
PSALM 22:3, EMPHASIS ADDED

*You will not need to fight in this battle. Position yourselves, stand
still and see the salvation of the LORD, who is with you, O Judah
and Jerusalem! . . . And Jehoshaphat bowed his head with his face
to the ground, and all Judah and the inhabitants of Jerusalem
bowed before the LORD,* **worshiping** *the LORD . . . Jehoshaphat . . .
appointed those who should* **sing** *to the LORD, and who should*
praise *the beauty of holiness, as they went out before the army and
were saying:* "**Praise** *the LORD, for His mercy endures forever."
Now when they began to sing and to praise, the LORD set ambushes
against the people of Ammon, Moab, and Mount Seir, who had
come against Judah; and they were* **defeated.**
2 CHRONICLES 20:17-22, EMPHASIS ADDED

One day in February 2005, I was sitting in my room when the Holy
Spirit's presence came upon me intensely. As I prayed, I saw a
vision of students on campuses everywhere, worshiping and
prophetically praising God in courtyards. Then I saw students
boldly preaching the gospel in the open air. Finally, I saw multitudes of lost students on university campuses all over the world,
forcing their way into the kingdom of God. After being caught up
in this vision, I immediately wrote an article on my personal blog.
Below is an excerpt.

Blog Entry:
Apostolic Preaching and Prophetic Worship on Campus!

I am writing this message because I sense strongly in my spirit that God wants to release another Great Awakening, this time on the university campuses of America. We are coming upon the wake of another Jesus People movement. In the late 1960s there was a major move of God among young hippies all over California. Radical hippie preachers like Lonnie Frisbee preached on campuses, street corners, in bars on Hollywood Boulevard and baptized thousands of hippies in the ocean beaches. What happened in those days was like it came straight out of the book of Acts. I read that there were signs, wonders and miracles, speaking in tongues, thousands of young people swept into the kingdom of God. They were living in 24/7 communes together, sharing all things together and enjoying fellowship while radical street preaching was bringing in the masses to Christ. *Do it again, Lord! I know You will; now is the time!*

In the last six months, the Holy Spirit has been impressing heavily upon me to see the book of Acts happen again on college campuses. There is too much timidity among Christians on every campus I visit. There is a fear of what others think . . . and it is justified by an "I don't want to offend others" mentality. It is compromise.

The national average of Christians at each university is less than 5 percent, and more than 90 percent of those 5 percent come from Christian backgrounds.[1] In other words, Christians are mainly reaching Christians on campus. If we don't see revival now, we will have a post-Christian generation tomorrow. It's time for radical Christianity . . . or should I say "normal Christianity" to be released on this generation with power.

Like I said, I've been studying the book of Acts. The more I read, the more I am challenged. Church was never meant to be in a temple or a building; it was meant to be on the streets. It was meant to be in the marketplace, 24/7, where the people are. Where do you think Jesus would be preaching if He were here today? Where would Peter and Paul be preaching if they were still around?

I highly doubt they would be preaching in a Sunday morning church service or the next large-group fellowship meeting. I know exactly where they would be preaching . . . in the middle of the campus where all the student organizations are promoting their beliefs.

It's sad, but there is too much preaching within the four walls of the church and not enough preaching to the lost. Preaching was meant for the lost! Yet we have turned the powerful art of preaching into "sermonizing." *Lord, have mercy, and turn us back to the power of God unto salvation!*

The Spirit of the Lord GOD is upon Me, Because the LORD has anointed Me to *preach* good news to the poor; He has sent Me to heal the brokenhearted, to proclaim liberty to the captives, and the opening of the prison to those who are bound; To proclaim the acceptable year of the LORD and the day of vengeance of our God! (Isa. 61:1-2).

What am I getting at? There is a move of God that will sweep thousands of young people into His kingdom, beginning on university campuses across California and then all over the United States of America. What is this move? It will be a move of two things: (1) prophetic worship and (2) apostolic preaching.

Last week, a student leader in our campus church network was inspired during his early morning quiet times to bring his guitar to school at San Jose State University. Not sure why, he went with his guitar to the middle of campus—the place with the most student traffic. He sensed that the Holy Spirit wanted him to break out his guitar and worship at the top of His lungs. He did. At first, he was scared out of his pants, but as he continued to worship, the manifest presence of God began to descend on the ground on which he was worshiping. He later told me that all he was asking God for that morning was one thing: *Lord, I want to see heaven come down on this campus!* Well, he got what he was praying for.

As the Holy Spirit prophetically led him to sing new songs by proclaiming Jesus over the campus, this same student sensed that he was to pull out his Bible and read it out loud. With authority, he began to read out loud, at the top of his lungs, the written Word of God. Students began to look at him, stare at him, even laugh at him. But he didn't care, because he was in the zone with Jesus. As students gathered around to watch this Jesus freak, he began to read the Scriptures and he prayed for students who the Holy Spirit was pointing out to him.

While praying for students, he saw a fraternity table with a frat brother sitting there, completely gripped by the Scriptures being read. All of a sudden, the frat brother left the table and walked up to my friend.

He said, "I don't know who you are, but while you were singing those songs to God, I felt His presence touch my body. You see, I've been a backslidden Christian for over three years, and this weekend our fraternity house burned down. Everything I've ever owned burned down in that house this weekend, but there was only one thing left . . . my Bible!"

This fraternity brother broke down under the conviction of the Holy Spirit and the spoken Word of God. He encountered the presence of the living God in the middle of the day on a university campus while sitting outdoors at his fraternity table. Now, that's what I'm talking about!

"Enter into His gates with thanksgiving, and into His courts with praise" (Ps. 100:4). We don't need more persuasion evangelism in this postmodern generation. What we need more is presence evangelism and encounters with an Almighty God. How do we bring the presence? It is only through worship and prayer. It's prophetic worship that sings to Jesus from the heart, not from a PowerPoint slide. It's passionate, raw, unplugged worship that touches the heart of God and ends up touching the heart of a generation.

Thousands of new prophetic worship bands will hit the shores of the college campuses during the day and into the night. Bands of young radicals who pull out their guitars, djembes, drums and all kinds of instruments will worship at the top of their lungs in the middle of campuses. It's a prophetic band of worshipers who aren't just singing the latest hit worship song but are worshiping in their own way, singing new songs, creating new lyrics, going all out, undignified like King David.

It's a sound that even the Christian world has never heard. They are the new sounds that come from the streets of heaven. Get ready, because the sons of thunder are coming! They worship in spirit and truth; and while students are passing by, while others are gathering at tables, while others are watching . . . the presence of God comes. The lost have never heard this kind of worship, with such passion, with such beauty and attraction. It's prophetic, for the spirit of prophecy is the testimony of Jesus.

This prophetic presence all of a sudden invades and touches the hearts of young people, and they begin to come under the overwhelming love of God. This generation is waiting to see true passion. But where is it? True passion is only revealed when we passionately worship the passionate One . . . our suffering King Jesus. When this generation sees true worship, they will come to worship God.

After I posted this blog, an outdoor prophetic worship movement broke out all over Southern California. In Los Angeles a prophetic worship movement called Strike LA was birthed by students on the UCLA and University of Southern California (USC) campuses. Hundreds of students have been striking in outdoor worship warfare and praise, breaking open the heavens over the city of Los Angeles for revival and reformation. Students have been gathering in small prophetic worship bands, releasing public praise during the noonday and at other times on different college campuses, high schools and strategic high places in the city. Check out www.strikela.org. Let the prophetic worship movement begin!

Prophetic Worship in the Old Testament

In 2 Chronicles 20:1-22, God gives King Jehoshaphat an unusual battle plan. The battle plan was not to fight with swords, but to fight with prophetic worship. To be prophetic is to hear the voice of the Lord and declare what is to come. To be a worshiper is to

humbly submit our will to God and love Him with all our heart—
with our entire being—in order to glorify His name. King
Jehoshaphat and the army of Judah did just those things and they
won one of the greatest military victories in biblical history.

God grants victory to those who trust Him. Jehoshaphat was
facing the greatest enemy threat of his reign. A great multitude of
Moabites, Ammonites and others from Syria were plotting to
annihilate Judah (see 2 Chron. 20:2). Being completely outnum-
bered, King Jehoshaphat gathered all the cities of Judah and
called a fast, and together the people of the cities cried out to the Lord
for deliverance from their enemies. As they were seeking the
Lord for mercy, the prophet Jahaziel gave a prophetic word to
King Jehoshaphat:

> Thus says the LORD to you: "Do not be afraid nor dis-
> mayed because of this great multitude, for the battle is
> not yours, but God's . . . You will not need to fight in this
> battle. Position yourselves, stand still and see the salva-
> tion of the LORD" (vv.15,17).

The victory came in a strange but powerful way. King Jehoshaphat sent the Levitical priests in front of the army to stand and
praise the Lord God of Israel "with voices loud and high" (v. 19).
Then others were appointed to sing to the Lord and praise Him in
the beauty of His holiness. They went out before the army saying,
"Praise the LORD, for His mercy endures forever" (v. 21).

> Now when they began to sing and to praise, the LORD set
> ambushes against the people of Ammon, Moab, and
> Mount Seir, who had come against Judah; and they were
> defeated (v. 22).

The Lord destroyed the enemies of Judah when the Judeans
set out to trust God in prophetic worship. As Judah prophetically
declared God's power and reign, God fought their battle. Through
this mighty victory, we learn that a key principle and strategy to

winning the battle on our campuses and in our cities is through prophetic worship power.

Frontline Spiritual Warfare

Ephesians 6:12 says, "For we do not wrestle against flesh and blood, but against principalities, against powers, against the rulers of the darkness of this age, against spiritual hosts of wickedness in the heavenly places." Some people ask me, "Why do you do outdoor worship on campuses? What is the point?" The point is this: There are spiritual principalities that wage war over the minds of students and faculty on our campuses. These principalities cannot be taken down by mere human strategies. They can only be taken down by supernatural strategies born of the spirit of God. Prophetic worship is an act of spiritual warfare. It invades the darkest regions of a campus or a city and declares the name of God boldly in the face of satanic opposition in the unseen realms.

There is one thing demons can't stand—praise and worship. When we sing praise like the priests sang praise in 2 Chronicles 20:21, all heaven breaks loose and all hell disappears. Prophetic worship is warfare. It is not for the fainthearted. It is not singing nice praise songs in a classroom or in a church building. Prophetic worship is prophetically declaring God's praise in the public, in the darkest of areas where Satan has a stronghold. It is when we lift up a shout of triumph (see Ps. 47:1) that the walls of darkness begin tumbling down and the enemies are defeated. The victory won't come easily; there are age-old principalities on our campuses that won't go down without a fight. We must prophesy and worship and praise non-stop until we know in our spirit that the victory is won.

Trusting God to Win the Battle

In prophetic worship, we must trust God to win the battle and not rely on our own strength, strategies or ideas. King Jehoshaphat recognized that without God's supernatural intervention, there was no way Judah could win the battle. God wanted Jehoshaphat and everyone else to know that His ways are above our ways and that only His presence can bring about victory.

We see so little effective evangelism on our campuses because we don't fully rely upon God's power to do the job. When we prophetically worship in public, we are putting our full trust in God's presence and the power of the Holy Spirit to convict students of righteousness, sin and judgment. We believe that as we prophetically worship, warring angels are being sent out to do battle to bind the demonic principalities and open up the heavens over our campuses for revival. We believe that when students walk by, they are walking into the very presence of God and encountering Him. It may seem ridiculous, but this is what God wants—for us to lose our reputation and be fully reliant on Him for breakthrough. For the battle is not yours, but God's (see 2 Chron. 20:15).

Praise Releases His Manifest Presence

King Jehoshaphat knew that the key to winning the battle was to release God's presence over his enemies so that God would take it from there. This mighty presence of God in Jehoshaphat's time could only be released through the high praise and worship of the Levites and priests. But today, we are a royal priesthood, a chosen generation called to give God praise night and day for all to see (see 1 Pet. 2:9).

What do you think will happen when all Christ followers on every campus gather daily to praise God out loud in the courtyards of our universities? I'll tell you what will happen: When we worship and praise, the presence of God has to come in power! Praise and worship enthrone the Holy Spirit. They form a resting place or platform for the Holy Spirit (see Ps. 22:3-5). When we love Him with all our hearts, when we give up our reputations and say, "I will be even more undignified than this," like King David did, something in God's heart jumps, and we get His attention.

This generation doesn't need another explanation of the gospel; what it needs is an encounter with God's manifest presence. Through prophetic worship we bring heaven down to Earth and His light into the darkest areas of our campuses. The multitudes will have to bow down to His manifest glory, because it is not only powerful, but also so irresistibly beautiful.

Declaring God's Victory Before the Battle

God wants us to be a people of great faith. Prophetic worship prophecies by calling those things that are not as though they were (see Rom. 4:17). It is faith. It believes that the battle is won before we even step onto the battlefield. The army of Judah wasn't sent out first. The priests were sent out first to declare victory to God before the battle even began. On your campus, the enemy might seem to outnumber you, seem to be intimidating and seem to be in control. But it only "seems" this way. It is a front. It is not real. It is your duty to go out, trust in God's promise, and prophetically declare the victory out loud over your campus, because the demons have to hear you (see Eph. 3:10).

"Do not fear or be dismayed; tomorrow go out against them, for the LORD is with you" (2 Chron. 20:17). The first response of Jehoshaphat to the prophetic instruction given him was to kneel down and worship the Lord. So must we. By faith, he received the victory in His spirit-man and thanked God for it. We must do the same. Next, as we go out, we must clap our hands and shout with triumph! We are instructed in Psalm 47:1 on how to praise God: "Oh, clap your hands, all you peoples! Shout to God with the voice of triumph!" The word "clap" is *taqa* in Hebrew, meaning "to strike." It describes pitching a tent or fastening a nail through the striking of a hammer. *Taqa* is also used to describe blowing a trumpet or sounding an alarm.[2] It depicts a supernatural energy and enthusiasm when engaged in praise and worship.[3]

Prophetic worship is not quiet worship or clapping hands in a circle. No, prophetic worship is boldly declaring and loudly praising God with all our heart, soul, strength, body and mind in the public high places to tear down strongholds and release God's victory! If we can shout for our school sports team, how much more should we shout for the glory of God? Declare His victory through bold, public prophetic worship and watch God defeat His enemies before you.

Prophetic Worship Strategies

1. Gather a team to prophetically worship outdoors on your campus.

2. Ask the Holy Spirit where to publicly praise Him on your campus. (Target places where there are satanic strongholds, where there are masses of students or places that are open for students to march or to assemble and worship.)

3. Begin your time in prayer for faith and protection from the enemy.

4. Worship with simple instruments (guitars, djembes, and so on) or a cappella.

5. As you prophetically worship, don't focus on those around you or the spiritual warfare; focus on the beauty of the Lord's holiness.

6. In the beginning it may be difficult to worship because of the satanic opposition, but keep pressing in. Don't give up. Boldly praise until you sense together in your spirit that there is breakthrough and an open heaven over the area.

7. Once you sense the victory in your spirit, declare the Lord's praise and do as the Holy Spirit leads you.

Notes
1. http://www.ivyjungle.org.
2. Francis Brown, S. R. Driver and C. A. Briggs, eds., *A Hebrew and English Lexicon of the Old Testament* (Oxford: The Clarendon Press, 1951), p. 1075.
3. Jack Hayford, *Spirit Filled Life Bible* (Nashville, TN: Thomas Nelson, 1991), p. 794; James Strong, *The New Strong's Exhaustive Concordance* (Nashville, TN: Thomas Nelson, 1984), Hebrew #8628.

CHAPTER EIGHT

APOSTOLIC PREACHING POWER

And my speech and my preaching were not with persuasive
words of human wisdom, but in demonstration of the Spirit
and of power, that your faith should not be in the wisdom
of men but in the power of God.
1 CORINTHIANS 2:4-5

Prophetic worship ushers in the presence of God, but it is apostolic preaching that ushers in the power of God:

And Joshua rose early in the morning, and the priests took up the ark of the LORD. Then seven priests bearing seven trumpets of rams' horns before the ark of the LORD went on continually and blew with the trumpets. And the armed men went before them. But the rear guard came after the ark of the LORD, while the priests continued blowing the trumpets (Josh. 6:12-13).

Joshua followed the strategy of the Lord. He sent out the priests (who represent prophetic worshipers) into battle first, while the armed guards (who represent apostolic preachers) stood prepared to attack. The presence of God must be ushered in first, in order for His presence to anoint the army for war. This also applies to prophetic worship and apostolic preaching needed for transforming the campuses.

We experienced a breakout of prophetic worship and apostolic preaching firsthand at UCLA in October 2005, months after the Holy Spirit had given me the vision of students worshiping and preaching on campuses. The record of the encounter was posted to my personal blog.

Blog Entry:
Prophetic Worship and Apostolic Preaching at UCLA

God is asking us to press in at this hour and to pray and war for "heaven on earth" to come to our university campuses. Do not relent; press in. The breakthrough is waiting to break out! But a divine break-out is dependent on the level of our spiritual hunger and violence. The kingdom of heaven already suffers violence, and it is the violent who will take it by force (see Matt. 11:12).

This past Wednesday at UCLA, we experienced a taste of heaven on Earth, but it came with a cost. We got onto campus and sensed that the Lord was asking us to go into the middle of campus and to lead prophetic outdoor worship and outdoor proclamation of the gospel. As we walked up onto campus there were thousands of students walking up and down Bruin Walk. Normally, we would sit at the patch of grass where there were not many onlookers (the free speech area), but on Wednesday the main steps at the top of Bruin Walk were open, with no student organizations tabling. We took it by faith.

There were only eight of us (Matt, Caleb, Josh, Alyson, Jumpei, Neil and Sam). As we sat on the steps, we began to pray. It was difficult. The enemy immediately began to intimidate us with fear and self-consciousness, and I could tell many on our team were distracted. I could sense the spiritual darkness/forces right there in the middle of campus opposing our prayers, as hundreds of students were standing/tabling and hanging out around the Bruin Walk sidewalk. It was almost as if we could hear the devil say, "Come on, what are you going to do? Worship in the middle of campus? With your little guitars and make a fool out of yourself? Don't you know I own this campus?" But greater is He that is in us than he that is in the world (see 1 John 4:4).

As time passed, it became more difficult. Yet, my heart began to break as I saw thousands of students walk past us with no sense of hope or direction. On the outside, these UCLA students all look like they've got it together. They go to UCLA, they have the status, the image, the self-confidence. They look cool and they look like they've got it together. Then I heard the Spirit of the Lord shout to my spirit, "Stop looking with your physical eyes! Look with your spiritual eyes. They are all lost, dying and headed toward eternal separation from God!" I had to remind myself that the battle is not against flesh and blood. The battle is against spiritual powers, principalities and darkness in the air. The god of this age has blinded their eyes so that they cannot see (see Eph. 6:12; 2 Cor. 4:4).

In the natural, seven Asian nobodies with two guitars, and a big white guy—all worshiping at the top of their lungs in the middle of the day at UCLA would seem like the most foolish strategy anyone could devise to advance God's kingdom on Earth. Yet, God chooses to use the foolish things of the earth to confound the wise (see 1 Cor. 1:27). We began to worship not for them, but for Him, with all of our hearts. It was extremely difficult. Alyson all of a sudden got sick in the stomach and wanted to throw up. Caleb and Josh both started to feel out of it and were having negative thoughts. I knew it was the enemy's attack. "Guys, focus! Pull it together! The enemy wants to make us think this is pointless. We might not look cool singing hallelujah songs, but this isn't about being relevant or cool. This is a spiritual war. Don't look at the students laughing. Don't look at the physical circumstances. Look at God, press in, worship God and He will come! Angels and demons are right here, right now. We need to press in and worship till heaven comes down to UCLA!"

The Holy Spirit began to help us. We began to sing a cappella "I love You, Lord, and I lift my voice, to worship You, Oh my soul rejoice. Take joy, my King, in what You hear. Let it be a sweet, sweet song in Your ear!" Over and over again, we began not just to sing, not just to worship but to also prophetically declare to the spiritual powers and principalities at UCLA an authentic and genuine heartfelt cry of love to Jesus! We began to enthrone Jesus over UCLA, looking to God, not to man. Many people began to watch. It was like time stopped and the presence of God began to descend—

it was felt. I knew in my spirit that angels had descended and that God was with us! We kept shouting it out as hundreds of students walked by and were looking at us, some stopping and watching, others turning their heads back. The Holy Spirit—yes, the Holy Spirit—comes to convict hearts with righteousness, sin and judgment (see John 16:8)!

Sam from CCM fellowship began to lead us into worship (thank God for Sam—if he wasn't there we wouldn't have made it) and we sang in the middle of Bruin Walk for two hours. We kept pressing in. We were contending for heaven on Earth. We were contending for the power of God to be released. If His presence would not go before us, we had no hope. After two hours of worship warfare, we began to sense that it was time to preach. The spiritual air had been cleared. The heavens were open, blinders were removed and the Bruin Walk area we stood upon was consecrated holy unto the Lord.

Caleb had to go to class, so he got up and began to preach to the students walking by. He could only preach for a few minutes and then said, "I'm passing the baton. Who's taking it up next?" This was my first time on campus at UCLA during school. I'll tell the truth: I was intimidated, but I knew the Holy Spirit was with us. He was anointing us for the task (to preach the gospel and proclaim the good news of Isaiah 61)!

Let me tell you something—no matter how many times you have preached in public to masses of unbelievers, you never get used to it. You never feel confident right away. Apostolic preaching is not for the fainthearted. It's not a Sunday sermon. It's for those who dare to completely lose their own reputation and be completely and utterly dependent on God! I wanted to pee in my pants; I looked at the hundreds of students walking up and down where we were worshiping and I wanted to run and hide. But then I closed my eyes, I asked God for grace and again He showed me, "It's not by might, nor by power, but by My Spirit (see Zech. 4:6)! Don't look with your physical eyes. There is more with you than there is with them. Open your mouth and I will fill it with My words to follow!" Without opening my eyes, I jumped into the middle of Bruin Walk and I began to preach at the top of my lungs . . .

My voice was almost gone, but as I preached I could sense the unction and anointing of the Holy Spirit and His power. Students walking by began to stop dead in their tracks! Five here; 12 there. Two tour groups stopped at the top of the college above us, an entire Asian fraternity sitting on the steps stopped talking and began to listen; an entire group of African Americans who just moments before had their boom boxes blasting stopped and began to listen; those tabling turned around and within moments there was a crowd of students standing in wonder, gripped by the Spirit all over Bruin Walk, listening to me preach the gospel of repentance and love toward God! There had to have been at least 120 students standing still and listening for almost a half hour as I shared my testimony and proclaimed the death, burial and resurrection of Jesus Christ! Ask Josh, Alyson or Matt—the entire Bruin Walk moments before had been full of noise, conversations and hustle and bustle, but all of a sudden, the entire Bruin Walk was silent. God supernaturally amplified my broken voice with no microphone! People said they could hear the preaching from the third story of the building above us.

What happened? To tell the truth, I don't know exactly what happened, but all glory be to the name of God! I called the students who were listening to repentance and to commit in prayer to give their lives to Christ. At least six hands rose into the air, and I asked the crowd to shout out the sinner's prayer with me. We could hear students' voices all over shouting out the sinner's prayer in repentance and commitment all over Bruin Walk! Students began to pray for the infilling of the Holy Spirit, and others were weeping under the presence. It could only have been God!

The presence of God was present, so present that we didn't even know what to do once we were done praying the prayer. We prayed for those oppressed by darkness, casting out the evil spirits. As this was happening, one student began to question what was preached and started to begin a debate. I could tell it was a distraction, but God helped us by using a smoking skater sitting on some steps to defend me and to debate with this atheist. Then, the

Holy Spirit led our team to go two by two to begin talking with the students who responded.

One student who came from a Hindu background said, "I'm jealous for what you have! I want it, but I don't know how to get it!" We began to converse, answer his questions and immediately prayed with him.

There was also an African American student who was extremely angry. He looked demonically possessed and began to tell us, "You are full of @%#$!" We listened to him say how Christians could not be trusted; he told us he was a servant of the devil, that Christians had done too much wrong in this world and that millions were victims of genocide in the name of Christ. My heart began to break as I listened to him. I prayed, *Holy Spirit, give me wisdom to respond!* And He did. I responded to the African American student's anger by asking for forgiveness on behalf of myself and all Christians. He responded with, "I have no response for that one." He almost began to cry; his entire countenance changed. We prayed for him and he said, "I don't know what it is about you all. I'm the only one in my family who isn't a Christian, but if there is one church I'll go to, it's the one you go to." We gave him the info to Passion Church, which met on campus. It was the power of Christ's forgiveness that He could not resist.

Next to him was the large Asian fraternity group. They had been listening and responding to the preaching the whole time. There was one fraternity brother in particular with a white hat on. I saw him while I was preaching and knew God's hand was on him. I walked right up to him, and it was like he was waiting for me to speak to him. He shook my hand and said, "I heard your message; it spoke to me. I almost went to jail too; I'm actually a PK [Pastors Kid] and I'm the president of this fraternity. I feel like God may be calling me back to serve Him after all these years." We kept talking. God was moving upon his heart; he wanted to talk more, so I asked him if we could get together for coffee and to study the Bible. He wanted to eagerly . . . he is definitely a student of peace. (Later in the year, this fraternity brother was radically transformed and God used him to bring revival and to start a simple church in his fraternity.)

The stories go on and on. All I can say is, glory be to God! This is just the beginning, friends, soldiers, army of God. We praised God for what He did; we regrouped and ended with a prayer. But the enemy was not happy. We immediately began to feel uneasiness in our spirits. Alyson got sicker; others were battling negative thoughts. We continued to pray and intercede throughout the rest of the day and night.

Some of the giants at UCLA went down that day, but not all. Yes, God established His throne on the Bruin Walk steps on Wednesday, but the battle has just begun. The battle has just begun. We saw only a glimpse of heaven on Earth, a glimpse of His light breaking into the darkness. We must press forward, saints!

Yes, Wednesday at UCLA we encountered the intimate presence of Christ in worship. Yes, we operated and experienced the power of His anointing upon the preached Word, resulting in repentance and salvation. Yes, we also experienced the spiritual warfare, demonic attack and the grace to fellowship in the sufferings of Christ Jesus our Lord. In John 16:33, Jesus says, "In the world you will have tribulation; but be of good cheer, I have overcome the world." Do not relent, we must press in and contend for the perfect will of God to be established upon the earth, upon our campuses. Do not relent, do not give up, continue to pray, prophesy, seek His face, prophetically worship and apostolically declare to every university campus in this nation, *Repent, for the kingdom of God has come!*

The Power of Apostolic Preaching

Prophetic worship is what opened the heavens over Bruin Walk that day, but it was apostolic preaching that God used to reap the harvest. There is a great need in the Body of Christ in our nation to understand and, once again, have a burning vision for apostolic preaching. But what is apostolic preaching? Let the book of Acts explain:

Now when they heard this, they were cut to the heart, and said to Peter and the rest of the apostles, "Men and

brethren, what shall we do?" Then Peter said to them,
"Repent, and let everyone of you be baptized in the name
of Jesus Christ for the remission of sins; and you shall
receive the gift of the Holy Spirit . . ." And with many
other words he testified and exhorted them, saying, "Be
saved from this perverse generation." Then those who
gladly received his word were baptized; and that day about
three thousand souls were added to them (Acts 2:37-41).

Apostolic preaching is preaching the gospel so powerfully that
it cuts the hearts of men, resulting in deep repentance and mass
conversions. It happened in Peter's time when 3,000 came to Christ
in a day. A few days later, in the book of Acts (4:4), 5,000 more are
recorded as being saved and whole cities pushed their way into the
Kingdom through Paul's apostolic preaching. We may say, "This
happened in the days of old, but certainly it cannot happen in highly sophisticated campus cultures like Yale or Stanford." Why not? It
happened in the First and Second Great Awakenings of America.

Jonathan Edwards, a young preacher who attended Yale,
preached an unapologetic message in 1741, called "Sinners in the
Hands of an Angry God," that sent all of the East Coast into repentance and ushered in a sweeping revival to a hell-bent America.
Later, in the 1790s, Yale University had totally forgotten about the
great revival just decades before. The student body had fallen into
drunkenness and blasphemy, and the majority of students were
attacking the Christian faith because they had turned toward athe-
ism and deism. During that dark hour, a young man named
Timothy Dwight, the president of Yale and one of the few
Christians on campus, began to preach on the infallibility of God's
Word and His moral standard. By the end of the year more than
one half of the entire Yale University campus had turned in repentance toward God.[1]

When I was in Bible college, I read the biography of another
great revivalist, Charles Finney. His preaching was so powerful
that people would tremble, literally shake, before he even opened
his mouth:

Finney seemed so anointed with the Holy Spirit that people were often brought under conviction of sin just by looking at him. When holding meetings at Utica, New York, he visited a large factory. At the sight of him one of the workers, and then another, and then another broke down and wept under a sense of their sins, and finally so many were sobbing and weeping that the machinery had to be stopped while Finney pointed them to Christ . . . Finney seems to have had the power of impressing the conscience of men with the necessity of holy living in such a manner as produced lasting results. Over eighty-five in every hundred persons professing conversion to Christ in Finney's meetings remained true to God. Whereas seventy percent of those professing Christ in meetings of even so great an evangelist as Moody afterward became backsliders. Such results were the fruit of hours and hours of prayer.[2]

Beginning with the 1830-1831 Rochester, New York, revival, historians recorded through the preaching of Charles Finney that more than 100,000 people were converted to Christ as a result of his meetings—in only one year.[3] *Lord, do it again! We desperately need apostolic preaching released in this generation.*

I'm passionate about this kind of preaching coming on the scene again, coming into the public squares of our university campuses, because I've experienced it, just a taste of it. I know this is what God is after: men and women who will apostolically preach His Word in these end times on the campuses and in the cities of the nations to reap a great last-day harvest.

What Is Apostolic Preaching?

One of the most powerful books I've ever read on apostolic preaching is *Apostolic Foundations* by Art Katz.[4] Through this book and my own life encounters, I learned what apostolic preaching truly is. Below are a few key principles I've learned and experienced.

The Word of God Spoken in Humility

"For the word of the cross is foolishness to those who are perishing, but to us who are being saved it is the power of God" (1 Cor. 1:18, *NASB*). True preaching is humiliation. True prayer is humiliation. True witness is humiliation. Apostolic preaching is experiencing the word of the cross, the humiliation of the cross, and the reenactment of the cross when the word of God is being delivered. We never get used to it. It puts fear in us and it makes us utterly dependent on God.

Open air and street preaching is humbling. It is one thing to preach to a congregation that is there to listen; it is another thing to preach in the middle of a campus to students who are hostile to the Word being preached. At that moment, it becomes clear that if God doesn't show up when we open our mouths, we will fall flat on our faces—but it doesn't matter, because our only desire is to be obedient to delivering the heaven-sent Word.

Preaching that Comes from God

In the Western Church we have preaching, but we lack power. True preaching was never meant to be devoid of God's power. We have many sermons, many facts, much knowledge, good theologies, but again, no power. Preaching *about* God is not the same as preaching *a word that comes from* God. A preached word that comes from God cannot come from our own human ability. Apostolic preaching comes when a person does not rely on his or her own eloquence of speech, experience or ability, but when the preacher is completely abandoned to the leading of the Holy Spirit.

An apostolic Word cannot be figured out in the mind; it originates in the spirit, is received in humility and is released with heaven-sent authority. The heaven-sent Word is released like a hammer that comes out of heaven and shatters the listening hearts like a rock. We know the Word is from God. Apostolic preaching is to hear His prophetic Word and to deliver it, no matter the cost or humiliation.

Words that Produce a Lasting Work

"When you received the word of God which you heard from us, you welcomed it not as the word of men, but as it is in truth, the word of God, which also effectively works in you who believe" (1 Thess. 2:13). The Word that comes from the Lord is a word that produces lasting fruit. Why do we have so much preaching in our churches but so little transformation? Believers are merely sermonized from Sunday to Sunday or from one campus fellowship meeting to another. A true word, on the other hand, will produce a reaction.

When Jesus and Paul preached, there were only two reactions: revival or riot. Today, we have seeker-friendly sermons to satisfy Christian consumers. God is looking for those who will not cater to man but appeal to God and speak a true word of repentance. A true word spoken from God will produce change in the hearer and create a reality that was not there before the speaking of that word. It has lasting power. As mentioned above, more than 80 percent of Charles Finney's converts stayed soundly converted decades after their conversions. God, raise up apostolic preachers on campuses who will bring us the word and reestablish our foundations!

Words that Come from Deep Communion with God
"Him we preach, warning every man and teaching every man in all wisdom, that we may present every man perfect in Christ Jesus. To this end I also labor, striving according to His working which works in me mightily" (Col. 1:28-29). Paul was a man of deep communion with God, in whom the power of the Holy Spirit was working mightily. "Working," in this sense, literally means supernatural energy or operating power.[5] The source of Paul's strength was his prayer life. He prayed incessantly.

If God is birthing in you a vision to be an apostolic preacher, then you must live a life of radical intercession and intimate communion with God. The great reformers like John Wesley, George Whitfield, Charles Finney and David Brainerd all prayed for hours upon hours before preaching to any crowd. The power in their preaching was not in their eloquence of words or delivery. The power in their preaching was in how much they prayed. Intercession was their place of preparation.

I didn't tell anyone, but when the divine outbreak happened at Bruin Walk, I had spent the whole day before on my face in intercession. Personal, fervent intercession is required for anyone who desires to preach apostolically, for when the word goes out, it is full of weight. It puts a demand upon our attention and requires from the hearer an obedience that produces a fruit that remains.

Holy Spirit, from every campus in every city, raise up
new apostolic preachers like the reformers of old, who will deliver
Your prophetic word to this generation and turn their hearts
fully back to You. Let me die a street preacher, one whose
feet are shod with the gospel of peace.
In Jesus' mighty name,
Amen.

Apostolic Preaching Revisited

1. Get a vision to be an apostolic preacher by reading biographies of apostolic preachers and reformers of old (biblical and historical).

2. Give yourself to a life of deep communion and intercession with God at a minimum of one hour a day (see Matt. 26:40). If you know you are going to outdoor preach, make sure you pray in the spirit for at least two hours beforehand.

3. Ask God for His heart, and fear Him, not man, to deliver the true Word of God.

4. On campus, find a free-speech area for open air preaching, open your mouth and trust the Holy Spirit to fill it with His words and confirm it with signs and wonders. Remember, don't preach *at* them but *to* them. Create dialogue when necessary (see Acts 17:16-34).

5. After preaching, look for open doors in students or people who are listening. Engage in conversation, pray

for them and follow up on them. Some of the best fruit that comes out of open-air preaching is talking afterward to those who listened.

6. Gather those who believe into new churches by starting a Bible study for them that results in the formation of a simple church. Apostolic preachers start churches!

Notes

1. Erwin Lutzer, "Will God Send Revival to America Once Again?" Sermon Index, March 10, 2006. http://www.sermonindex.net/modules/newbb/viewtopic.php?topic_id=12679&forum=40 (accessed January 2007).

2. David Smithers, "Charles G. Finney," Awake and Go! Global Prayer Network. http://www.watchword.org/index.php?option=com_content&task=view&id=22&Itemid=22 (accessed January 2007); Charles Grandison Finney, "An Autobiography or, The Memoirs," WhatSaithTheScripture.com. http://www.whatsaiththescripture.com/Voice/Finneys.Autobiography.html (accessed January 2007).

3. Elmer Towns and Douglas Porter, *The Ten Greatest Revivals Ever* (Ann Arbor, MI: Servant Publications, 2000), pp. 100-104.

4. Arthur Katz, *Apostolic Foundations* (Laporte, IN: Burning Bush Press, 1999), n.p.

5. James Strong, *The New Strong's Exhaustive Concordance* (Nashville, TN: Thomas Nelson, 1984), translating *energeia* as "energy," Greek #1753; G. Bertram, "*energeo*," in G. Kittel, *Theological Dictionary of the New Testament* (Grand Rapids, MI: Eerdmans, 1964-74), vol. 2, p. 652; C. H. Powell, *The Biblical Concept of Power* (London: Epworth Press, 1963), p. 136.

CHAPTER NINE

DEMONIC DELIVERANCE POWER

And these signs will follow those who believe:
In My name they will cast out demons.
MARK 16:17

When the enraged African American student walked up to me that day we preached on Bruin Walk, I was a bit intimidated. When I looked into his eyes, they were bloodshot and I could barely see his pupils. He was so angry that I thought he would literally take his fists and beat me into the ground. He was cursing and swearing at me at the top of his lungs, and his face was gripped with a spirit of rage.

But as I looked at him not with my physical eyes, but with my spiritual eyes, I could discern that he was demonically oppressed. At that moment, as he continued to threaten me, proclaiming that he was a son of Satan and saying he would kill me or call the police on me, I whispered a prayer under my breath, "Holy Spirit, I arrest this spirit of violence in Jesus' name. I command it to be bound and broken. I take authority over this evil spirit of antichrist that comes against Your name and command it to be silenced. Holy Spirit, show me what I am to do in this situation."

Immediately after I finished praying this prayer under my breath, he stopped screaming at me and became quiet. He just stared at me, still furious, but silenced. The Holy Spirit immediately showed me that this African American student was hostile against Christians because of past hurts he had received from other believers. I knew the Holy Spirit was telling me to ask him for forgiveness as a Christian, not only for myself, but also for all Christians.

I said, "Bro, I don't know you and you don't know me, but I want to ask you for forgiveness on behalf of any wrong or offense I have brought against you and on behalf of all those who say they are Christian."

He looked shocked and exclaimed, "What did you say? I don't know what to do with that! No Christian has ever told me that before!" His facial expression immediately changed. He was no longer full of rage, but he was willing to listen and even began to weep. Then he said, "When you were preaching, I literally wanted to grab your head, throw it into the concrete and step on your face till you were bloodied and dead. But while you were preaching, it felt like something arrested me and I was forced to listen. I don't know what it is about you—you're different than other Christians. I want to know more. I told myself I would never go to church, but if you have one, I'd like to go to yours!"

Right then and there, my friend and I prayed for him. We bound the demonic presence in his life and shared the gospel with him. He received our prayers and we cast out the demons in his life. Something radically changed in his heart at that moment. His entire countenance changed from anger to peace. Today he is a born-again believer, no longer serving Satan, but worshiping God and serving His purposes.

The Believer's Authority and Power

In Luke 10:19, Jesus declares, "Behold I give you the *authority* to trample on serpents and scorpions, and over all the *power* of the enemy, and nothing shall by any means hurt you" (Luke 10:19, emphasis added). In Greek, the words "authority" and "power," *exousia* and *dunamis,* are virtually interchangeable.[1] Jesus has given His authority and His power to every believer to cast out every kind of demon.

When talking about "serpents and scorpions," Jesus is talking about the power of the devil—of demons, evil spirits and all of Satan's cohorts. As believers, we must recognize that each of us has authority over every one of these demonic forces. For we know that our battle is not physical but spiritual (see Eph. 6:12). The enemy has blinded the eyes of unbelievers from receiving the gospel through the deceptive work of spiritual principalities (see 2 Cor. 4:3-4; Eph. 6:12). Because of this, it is now our responsibility to exercise the authority Jesus has given us to cast out these demonic powers in order to set the captives free (see Matt. 10:1,7-8; Mark 3:14-15; Luke 9:1-2; 10:9; and compare Matt. 28:18-20; John 14:12). The power of our authority rests on the authority of Him who is behind us, backing us up. We must recognize that it is God who is the power behind our authority! The devil and his forces must fully submit to the authority God has given us (see Luke 10:17-19 and Eph. 1:20-21; 2:6).

When we as believers understand that the power of God is backing us up, we can exercise the authority given us and confront the enemy without fear. Authority, in this sense, means "delegated power." For instance, during rush hour traffic a policeman or policewoman only has to lift his or her hand, and cars will stop. They have no physical power to stop cars from not driving on; they use the authority invested in them by the government they represent. People recognize their authority and obey the law. In the same way, Jesus has given us "delegated power" to hold up our hand against the devil, to stop his activity and to cast him out of people and places. All heaven is behind us. We must exercise this authority![2]

As Christ followers, we must cast out demons to deliver this generation from the grip of Satan. Jesus' entire ministry consisted of "healing all who were oppressed by the devil" (Acts 10:38). Jesus came to destroy the works of the devil and so must we (see 1 John 3:8). The book of Acts is full of demonic deliverances through the ministry of the early disciples (see Acts 5:16; 8:7; 19:11-12). If the Early Church had great authority over the demonic powers, how much more do we need to have greater authority today?

Have you ever considered that there is not one instance in the New Testament where the Church is ever told to pray and ask God the Father or Jesus to deal with demons? That is a waste of time. It is the *believer* who is told to do something against the devil. Jesus said, "All [power] authority has been given to Me in heaven and on earth" (Matt. 28:18). Jesus delegated His power and authority to the Church to accomplish His work (see Luke 10:17-19; 9:1-2; Matt. 28:18-20; John 14:12). He is the head and we are His body (see Eph. 1:22-23)—His very hands and feet! Jesus said in Mark 16:17-19:

> And these signs will follow those who believe: In My name they will cast out demons; they will speak with new tongues; they will take up serpents; and if they drink anything deadly, it will by no means hurt them; they will lay hands on the sick, and they will recover.

The very first sign mentioned in this verse about followers of Christ is that "they will cast out demons." It means that Jesus has given every believer the mandate to exercise authority over the devil.

I've experienced this authority operating in my life many times, having cast out demons in Jesus' name in the lives of countless students on different campuses. Demons are real. We must deal with them on our campuses to set the captives free and to release God's justice.

Demonic Deliverance Process

As a new believer, I used to be afraid of demons. But one day I read, "You are of God, little children, and have overcome them, because He [God] who is in you is greater than he [the devil] who is in the world" (1 John 4:4). This verse radically changed my perspective. I realized that God in me is greater than the devil against me. I now had faith to cast out demons.

Throughout college, I prayed on the armor of God (see Eph. 6:10-18) and asked the Holy Spirit daily to open doors for me to pray for others who were demonically oppressed and who needed deliverance. Nearly every day or week after I prayed, I would be led to students on and off campus who were tormented by evil spirits (many leaders use the term "demonized," derived from the Greek *daimonizomai*: "to be influenced by a demon"), some oppressed

and others possessed (almost totally controlled by demons). The
Holy Spirit taught me principles to cast out each of these demons
through prayer.

Jesus, when being questioned about exorcism, explained the
process of demonic deliverance:

> But if I cast out demons with the finger of God, surely the
> kingdom of God has come upon you. When a strong man,
> fully armed, guards his own palace, his goods are in peace.
> But when a stronger than he comes upon him and over-
> comes him, he takes from him all his armor in which he
> trusted, and divides his spoils (Luke 11:20-22).

Jesus goes on to describe in Luke 11:24-26 how once an evil
spirit is cast out, if the house is empty, the evil spirit will try to
come back seven times stronger. But Jesus is the stronger man
even in this passage, and He has given us authority to overcome
every other strong man or demon. Also, when Jesus cleans house,
we must be prepared to keep our house in order so that stronger
demons cannot come back. How do we do this?

In my personal experience, I have witnessed both very dramatic demonic deliverances and other more subtle ones. However, in
either case, it is important to follow a general strategy of deliverance. The steps below are a systematic process for demonic deliverance that I learned from training under the ministry of Carlos
Anacondia, the powerful Argentinean revivalist, who is known for
casting out thousands of demons in his evangelistic crusades.[3]
I have practiced these steps in ministry for years on different campuses and in different cities. It is not the only method, as each case
of deliverance will be different, but this step-by-step process has
proven fruitful for me time and again.

Step 1: Verify the Demonic Possession

As a rule, do not handle demonic deliverance alone. Minister as a
team. We must first ask the Holy Spirit to give us discernment
about whether the person we are delivering (Christian or non-

Christian) is being tormented, oppressed or possessed by an evil spirit(s). In every biblical instance, the oppression of those who were demonized manifested in an obvious way, revealing that they were held in bondage. These were the ones that Jesus delivered (see Matt. 8:16).

Step 2: Exercise Authority over the Evil Spirit

Many times, an evil spirit will rebel and overcome the person it is tormenting. We must remember that we have power from God to exercise authority over all demons (see Luke 10:17). Jesus said, "Or how can one enter a strong man's house and plunder his goods, unless he first binds the strong man?" (Matt. 12:29). He said we are to bind (or "tie up") "the strong man," or the evil spirit occupying the person who is in bondage. It is only the name of Jesus to which demons are subject and by which they are bound. As with the African American student who was demonically oppressed, I prayed, "In the name of Jesus I bind this evil spirit that is manifesting and command it to stop and to be silenced!" and the student immediately stopped cursing at me. By exercising our authority to bind and loose (see Matt. 16:19), we can neutralize the manifestation and activity of the enemy's attack on a person.

Step 3: Pray for the Person's Return to His or Her Right Mind

In Luke 8:26-36, Jesus delivers a demonized man who was living in the tombs and who was daily tormented by at least a legion of demons (2,000 demons). When the man saw Jesus, he begged for mercy and Jesus immediately cast the demons out of the man. But it says that before he cast the demons out fully, "Jesus asked him, saying, 'What is your name?' " (v. 30). Instead of the man answering, the demons answered with "Legion" (meaning "many"). I believe Jesus wanted to talk to the person first, not the demons, for the Bible says He *asked him.*

In deliverance, we must bind the evil spirits in order to talk to the person, because it is only the person's will that decides whether or not he or she can be delivered. If a person does not want to be delivered of demons, he or she won't be. We cannot

exercise authority over a person's will; we can only exercise authority over demons. If the person is unwilling to receive deliverance,
the demons will not leave no matter how many times we try. After
binding the evil spirit(s), I simply pray, "In the name of Jesus I
command this person to come into their right mind!" Believe it is
done by faith and then speak to the person in love.

Step 4: Ask the Individual, "Do You Want to Be Set Free?"

In many instances, after casting out demons, Jesus would ask
those who had been demonized or those who had been physically
sick if they wanted deliverance or healing. He asked the man with
the lifelong infirmity at the pool of Bethsaida, "Do you want to be
made well?" (John 5:6). Jesus will never infringe or force Himself
upon anyone. It is always one's own choice to choose Christ or not.
In the same way, once the person tormented by evil spirits is in his
or her right mind, we must share with him or her how Jesus desires
to bring deliverance, but we must also share that it is his or her
choice if he or she wants to be set free.

Normally, I will share Scriptures and stories with the demonized person of how Jesus was willing to deliver and how He delivered many who were tormented by the devil. This gives the person
faith and hope to believe and choose to be set free. If the person
does choose to be delivered, then proceed forward.

Step 5: Introduce the Person to Jesus as Savior and Lord

If the person is willing to be delivered, then we must introduce
him or her to Jesus as Savior and Lord. The person being delivered
may be an unbeliever, in which case we must make sure he or she
understands the message of salvation, and we must lead that person in a prayer of salvation first. Once Christ is resident in the person's heart, the enemy has no legal grounds to stay. But it is not
enough for Christ to be Savior—He must be made Lord over every
area of that person's life.

I don't believe Christians can be possessed by demons but I do
believe they can be demonized (oppressed or tormented and having
demons in them) because Jesus is not Lord over their whole lives.

For example, Ananias and Sapphira were *bona fide* believers—there is no other way they could have been among the community of believers, since the boundary between believers and unbelievers was stark according to Acts 5:13-14 ("None of the rest dared joined them"). But Ananias's and Sapphira's hearts were *filled* by Satan through acting out of greed and deceit ("Why has Satan filled your heart?" [Acts 5:3]).

Like Ananias and Sapphira, if a Christian decides to be involved in witchcraft, adultery and other such sins, this opens doors or forms of "footholds" for the enemy to come into their lives (see Eph. 4, especially Eph. 4:27, *NIV*: "Do not give the devil a *foothold*," emphasis added). A believer can actually be held captive by Satan and be made to do his will, according to 2 Timothy 2:26. Paul even warned the believers of Corinth that they might "receive a different spirit"—obviously a demonic spirit opposed to the Holy Spirit[4]—by receiving a different gospel, according to 2 Corinthians 11:4 (recalling the warnings of 1 Tim. 4:1 and 1 John 4:1-3). Therefore, we must pray with every person to make sure he or she truly repents of his or her sins and makes Jesus Lord of all (see Luke 6:46; Acts 10:36).

Step 6: Investigate the Different Areas of Spiritual Problems

Many times people get saved, but they don't get fully delivered. This is a result of that person not making Jesus Lord and not renewing his or her mind according to His Word and ways (see Rom. 12:2). When casting out demons, we must understand the root causes of the affected person's sinful bondage and torment.

There are many ways people open up doors and give the devil authority in their lives. We must find the cause, expose the false legal agreements the person has made with the enemy, and acquit each one case by case, by the blood of Jesus. In Deuteronomy 18:9-14, the Bible warns God's people about being involved in witchcraft and abominable sins. In Galatians 5:19-21, it warns us of the works of the flesh that will open doors for demonization. By abiding in sin we make legal agreements with the enemy and give him permission to accuse and torment us (see Acts 5:3; Eph. 4:27; 2 Tim. 2:26; Rev. 12:11).

At UCLA, I discerned through talking with the African American brother that he had major issues with unforgiveness, bitterness and a spirit of the antichrist. When praying for demonic deliverance, we need to talk to the one being delivered and ask that person investigative questions to find out what may be the cause for demons to have gained a foothold in his or her life. You may ask the person questions like, "When did this oppression start happening? What happened? What sins have you committed? What possible agreements have you made with sin?" Then come against the sins with the opposite spirit. For example, if the person has hatred in his or her heart, ask that person to forgive the one who has offended him or her; or if he or she has a spirit of doubt, ask that person to repent and receive a spirit of faith.

Step 7: Lead Them to Pronounce Words of Renunciation
"But we have renounced the hidden things of shame, not walking in craftiness nor handling the Word of God deceitfully" (2 Cor. 4:2). Once you have identified the root cause of the person's demonic oppression or possession, that person must confess and renounce each specific sin (see Jas. 5:15-16). Lead the person in a prayer to ask for forgiveness and renounce out loud the specific sins he or she has committed. Also, have the person renounce the pacts he or she has made with the enemy through sins or through any agreements consciously made with the enemy that opened doors for demons to come into his or her life.

We pray out loud because demons can only hear what we say; they cannot read our minds. (Only the Holy Spirit dwells within the spirit of a believer and knows the thoughts of a believer, according to Rom. 8:9; 1 Cor. 2:11-12; 6:17; and there is no instance in Scripture where demons leave without being verbally commanded to leave.) Just as we confess that Jesus is Lord with our mouths (see Rom. 10:9), to be freed and healed from demonic influence, we must also confess our specific sins and renounce our old ways with our mouths to declare that they are no longer a part of our lives (see Jas. 5:16: "Confess your trespasses to one another . . . that you may be healed"). Once renounced, the sin agreement is broken and put under the blood of Jesus (see Rev. 1:5). The devil has no more authority and he must leave because all the ties and commitments the person had with Satan are broken. The enemy's activity is terminated.

Step 8: Break All Bondages and Cast Out the Demon(s)

After the person has confessed his or her sin and renounced his or her sinful practices and agreements, you can declare in Jesus' name that the yokes of bondage are broken, and you can cast out the demons. We must understand that demons are spirits and that the Bible clearly shows that demons have specific functions and assignments. For example, the "spirit of fear" functions by causing fear (2 Tim. 1:7); "deceiving spirits" cause deception (1 Tim. 4:1; 1 Kings 22:22); the "spirit of error" leads one into error (1 John 4:6); the "spirit of bondage to fear" keeps one locked up in fear (Rom. 8:15); "the spirit of infirmity" causes sickness or physical malformations in one's body (Luke 13:11); the "spirit of divination" draws one and empowers one in divination and in receiving demonic revelation (Acts 16:16); a "deaf and dumb spirit" causes inability to speak and deafness in a person (Mark 9:25); the "spirit of prostitution" causes sexual immorality and idolatry (Hos. 4:12, *NIV*); and there are many other functions that demonic spirits can have.

Here is a simple prayer guide that will help you lead people in a prayer of deliverance:

<u>Demonic Oppression</u>

1. Include the following steps if not yet accomplished:
   - I *confess* my sin of _____ and *forgive* all who may have influenced me to sin.
   - I *repent* for giving place to the demons of _____ _____.
   - I *forgive* myself for the pain and limitations I have allowed the demons to inflict upon me.

2. In the name of Jesus, I *renounce* and *break* all agreements with the demons (stronghold) of _____ _____. I take *authority* over the demons (stronghold)

of _____ and *command* you to leave
me now based on the finished work of Christ on the
cross and on my authority as a believer.[5]

Once you have led the person through confessing and renouncing sins and demonic strongholds, now pray, "I break the stronghold of _____ out of your life in Jesus' name and I command every evil spirit of _____ to leave now in Jesus' name!" Break each sin bondage specifically, destroying the legal agreement with sin, and cast out each specific sin/demonic stronghold in the person's life.

Step 9: Give Thanks to God and Ask to Be Filled

Often throughout the gospels, whenever a demonized person was set free, he or she would give praise and glory to God for deliverance. Lead the person who has been set free into giving thanks and praise to Jesus so that he or she recognizes it is Jesus who delivered him or her and so that the person gives all the glory to Him.

Also, in Matthew 12:44, we learn that the demons will try to come back if the person's life is "empty"—that is, unless the person who has been delivered is filled with God's Spirit and truth, the demons will be free to return in greater strength. It is crucial that you teach the person not to return to old sins and to no longer believe the false lies of the enemy. This can only be done by praying immediately with the person to be filled with the Holy Spirit. Then, he or she must daily meditate upon the Word of God, replacing the lies he or she believed with God's truth. Help the person to find specific Scriptures to meditate daily upon, which will displace the lies of the devil he or she once believed. Finally, the person must be devoted to meeting regularly with a community of believers—God's Church.

Step 10: Verify the Effectiveness of the Deliverance

The last step of casting out demons is to verify that the deliverance was effective. Usually, once a person is delivered, his or her countenance changes. There is a spirit of rest, peace and joy upon his or her face (see Rom. 14:17). You know that something has changed and lifted. The person will be back in his or her right mind and will acknowledge Christ as Lord and no longer reject Him. At this point, the team praying should rejoice, give praise to God and plead the blood of Jesus over themselves for protection from any other spiritual warfare.

For example, the countenance of the newly converted African American brother on Bruin Walk, who was delivered of demons, was instantly changed. He went from rage to peace. He is now in a growing process of reading the Word, praying, being part of a simple church and praising Jesus! Let us pray on the armor of God daily as we engage in the reality of spiritual warfare on our campuses and in our cities.

Heavenly Father, I desire to be obedient by being strong in the Lord and the power of Your might. I recognize that it is essential to put on the armor You have provided, and I do so now with gratitude, praise and by faith as effective spiritual protection against the spiritual forces of darkness. I confidently put on the belt of truth. I take Jesus who is my truth, my strength and my protection and ask for wisdom and discernment to believe, live, speak and know only the truth.

Thank You, dear Lord, for the breastplate of righteousness—I appropriate the righteousness of Jesus Christ and ask You, Jesus, to help me walk in Your holiness in my life today. Thank You, Jesus, for the shoes of peace—I stand on the solid rock of peace. As I walk in obedience to You, the God of peace, You promise to walk with me. Eagerly, I lift up the shield of faith. By faith, I trust in You to be a complete and perfect shield against the flaming arrows of the serpent.

I recognize that my mind is a target of Satan's deceiving ways. I take Jesus who is my salvation and I shield my head with Him and invite His mind to be in me. Finally, I take the sword of the spirit, which is the Word of God, affirming that

it is the infallible Word of God. Enable me to use Your Word
to not only defend myself from Satan but also to claim
its promises. Thank You, dear Lord, for prayer. Help me
to keep this armor well oiled with prayer.

I desire to pray at all times with depth and intensity as the Holy
Spirit leads me. Grant me a burden for others in God's family
and enable me to see their needs and assist them in prayer as the
enemy attacks. All these things I ask in the mighty name of
Jesus Christ our Lord. Amen! (See Eph. 6:10-18.)

Notes

1. Bauer, Arndt, Gingrich and Danker, *A Greek-English Lexicon of the New Testament and Other Early Christian Literature* (Chicago: University of Chicago Press, 1979), pp. 207, 278.
2. Kenneth Hagin, *The Believers Authority* (Tulsa, OK: Faith Library Publications), pp. 7-8.
3. Carlos Anacondia, *Listen to Me, Satan!* (Lake Mary, FL: Charisma House, 1998), pp. 79-88.
4. Bauer, Arndt, Gingrich and Danker, *A Greek-English Lexicon of the New Testament and Other Early Christian Literature*, p. 678.
5. Chester and Betsy Kylstra, *Restoring the Foundations: An Integrated Approach to Healing Ministry* 2nd ed. (Hendersonville, NC: Proclaiming His Word Ministries, 2004), n.p.

CHAPTER TEN

PROPHETIC EVANGELISM POWER

*But if all prophesy, and an unbeliever or an uninformed person
comes in, he is convinced by all, he is convicted by all. And thus the
secrets of his heart are revealed; and so, falling down on his face,
he will worship God and report that God is truly among you.*
1 CORINTHIANS 14:24-25

That day in April 2006, when I carried the seven-foot cross onto
Bruin Walk and the Holy Spirit gave me a word of knowledge (prophetic insight; see 1 Cor. 12:8) that the fraternity brother's mother
had cancer, the impact of that word was threefold.[1] According to
1 Corinthians 14:24-25, the prophetic anointing has the power to
do three things: (1) convince, (2) convict, and (3) reveal.

The prophetic anointing convinced this fraternity brother
that God was real. It then had the power to convict him of his need
for God. It also revealed the secrets of his heart so that he realized
that God knew him personally. Not only was the fraternity brother encountered that day but also his frat brother who was sitting
next to him began to shake uncontrollably under the presence of
God, weeping because he knew that what had just happened was
supernatural. Both had had the gospel preached to them before,
but to no avail; it was prophetic evangelism that finally opened
both their hearts to the gospel.

The Holy Spirit is releasing the gift of prophecy in abundance
at this hour to win an unbelieving generation to Him. It is a movement of prophetic evangelism that will supernaturally capture the
hearts and minds of students on every campus for Christ!

And it shall come to pass afterward that I will pour out
My spirit on all flesh; Your sons and your daughters shall

prophesy, Your old men shall dream dreams, Your young men shall see visions (Joel 2:28).

In the last days, God will pour out the Spirit in fullness upon all flesh, beginning with young people—the "sons and daughters." This is a prophetic generation where all can prophesy as long as we are hungry enough to pursue God in intimate friendship. To be prophetic, to hear God's voice, to know His secrets, to declare His will and what is to come, is about one thing: being His intimate friend. "Surely the Lord GOD does nothing, unless He reveals His secret to His servants (or friends) the prophets" (Amos 3:7). Abraham, for example, was a prophet and an intimate friend of God (see Gen. 20:7; 18:17-33; Isa. 41:8). This is the requirement. If we are a friend of God, we can hear His voice, and we can prophesy so that the lost in this generation may come to know Him (see 1 Cor. 14:31)!

What Are Prophecy and Prophetic Evangelism?

When God poured out His Holy Spirit on the Day of Pentecost, believers were given power to witness about Jesus (see Acts 1:8). One of the gifts that God gave to His Church that day was the gift of prophecy (see Acts 2:17). Prophecy is the ability to receive and declare revelation from God to others.

When God empowered His Church, He gave the gift of prophecy to help us. While the gift of prophecy can be used within the Church to build up and edify one another, it also carries supernatural power and anointing for reaching the unchurched through prophetic evangelism (see 1 Cor. 14:24-25). Prophetic evangelism is when God uses revelatory phenomena to speak to the hearts of those who don't know Jesus so that they may come to know Him in a radical way.

Two Forms of Prophetic Evangelism

There are two forms of prophetic evangelism that every believer can believe for, experience and move in. The first form is *prophetic words of knowledge*. This is when a believer receives revelation about an unbeliever that he or she doesn't personally know. This can happen through a vision, a dream, an impression, a picture or through any number of other ways revealed by the Holy Spirit. In the first form, the person receiving the prophetic revelation is the believer. The believer shares this revelation sensitively with the unbeliever and the result is that the unbeliever recognizes that God is real, that He is alive and that He speaks today. The prophetic word of knowledge has a huge impact on that person's openness to hearing and receiving the gospel. It boggles that person's mind, breaks open his or her hardened heart and releases an encounter with the living God!

Once I was ministering at a college-age/young adult church. After I preached one morning, a young woman, eyes full of tears, walked up to me and said, "I don't know why I walked into this church building today. I have given up seeking God. My mother just died of cancer this week and I can't believe in a God that would let my mother die such a horrible death. For some reason, I felt I should share this with you." I didn't know what to say to her, so I asked the Holy Spirit to give me a prophetic word of knowledge. At that moment, I saw a picture of a yellow banana and a golden picture frame. Then I heard the Holy Spirit say to me, "Tell this young lady you see a yellow banana in a golden picture frame and tell her that this is proof that her mother is safe in heaven with Me." This seemed ridiculous, but oftentimes when giving prophetic words, the Holy Spirit will give me ridiculous things to say so that my faith will be in Him and not in my logical mind. Stepping out in faith, I shared this prophetic word with her.

Immediately, her jaw dropped. She looked at me, shocked, and said, "That's impossible. How did you know?"

I asked, "Know what?"

She replied, "The reason why I don't want to believe in God is that I thought God sent my mom to hell." Then she said, "How did you know that in our living room is a picture of my mom holding a yellow banana in a golden picture frame? Bananas are her favorite fruit and that picture is our family's favorite picture of her!"

I told her, "I don't know, but God knows and He wants you to believe in Him."

She immediately smiled, gave me a hug and later e-mailed me about how she shared this news with her family, knows her mom is in heaven and has put her faith in Christ!

God used a believer (me) to receive revelation for the unbeliever (the young lady) so that her heart was convinced, convicted and revealed and so that she believed in the goodness of God and put her faith in Jesus.

In the second form of prophetic evangelism, *prophetic encounter,* the Holy Spirit reveals something about Jesus directly to an unbeliever (see Matt. 27:19; Acts 9:3-7; 10:4-7). This may come in the form of a vision, a dream or an impression—it can come in many different ways. In whatever way it comes, the unbeliever realizes as a result of this prophetic revelation that Jesus Christ is alive and that He is appealing to the unbeliever to follow Him. Revelation 19:10 says, "For the testimony of Jesus is the spirit of prophecy." The purpose of prophetic revelation is to encounter and awaken the person to the truth of the gospel. Once this power encounter happens, the challenge then is for the person to connect with a Christian who can disciple and integrate him or her into a simple church.

Missionaries have recorded dramatic stories of how entire Muslim villages in Northern Africa are coming to Christ through receiving prophetic dreams of Jesus Christ. There are reports of entire villages of people receiving the same dream of seeing "a Man in a white robe" on the same night. The very next day, missionaries come into the village showing the Jesus film.[2] This is an example of the second type of prophetic evangelism, where, because of the prayers of saints, God reveals Himself directly to lost peoples so that they might come to Him by faith.

One student in our campus church network at University of California, San Diego, has been praying in his biology lab for the professors and scientists to receive prophetic dreams or encounters from God. After praying these prayers for weeks, the head professor over his lab department received a dream of a racehorse breaking its leg in a race and the number "8" horse going on to win the race. A few days later on TV, the dream actually transpired in real life when a favored horse was supposed to win a race but fell and broke his leg while the number 8 horse went on to win. The professor, who is an atheist, told some others in the lab, "This can't be possible for me to receive a dream that foretold the future. What is the probability of this happening?" Since that time, the student has been witnessing and interpreting the dreams of many in this biology lab and has also started evangelistic Bible studies to win faculty and students to Christ. He is operating in the *prophetic encounter* form of prophetic evangelism, where he prays and God reveals Himself directly to the unbeliever(s).

Here is a summary of the difference between the two approaches of prophetic evangelism:

Form 1
Prophetic words of knowledge involve God speaking to a believer about an unbeliever. This is "mediated revelation" (i.e., revelation given through a human intermediary):

God > Believer > Unbeliever

Form 2
Prophetic encounters are "immediate revelations." In other words, they are revelations given directly by God to an unbeliever, without a human intermediary:

God > Unbeliever

We must understand that both types of prophetic evangelism are entirely biblical. The Holy Spirit is using prophetic evangelism more and more today to encounter and win lost souls to Christ. We still use all other forms of evangelism, but we must step out in faith with what the Holy Spirit is restoring in this hour to reach this millennial generation. This generation is hungry for the voice of God. This generation doesn't want to know about God; it wants to encounter God. We can bring them into an encounter with God through exercising our gift to prophesy!

Prophetic Evangelism in the Bible

There are many cases in the Bible where God uses prophetic evangelism to further His kingdom. In the Old Testament, there is at least one story where we see both forms used: God gives Daniel a *prophetic word of knowledge* to interpret King Nebuchadnezzar's *prophetic encounter* that he had in a dream in order to bring the pagan ruler to repent and acknowledge God (see Dan. 2:30; 4:2-3). Because God's power was upon him, Daniel had more wisdom, revelation and supernatural power than all the psychics and wizards in King Nebuchadnezzar's court. His prophetic insight prevailed over the false psychics of his day and resulted in the pagan king turning to God!

Today in America, the psychic business is a one billion dollar industry. Unbelievers are hungry for the supernatural. God wants to give this prophetic generation supernatural insight into the heart of man so that we will have more wisdom and revelation than professors who shun God in our universities and psychics who deceive as false prophets. We are a new prophetic breed—the new Daniels of our day. Let us exercise the prophetic gift in us!

Not only in the Old Testament but also in the New Testament, God uses prophetic evangelism to spread the gospel. For instance, Jesus' words of knowledge to the Samaritan woman at the well result in her entire town being saved (see John 4). Later, in Acts 10, the Holy Spirit utilizes prophetic evangelism to spread the gospel outside the confines of Jerusalem, Judea and Samaria, and to the ends of the earth. The apostle Peter received revelation through a prophetic vision about Cornelius that led not only to Cornelius's household being saved but also confirmed the movement of the gospel from the Jews out to the Gentiles.

As we study other accounts through Scripture, we see the Holy Spirit from the beginning of time revealing the gospel through prophetic revelation and intervention. The Holy Spirit has not stopped. We must move in the prophetic even more so today to reap the last days' harvest!

How to Move in Prophetic Evangelism

For you can all prophesy one by one, that all may
learn and all may be encouraged.
1 C ORINTHIANS 14:31

The Holy Spirit desires "all prophesy," not because it's cool but because it is effective for evangelism. This is why we are exhorted to desire spiritual gifts, especially that of prophesy (see 1 Cor. 14:1). When we prophesy, it is not for us but for others. It is to edify, exhort and comfort people (see 1 Cor. 14:3). It is to put a smile on someone's face. Prophecy makes people feel honored and special. It lets them know that an infinite God is interested in the most intimate details of their life and desires an intimate relationship.

In our prophetic evangelism trainings, I always ask students, "Do you want to make people smile?" They always nod their heads yes. Then I say, "Then learn to prophesy!" I love to pray for others because it brings them hope. I love prophetic evangelism because it is about making people smile by introducing them to Jesus.

Through prophetic evangelism, the Holy Spirit can open up the hardest hearts on our campuses to know the love of Christ. Taking a risk, stepping out in faith and giving a lost person a prophetic word can change a life eternally. Like the story of the woman at the well, it can flip our campuses upside down for God's glory. Let's make some people smile, yeah? Here is how to begin to operate in prophetic evangelism to bring benefit to others and glory to God:

1. *Be filled and led by the Holy Spirit.* Ephesians 5:18 tells us to be continually filled with the Holy Spirit. We must be dependent on the Holy Spirit when it comes to any kind of evangelism, but especially prophetic evangelism. Ask Jesus to fill you up with more of the Holy Spirit before you go out to prophetically evangelize. Wait upon the Lord daily until you are filled again to overflowing with His transforming and empowering presence. Remember, evangelism is overflow!

2. *Ask the Holy Spirit for open doors and divine appointments.*
   Write down what you hear, see or feel when you are
   praying, then go out to look for it! It is through prayer
   and divine revelation that the Holy Spirit opens doors
   for us to evangelize the lost. Get into small groups of
   two to five people and first pray for the Holy Spirit to
   give you open doors, divine appointments and prophetic clues about whom you should pray for.

   After you do this, wait on the Lord as a group and listen to the Holy Spirit. Write down what you see, hear and
   feel (people, places or things). Once you write them
   down, trust the Holy Spirit to confirm what was spoken
   and to show you for whom you should pray as you go out
   on campus or in the city. It's a prophetic treasure hunt.

   Whatever the outcome, be obedient to the Holy
   Spirit to pray blessings for those people the Holy Spirit
   brings to you. (If you are alone, just ask the Holy Spirit
   to give you opportunities daily to pray and prophesy
   over lost people you encounter.) We followed this strategy while training university students in Taiwan. Many
   teams of students received specific pictures of specific
   places, people and things. When they went out on campus and into the city to look for them, many prophetic pictures were confirmed, so accurately so that many
   lost people were prophetically encountered and came
   to Christ as a result![3]

3. *Ask someone if you can pray for him or her.* When the Holy
   Spirit leads you to prophesy over someone, whether it
   is your roommate, a random person on campus or
   your professor, simply tell that person that you are a
   Christian who believes in the power of prayer. Then,
   ask him or her if he or she has any needs you can pray
   for or if you can just bless that person. Most people
   are not resistant to prayer. If they say yes, stop to listen
   to the Holy Spirit for any words, Scriptures, pictures,

images, thoughts, sentences, visions or other divine revelation for the person. (This can be done before or after you ask them if they would like prayer.) Take note of the revelations, ask the Holy Spirit for insight and discern how to share the word with them.

4. *Step out in faith.* Once you have a prophetic word, you must step out in faith to share the word of knowledge, prophecy and blessing with the person or persons you encounter. Faith is spelled R-I-S-K, as John Wimber used to say. Remember, there is no failure; simply relate with sensitivity and take a chance opportunity to bless the person! Tell that person you are practicing hearing God's voice for others and would like to practice with that person to bless him or her.

5. *Release the prophetic word.* When you release the prophetic word, never say, "Thus says the Lord." Rather, share with sensitivity and discernment. In the story I told you earlier about the young woman whose mother died, I simply said to her, "Does a yellow banana and golden picture frame have any significance for you, because I believe . . .?" The more you step out in faith and do it, the more faith you will have, and you will begin to give more accurate words each time!

Finally, remember that all prophecy is to be tested (see 1 Thess. 5:20-21) by God's Word, His will and His ways. If the prophetic word is true, it will agree with Scripture and be in accordance with God's will and character. It will also be confirmed in the person receiving the word immediately or sometime later. Check and see.

> *Holy Spirit, we pray that You will release an army of*
> *students to move out in prophetic evangelism on every*
> *campus and city in every nation to reap a great*
> *end-time harvest for Your glory!*

Notes

1. For the complete story about the fraternity brother whose mother had cancer, see the blog entry "UCLA Is Shaking!!!" at the beginning of Section 2.
2. Kevin Greeson, *Camel Training Manual* (Midlothian, VA: WIGTake Resources, 2004), pp. 7-8.
3. For a full report, see Jaeson Ma, "Heaven Full, Hell Empty in Taiwan," *Jaeson's Journal*, February 14, 2007. http://www.jaesonma.blogspot.com.

CHAPTER ELEVEN

DIVINE HEALING POWER

Then He called His twelve disciples together and gave them
power and authority over all demons, and to cure diseases.
He sent them to preach the kingdom of God and to heal the
sick . . . "Whatever city you enter . . . heal the sick there, and say
to them, 'The kingdom of God has come near to you.'"
LUKE 9:1-2; 10:8-9

Therefore go and make disciples of all nations, baptizing them in
the name of the Father and of the Son and of the Holy Spirit, and
teaching them to obey everything I have commanded you.
MATTHEW 28:18-20, *NIV,* EMPHASIS ADDED

Go into all the world and preach the gospel to every creature,
He who believes and is baptized will be saved; but he who does
not believe will be condemned. And these signs will follow those
who believe: In My name they will cast out demons; they will
speak with new tongues; they will take up serpents; and if they
drink anything deadly, it will by no means hurt them; they will
lay hands on the sick, and they will recover.
MARK 16:15-18, EMPHASIS ADDED

In March 2006, an intercessor friend of mine walked up to me and
said, "Jaeson, I've been meaning to share with you this dream I've
had for a few months. In this dream I saw you standing in the middle of a university with crutches in your hands. Empty wheelchairs
and stretchers were all around you. Then I saw Smith Wigglesworth,

the great healing evangelist, walk up to you and offer you his mantle. But this mantle wasn't just for you; it was a mantle for all the students you work with on different college, university and even high school campuses, to release the power of divine healing to this generation."

After he shared this dream with me, I was shocked, because just the day before I had pulled out my 500-page Smith Wigglesworth autobiography to read. I had asked God in prayer, "Lord, would You stretch out Your mighty right hand and release the healing anointing of Smith Wigglesworth over the campuses of America once again!" Wigglesworth was one of the greatest healing evangelists and preachers in history. He raised more than a dozen people from the dead and had faith like no other.[1] When praying for the sick, he would preach, "Fear looks, faith jumps! Only believe," and, "I am not moved by what I see. I am only moved by what I believe."[2] I knew this prophetic dream of Smith Wigglesworth was timely—a confirmation and prophetic sign that the Holy Spirit is releasing His healing power, right now, to this generation.

It was only a few weeks later that the outbreaks of divine healing occurred at UCLA on Bruin Walk. The fraternity brother miraculously started walking without his crutches in front of the crowd of on-looking students after we prayed for him. Many were weeping at the sight of it; the healing presence of God was so strong and the power of God was present for all to witness. The people were in awe of God's power and I knew it was a confirmation of the prophetic dream I had received weeks before.

Indeed, this is just the beginning. In the coming days we will see supernatural healings occur on our campuses night and day with regularity. What happens when the star basketball player gets his broken arm healed instantaneously because you prayed for him and news got out? What happens when the miracle-working power of Jesus breaks out so strongly in the middle of campus that students are being healed of sicknesses and infirmities daily in the campus courtyards? What happens when word catches wind, the entire student body comes to watch, the gospel is preached and hundreds, even thousands are saved? Why not? It happened when

Jesus walked the streets of Galilee; it happened in the book of Acts, when entire cities were shaken by the disciples (see Acts 19:1-20); it will happen again today. We owe this generation an encounter with God. It's not enough to talk a good theology; it's time to demonstrate God's power. It will happen when we become compassionate for souls and passionate for divine healing.

The Power of Divine Healing to Save the Lost

Scripture tells us, "Then Jesus went about all the cities and villages, teaching in their synagogues, preaching the gospel of the kingdom, and healing every sickness and every disease among the people. But when He saw the multitudes, He was moved with compassion for them, because they were weary and scattered, like sheep having no shepherd" (Matt. 9:35-36, emphasis added).

The word "compassion" in the Greek is *splanchnizomai*[3] and it means to be moved with deep compassion or pity.[4] It was Jesus' compassion and deep love for people that motivated Him to heal the sick. He saw them as "weary," or as another translation says, "harassed and helpless." Scholars believe this word can also be translated "pinned-down and molested."[5] Jesus was so hurt, so moved, so pained at the lost state of Jerusalem that it was like watching the devil pin down and molest God's children. He couldn't take it. His compassion moved Him to action. I pray that we too are moved with compassion when we walk the streets of our campuses and see the lost souls pinned-down, molested by the devil and on their way to eternal damnation.

In His great compassion, Jesus came to seek and save the lost. The word "save" in the Greek is *sozo;* it means "to heal, save, make well or whole."[6] The first and greatest miracle is always salvation. The greatest miracle happens when someone repents and commits his or her life to Christ. But to save (*sozo)* does not only mean to save the spirit; it also means to save the soul and body. Jesus' concern is to restore every part of a person's life. Our goal is not first to get to heaven but to bring heaven, which brings God's power to heal, down to Earth.

Jesus healed the sick because His nature is compassion. And Jesus is the same, yesterday, today and forever (see Heb. 13:8). Today He still desires to heal the sick. We follow Christ in doing greater works than Him (see John 14:12), such as healing, so that people will know the compassion of Jesus. Our nature must be like His. We must heal the sick because of love and for no other reason. We must be moved with compassion to operate in divine healing power to heal the sick and demonstrate the compassion of Jesus to this unbelieving generation. This is not a suggestion; it is a command of Jesus (see Matt. 10:1,7-8; 28:20; Luke 9:1-2; 10:9).

Consider this: When Jesus was on Earth, His purpose and work was to destroy the works of the devil (see 1 John 3:8). He did this by casting out demons, healing the sick, raising the dead and preaching the gospel of the Kingdom. We must do the same. To preach the gospel without casting out demons and healing the sick is not a full gospel.

In Luke 10:9, Jesus commanded the 70 disciples to go into the towns and villages to heal the sick and pronounce that the kingdom of God has come. There is a significant link between divine healing and the kingdom of God. It is through divine healing that people recognize the authority of God's power and that the presence of His supernatural kingdom has come. If we want heaven on Earth, we must expect signs and wonders to confirm the preaching of the gospel. Miracles and divine healing are signs that the Kingdom is near. We desperately need these signs in our evangelism on campuses today. However, it is up to us to release God's power for the lost to be saved. Jesus commanded:

Go into all the world and preach the gospel to every creature. He who believes and is baptized will be saved; but he who does not believe will be condemned. And these signs will follow those who believe; In My name they will cast out demons; they will speak with new tongues; they will take up serpents; and if they drink anything deadly, it will by no means hurt them; *they will lay hands on the sick, and they will recover* (Mark 16:15-18, emphasis added).

The words of Jesus are clear: Those who preach the gospel, who believe and who are baptized, *will* cast out demons and heal the sick. This mandate is for all believers—for you and me. It isn't only for the apostle, the ordained minister or the healing evangelist who will perform these signs, but for *everyone who believes* (see John 14:12). God has given us authority and power over sickness and disease. The Holy Spirit who was in the apostle Paul, who was in the apostle Peter and who was in Smith Wigglesworth is the same Holy Spirit who is in us.

As you go out onto your campuses preaching the gospel, look for the oppressed and sick people to heal. Hunt for the sick like a lion hunting for prey. The Word of God guarantees that He will show up: "And they went out and preached everywhere, the Lord working with them and confirming the word through the accompanying signs" (Mark 16:20). In our simple church network at UCLA, we challenge our students to pray for one sick person each day on campus to be divinely healed. Almost every week, we get e-mail praise reports of divine encounters that students have had when obeying the Holy Spirit to pray for the sick. Come on!

How to Pray for Divine Healing

There is much theology about divine healing, but I am not here to explain why God heals or doesn't heal today. I am here to say that I've seen it happen in my life, through my life and to others time and time again for the sole purpose of glorifying Jesus.

It is clear that the Bible commands us to pray for the sick to be healed (see Jas. 5:14-16). This is a grace available to every believer (see John 14:12; 1 Cor. 12:9). It is also clear that we are called to lay hands on the sick for their recovery (see Mark 16:18). Divine healing is a weapon in our arsenal to win the lost and bring revival. If we look throughout the Gospels and the book of Acts (see especially Acts 3:1-10; 5:12-16), divine healing was used by Jesus and the early disciples to gather large crowds, fill them with awe and shake entire cities so that multitudes would be saved.

I asked a Baptist missionary friend of mine in China, "How is it that the Church in China is growing so fast?" He replied, "It is mainly through signs, wonders, miracles and divine healing." God is releasing healing power in this hour and it's our responsibility to take it to our campuses. How do we use this spiritual weapon of divine healing power? My spiritual father, Pastor Ché Ahn, taught me how to pray for divine healing using the five steps below that were originally developed by John Wimber and the Vineyard.[7]

As you go out to your campus each day, look for sick people to pray for. Whether it is for a cold, a broken arm or leg or a serious disease, simply introduce yourself and ask them if you can pray for their divine healing—there is no prayer too big or too small that God can't answer. Then, follow the below steps on how to pray for the sick.

Step 1: Investigate the Sickness

Find out what the sickness is by asking questions. Simply ask the sick person what is wrong with him or her. Where does it hurt? How did it happen? When did it happen? It is not our goal to know the details of the illness; we are not doctors. But we do want to investigate enough to know what we are praying for. Prayer must be specific. Peter and John told the lame man in Acts 3 to take up his mat and walk. They knew his sickness and, therefore, they were able to be specific in their prayer for his healing.

The sick person's response may be anything from "I have a migraine" to "I just found out I have cancer." When I talked with the fraternity brother at UCLA, he told me exactly why he had crutches and a broken foot. By knowing what was wrong, I could pray for the divine healing with precision.

Step 2: Welcome the Holy Spirit

Once you know what the sickness is, invite the Holy Spirit into the situation before you engage in prayer: "Come, Holy Spirit,[8] rest on this person and increase Your power on his/her body where he/she needs healing." We can do nothing without the Holy Spirit and no healing can take place without the presence of the Holy Spirit to heal. Jesus healed the paralytic man in the house in Capernaum, and the text of Luke 5:17 says, "And the power of the Lord was present to heal them."[9] As this verse suggests, the Holy Spirit must be manifestly present in order for the power of the Lord to be released for healing. It is Jesus that heals, not us. We simply partner with the Holy Spirit to bring about divine healing to others.

Step 3: Diagnostic Decision

Now find out the cause of the condition. What is causing this sickness? There are three main causes for sickness: (1) physiological, (2) demonic and (3) sin. Some people are sick because of natural circumstances. Maybe they caught a cold, got into an accident or are not taking care of their health. Others may have a sickness where the root cause is demonic (see Matt. 12:22; Mark 9:17,25; Luke 11:14; 13:11).

There are also people who are sick because of hidden or harbored sin in their lives (see Luke 5:20,24-25). James 5:14-16 says:

> Is anyone among you sick? Let him call for the elders of the church, and let them pray over him, anointing him with oil in the name of the Lord. And the prayer of faith will save the sick, and the Lord will raise him up. And if he has committed sins, he will be forgiven. Confess your trespasses to one another, and pray for one another, that you may be healed.

We are called to confess our sins to one another in order to be physically healed. Sin opens a door for sickness and the demonic to enter into our life (see Pss. 32:3-4; 38:3,5; 1 Cor. 11:27-30; Jas. 5:16).

There are five factors or types of sin that can cause sickness:

1. Sins of emotion and attitude, such as unbelief and pride

2. Sins that we commit against others that cause bitterness and hatred in us, in the other person or in both

3. Sins that others commit against us, such as physical, verbal or emotional abuse that may cause trauma and hurt and may open a door to Satan

4. Sins of our generational fathers: generational sins and curses. Exodus 20:5 says that the sins of the fathers are visited upon the children to the third and fourth generations. A child may be born with a disease, such as cancer, or may inherit a tendency such as a weakness toward alcoholism because his parent had the same condition or sinful tendency.

5. Sins that we commit against ourselves: self-hatred, self-rejection, inferiority complex, guilt and condemnation

A rule of thumb to follow when praying for divine healing: If the pain is recent due to an accident, it is most likely physiological; if the problem is chronic and the doctors have no answer for the cause, it could very well be demonic. If you ask Him, the Holy Spirit can give you discernment as to what the root cause of the problem is. Finally, if it is neither physiological nor demonic, sensitively ask the person you are praying for if they may have committed any sin to open the door for the sickness to occur. If there is sin committed, lead them in a prayer of repentance, and then pray for healing.

Step 4: Select the Prayer Type

I generally use different kinds of prayer to apply to different causes of sickness. That day at UCLA, I used *command prayer* to command the student to rise up and walk. Jesus used command prayer most frequently in the Gospels.[10] Other times I will use *rebuke prayer* when I discern that the cause of sickness is demonic.[11] I'll pray, "In the name of Jesus I bind this spirit of infirmity and rebuke it out of this person's life now in Jesus' name!" If the sickness is not healed immediately, I use *intercessory prayer* and simply pray, "Jesus, I pray that You heal my friend of (name the sickness), in Jesus' name. Amen."

Step 5: Pray

Once you have chosen a kind of prayer, invite the presence of the Holy Spirit and engage in prayer. I have learned to pray with my eyes open so that I can discern what the Holy Spirit is doing. After praying, I will ask the person, "How do you feel?" Or I'll say, "Tell me what is going on now." Sometimes they are healed instantly; other times, nothing happens. If the healing does not immediately take place, I will ask the Holy Spirit how to continue in prayer, or whether there is a block to His anointing that I have not yet discovered. It is crucial that you follow the leading of the Holy Spirit throughout. Sometimes I will continue with *intercessory prayer*, asking Jesus to heal and having the person soak in God's presence.

Once, during a healing meeting in L.A., I heard the word "duck feet" and knew someone in the meeting had this problem. By faith, I gave the word of knowledge that there was someone in the room who needed to be healed of duck feet. In a room of about 200 students, suddenly one student walked up slowly to the platform. He had torsional deformities that caused his feet to point outward since birth. I prayed for him and nothing happened at first, but I prayed again and told him to soak in God's presence. Five minutes later he yelled out, "I'm healed." When we looked, his feet were completely straight, healed and he began to walk normally all around the room praising God!

Step 6: Check the Healing and Give Post-Prayer Direction

It is important after praying for someone's healing to first have that person check if he or she is healed. Ask him or her to try to do something he or she has not done before. Then give post-prayer direction. You can tell the person to thank God for the healing. Even if that person did not receive an instantaneous healing, encourage him or her to continually believe and thank God by faith for the healing (see Mark 11:22-24). Divine healing can be a process and may not always be immediate,[12] but as a general rule, it is the will of God to heal the sick. James 5:15 indicates that it is God's will to heal as a general rule: "the prayer of faith *will heal the sick person*" (the Greek future indicative *sosei* means "will heal" *not* "may heal" or "might heal if it's God's will").

The overall witness of the New Testament regarding God's attitude toward healing shows that God desires to heal. Any reader of the Gospels knows that God's Son, Jesus, healed the sick. Acts and the epistles show that the apostles and the Early Church also healed the sick. God gave the Church gifts of healing (see 1 Cor. 12:9), but He also commands the Church to pray for the sick in James 5:14-16. However, Scripture also makes it clear that in a minority of cases, for various reasons, the Early Church did not always see all the sick healed (see Gal. 4:13-14; Phil. 2:26-27; 1 Tim. 5:23; 2 Tim. 4:20).

So while Scripture makes it clear that it is generally God's will to heal, Scripture also shows us that we need to be ready for cases where for various reasons, people we pray for may not be healed over the short term or over the long term. And we need to keep in mind that there are many factors that can bring about or not bring about the healing. James 5:15 says that the "prayer of faith will save the sick," indicating that the faith of those praying is the faith that is most important for healing to occur.

We need to encourage those who are not healed that it is not necessarily any lack of faith on their part that is preventing healing. Also, we need to encourage those we pray for to study and continually confess the promises concerning healing found in God's Word (see Isa. 53:5). Finally, if they receive a manifestation of healing, ask them to have it verified by a doctor. The student who walked off the crutches at Bruin Walk went to a doctor the next day to verify the healing, and the doctor was amazed at how quickly he had recovered!

As we step out in faith to do what may seem ridiculous, God will do the miraculous. We do our part, which is to pray, and Jesus will do His part, which is to heal. It is not our job to heal; we only pray in the name of Jesus and expect God to show up. But we must pray in faith, believing that the sick will be healed, because whatever we ask for according to God's will, if we believe that we have received it, it will be ours (see Mark 11:22-24). In reality, Jesus calls us to heal the sick, not just pray for them, because it is an act of faith in which Jesus heals through our obedience to His command (see Matt. 10:7-8; 28:20; Luke 9:1-2).

I have prayed for many who were not healed instantly, but that has not deterred my passion to pray for the sick. We are to be a generation of faith, called to do greater works than even Jesus (see John 14:12). Step out in faith, go out two by two on your campus, look for the sick and pray for them by faith to be healed!

*Holy Spirit, I pray that You will move this generation with
deep compassion for the lost on our campuses and give us
a burning passion to pray for the sick with divine healing power.
In the name of Jesus.
Amen.*

Notes

1. Smith Wigglesworth, *Greater Works: Experiencing God's Power* (New Kensington, PA: Whitaker House, 1999), n.p.
2. Roberts Liardon, ed., *Cry of the Spirit: Unpublished Sermons by Smith Wigglesworth* (Laguna Hills, CA: Embassy Publishing, 1991), pp. 1, 10.
3. James Strong, *The New Strong's Exhaustive Concordance* (Nashville, TN: Thomas Nelson, 1984), Greek #4697.
4. Bauer, Arndt, Gingrich and Danker, *A Greek-English Lexicon of the New Testament and Other Early Christian Literature* (Chicago: University of Chicago Press, 1979), p. 762.
5. Ibid., p. 758, to see the original meaning of the Greek word *skullo*, "to flay, to skin"; p. 736, to see the meanings of the Greek word *ripto*.
6. Ibid., p. 798; also, Strong, *The New Strong's Exhaustive Concordance*, Greek #4982.
7. Ché Ahn, *How to Pray for Divine Healing* (Ventura: Regal Books, 2004), p. 129; John Wimber and Kevin Springer, *Power Healing* (San Francisco: Harper and Row, 1987).
8. In Hebrew, the phrase for "Come, Holy Spirit" is *bo'i haruakh*; see Ezekiel 37:9; Psalm 141:1, "O Lord, I call to you; come quickly to me" (*NIV*); 2 Corinthians 3:17, "Now the Lord *is the Spirit*" (emphasis added).
9. The Holy Spirit is always with us (see Ps. 139:7-10; John 14:16-19). But He comes especially and manifests distinctive anointing for particular purposes according to the following passages: Luke 5:17, "the power of the Lord *was present* to heal," implying that there were times when the power of the Lord *was not present*; 1 Corinthians 5:4, "When . . . the power of the Lord Jesus"; Isaiah 55:6, "Seek the Lord *while He may be found*; call upon Him *while He is near.*"

10. Examples of command prayer:
    "Be clean!" (to a leper), Mark 1:41, *NIV.*
    "Get up!" (to a lame man), Mark 2:11, *NIV;* John 5:8, *NIV;* Acts 9:34, *NIV.*
    "Stretch out your hand," Mark 3:5.
    "Get up" (to a dead person), Mark 5:41, *NIV;* Luke 7:14, *NIV;* Acts 9:40, *NIV.*
    "Be opened!" (to a deaf man's ears), Mark 7:34.
    Jesus "rebuked the fever, and it left her," Luke 4:39.
    "See again! [Greek, *anablepson]*" (to a blind man), Luke 18:42.
    "Lazarus, come forth!" John 11:43.
    "Walk!" (to a lame man), Acts 3:6.
    "Stand up!" (to a lame man), Acts 14:10.
11. An example of rebuke prayer: "Be quiet! . . . Come out of him!" (Mark 1:25).
12. See Mark 8:22-25, where Jesus had to lay hands more than once on the blind man before he was completely healed.

CHAPTER TWELVE

MARKETPLACE REFORMATION POWER

*Our Father in heaven, hallowed be Your name. Your kingdom
come. Your will be done on earth as it is in heaven.*
MATTHEW 6:9-10

"It was more church than church!" While in college, I was hired
part-time at a tech company in Silicon Valley, California. But this
was not your normal tech company; it was church in the marketplace. The CEO was a Korean businessman who started the tech
company with the purpose of giving 51 percent of the net profit to
student missions. They hired me to oversee the student mission
foundation and my task was to decide to which ministries the financial profits would be distributed.

Now, giving 51 percent of net profits to missions was radical, but
what was even more radical was what happened in the company on
a day-to-day basis. The vision of the CEO was not just to give money
to God's kingdom. His vision was also to bring church to the marketplace. Every morning the Christians would gather together to
pray for revival and welcome the Holy Spirit into the workday. Every
day we had Bible studies in the morning, afternoon and even after
hours with unbelievers in the company. Each employee was minis-
tered to and prayed for daily, and miracles happened in the office regularly. People were healed of sicknesses, and God's wisdom was
sought for business deals. When the company started, the majority
of the employees were not Christian. By the time I left the company,
more than 80 percent of the employees had found faith in Christ.

I remember going home one day after work and telling my
mother, "Mom, you don't understand, the company where I work—
it's more church than church!" Truly, this tech company was a
church without walls. Heaven had officially invaded the workplace.

Through this experience, God radically changed my paradigm of church. In my mind, the kingdom of God is no longer limited to the four walls of a church building; instead, the kingdom of God is everywhere at every time, wherever God's people are.

Working at this tech company also exemplified the dream I had with Pastor Bob Weiner about reforming society. We can't have revival without reformation of society. When revival comes, souls will be saved *en masse*, communities will flourish, laws will be changed, societies will be impacted and nations will be shaken. For too long the Church has had no impact or influence upon society and culture. The Church has separated itself from the world, even though Jesus prayed for us to be in the world (see John 17:18). In order to reform society, we must bring the kingdom of God into every sphere of society.

There are seven molders of culture, or seven influencers of society: *government, business, education, media, arts, religion* and *family*. Every person in a city or nation is shaped by one of these societal spheres. This is why it is so important that we reach college campuses for Christ, because the future leaders of society are found there. Nearly all of our future government leaders, business leaders, educational leaders, media leaders, community leaders and others will have gone to a college or university. If we can train them to do church on campus, they will carry this mentality with them into society and will bring church into the workplace. The Holy Spirit at this hour is raising up a missionary force from the college campuses that will bring God's presence into all of society, transforming it in the power of the Holy Spirit.

The Church is being called to reform society by transforming the seven areas of influence through power evangelism, making disciples and planting workplace churches. But first, we must have a new perspective on societal transformation.

Three Foundational Truths

In his audio teaching series *The Church in the Workplace*, Dr. Ché Ahn says that we must understand three foundational truths if we are going to reform society.[1]

1. We Must Understand the Kingdom of God

"For indeed, the kingdom of God is within you" (Luke 17:21). What is the kingdom of God? The kingdom of God is wherever Jesus is King. The kingdom of God is the exercise of God's kingship, His authority and His right to rule based on His might, power and glory.[2] It is the rule and reign of God. It is wherever Jesus is made Lord in the hearts of individuals. The kingdom of God is in *our* hearts. Wherever we go, the kingdom of God goes with us. Whether in a campus, in an office space or in the government of a nation, if Jesus is made Lord, the Kingdom is present to rule.

For Jesus, the kingdom of God means the abolishing of Satan's kingdom. The kingdom of God is not just a Sunday worship service; the kingdom of God is every place where Jesus is worshiped and made rightful King. *Lord, let Your kingdom come!* It is every believer's responsibility to contend for God's kingdom—His values, blessings, prosperity, rule and reign—to come into every sphere of society.

2. We Must Understand that We Are All Ministers

"But you are a chosen generation, a royal priesthood, a holy nation" (1 Pet. 2:9). In the Old Testament, only the high priest was able to enter into the presence of the Lord. He did this through blood sacrifice in order to make atonement for the sins of the people. In the New Testament, Jesus has become the blood sacrifice for all. Through the blood of Jesus we all can enter into God's presence. We are all called to be priests or ministers. Each of us is anointed and can hear from God—not just Billy Graham, our senior pastor or vocational missionary. No, each of us is called and empowered by God to win souls and make disciples wherever we are in society. Real ministry doesn't happen on Sunday only; it happens from Sunday to Sunday in our classrooms, our offices or wherever we are.

3. We Must Understand that Work Is Sacred

"And whatever you do in word or deed, do all in the name of the Lord Jesus, giving thanks to God the Father through Him" (Col. 3:17). Work is not evil; work is holy. We are on our campuses studying like crazy because God is preparing us for a holy work. Not necessarily a holy work in the pulpit, but a holy work in Hollywood, in the medical field, in politics, in business or any other sphere, because God wants His kingdom to rule there. We are agents of His kingdom.

We need to renounce the Greek idea of dualism, which places spiritual things above earthly things. John Beckett, a businessman and a major leader of today's church in the workplace, describes this concept well. In his book *Loving Monday*, Beckett writes:

> [Plato] sought to identify unchanging universal truths, placing them in the higher of two distinct realms. The upper level he called "form," consisting of eternal ideas. The lower level he called "matter." The lower realm was temporal and physical. Plato's primary interest lay in the higher form. He deemed it superior to the temporary and imperfect world of matter.[3]

This kind of dualistic thinking that separates the spiritual from material has plagued the Church for centuries and has caused the Church to separate itself from society. The Church has divided the sacred from the secular. But not any longer. God is equipping a new generation to take the Church back into society and to release signs, wonders and miracles just as Jesus did to bring about transformation.

Where Jesus Spent Most of His Time

Out of Jesus' 132 public appearances in the New Testament, 122 took place in the marketplace. Of the 52 parables Jesus told, 45 had a workplace context. Of the 40 miracles in the book of Acts, 39 took place in the marketplace. In addition, Jesus equipped 12 men from the workplace and spent more than 50 percent of his adult life as a carpenter before He went into a preaching ministry in the workplace.

Where do a *majority* of men and women spend a *majority* of their time interacting with a *majority* of the lost world? It's not in a church or even in a neighborhood: it is in the workplace.[4] A mentor of mine,

Pastor Ed Silvoso, wrote a book called *Anointed for Business* that changed my life and my paradigm of church. Through this book I learned that there is not a God-ordained division between clergy and laity. The Church is not called to operate primarily inside a building. People in the marketplace are just as spiritual as those serving in traditional church ministry. Moreover, the primary role of a marketplace Christian is not merely to make money to support the vision of those "in ministry"; their role is to be pastors to those in their workplace.

How to Transform Society

Every Christian is a minister. Every marketplace minister should have a vision to transform the marketplace with the gospel. "Workplace church" should happen all over the city, every day, all day, as we see in Acts 2:42. It should happen just as I experienced it when I worked for the tech company in California. If we are going to reform society by transforming the marketplace for Christ, then we must apply the following action steps.

We Must Transform Our Hearts

"That the genuineness of your faith, being much more precious than gold that perishes, though it is tested by fire, may be found to praise, honor, and glory at the revelation of Jesus Christ" (1 Pet. 1:7). Our success does not come from what we do; our success comes from who we are in Christ. He loves me, I love Him, and therefore I am successful.

The world's value system is based on works and how well we perform. It says, "You do, therefore you are." No, I don't think so. God says, "You are, therefore you do." God's value system is based on our value as His children, being His beloved son or daughter. There is nothing we can do to make Him love us more or less. We can do absolutely nothing and God will still love us. Reform society, because it is your destiny, but remember—your destiny is not your identity.

Our value is based solely on what Jesus has done for us, not what we can do for Him. We have priceless worth simply because we have relationship with Jesus. The glory that is in Jesus is the same glory that is in us (see John 17:22). We have it not because of what we can do—it can't be earned. We have it because it is who we are in Christ. To transform society, we must place intimacy with the Holy Spirit and our relationship with Christ as the true successes of our hearts. The success of our works is only a by-product of our intimacy with Him.

We Must Minister in the Power of the Holy Spirit

"But you shall receive power when the Holy Spirit has come upon you" (Acts 1:8). A friend of mine, Chuck Ripka, started a Christian bank in Elk River, Minnesota. The story of his bank made the front page of the *New York Times* magazine because of the miracles that have been taking place there.[5] When he started the bank, Chuck dedicated it to God for His purposes. Within the first year of business, the bank was the fastest-growing bank in its city. Not only this but also nearly 100 people were saved in the bank that year. Also, more than 100 instantaneous miracles, divine healings and answered prayers happened right inside the bank with customers! These miracles took place because Chuck had trained all his bank tellers to ask each customer if he or she wanted prayer after every business transaction.

Every believer has the power of the Holy Spirit within him or her. If we do power evangelism on the campus, we are to do power evangelism in the workplace. The Holy Spirit has given us the authority and power to cast out demons, heal the sick, prophesy over the lost and preach His kingdom in power to all of society.

We Must Plant Workplace Churches

"For where two or three are gathered together in My name, I am there in the midst of them" (Matt. 18:20). Church is not a building; it is people. If even two or three are gathered in Jesus' name, then all the authority of heaven is there, a church is established and the gates of hell will not prevail (see Matt. 16:18). It only takes two or three believers anywhere, at anytime, to start a revolution. Two believers on a campus can pray heaven down. Two believers in a workplace can bring revival if they will pray and release the power of the Holy Spirit. The Holy Spirit is sending students, upon graduation, from the campus into the marketplace of society to plant simple churches in every workplace.

Our ministry, Campus Church Networks, does a lot of work in East Asia. Right now, the church there is growing fast because church is happening everywhere, every day. Students start simple house churches in their apartments near campuses. Business people plant house churches in their homes, as well as at the office. I have partners who build factories in East Asia, where they hold evangelistic Bible studies with hundreds of workers. So many are getting saved that, in one of the factories, they made a baptism pool in the factory to baptize new believers!

Why not ask our coworkers if we can pray for them? Why not invite those we work with to an evangelistic Bible study during a lunch break or another time? We must win them, disciple them and do church with them in the power of the Holy Spirit by planting small workplace churches that multiply all over.

We Must Take Dominion

"And God said to them, 'Be fruitful and multiply; fill the earth and subdue it; have dominion over the fish of the sea, over the birds of the air, and over every living thing that moves on the earth'" (Gen. 1:28). God created us to take dominion—to rule, to master over, to be in charge—of the earth. We are the head and not the tail, above and not beneath (see Deut. 28:13). Our call is to rule the nations of the earth as representatives of God's kingdom. It is our responsibility to disciple nations. Jesus didn't tell us to disciple people, but in Matthew 28:19, He said, "Go therefore and make disciples of all the nations."

Church growth expert Peter Wagner, referencing Matthew 28:18, said:

It does not tell us to make disciples of individuals in all the nations, which has been our standard old paradigm interpretation. Instead, we are supposed to make disciples of

"panta ta ethne" which in Greek means all ethnic units or
social units or people groups. This is a term which denotes
sociological groupings of individuals. The whole unit, or
nation (including, of course the individuals who belong to
it), is supposed to be Jesus' collective disciple and observe
what Jesus commanded throughout their society. We now
see that the Great Commission's biblical goal is nothing
short of social transformation.[6]

The Bible makes it clear that the earth belongs to us. "The heav-
en, even the heavens, are the LORD's; But the earth He has given to
children of men" (Ps. 115:16). We are called to lead society by being
in society and changing it from the inside out. We are to apply biblical principles daily in the marketplace. We are to lead with
Christlike character, excellence and the power of the Holy Spirit.
Our campuses don't belong to Satan; they belong to us. Hollywood
doesn't belong to Satan; it belongs to us. Our economy and government don't belong to Satan; they belong to the Christ in us.

Mel Gibson, for example, took dominion when he started his
own production company (ICON Productions) and released the
movie *The Passion of the Christ*. Many in Hollywood and in the rest
of the world ridiculed him and tried to stop him, but he didn't
have to submit to the world's system. He had the authority to
overrule it because he had created his own production and mar-
keting distribution company. The movie was not only made with
excellence and was a box office hit, but more important, it also
continues to impact countless thousands of lives for the gospel.
It is time to take back what rightfully belongs to us. It is time to
take dominion and to transform and reform all of society!

Preparation for Societal Reformation

1. As a student, ask the Holy Spirit to help you identify
    your passions and gifts. What areas of society are you
    passionate to impact for Christ? What natural and
    spiritual gifts can you use for God's glory?

2. Understand that the ministry you do on campus is a time of preparation for you to do ministry and power evangelism in the marketplace and/or workplace.

3. Become a student who is daily filled with the Holy Spirit, and aim for excellence in your studies and work.

4. Begin to plan your future. Connect with Christian leaders in the marketplace who are transforming the workplace in your field of interest.

5. Begin to dream for God—start a company, invent a new technology, influence media, find the cure for cancer, eradicate poverty—and take dominion!

6. Once in the marketplace, have a vision to win souls, make disciples and plant workplace churches. Pray daily for your coworkers. Start evangelistic Bible studies where you work or live. Disciple these new converts and empower them to multiply the work.

Notes
1. Ché Ahn, "Ministers in the Workplace," The Church in the Workplace Audio Series (Pasadena, CA: Harvest Rock Church, 2005). This resource is available online at http://www.harvestrockchurch.org/store/home.php?cat=250.
2. Steven C. Hawthorne, *Perspectives on the World Christian Movement* (Pasadena, CA: William Carey Library, 1999), p. 20.
3. John Beckett, *Loving Monday* (Downers Grove, IL: Intervarsity Press, 2006), n.p.
4. Os Hillman, *The 9 to 5 Window* (Ventura, CA: Regal Books, 2006), n.p.
5. Russell Shorto, "Faith at Work," *The New York Times Magazine*, online edition, October 31, 2004. http://www.nytimes.com/2004/10/31/magazine/31FAITH.html?ex=1256965200&en=9a57b879c59fbe04&ei=5090&partner=rssuserland (accessed January 2007).
6. C. Peter Wagner, *The Church in the Workplace* (Ventura, CA: Regal Books, 2006), see the chapter entitled "Let's Take Dominion Now."

PASSION FOR PLANTING SIMPLE CHURCHES

*And on this rock I will build My church, and the gates
of Hades shall not prevail against it.*

MATTHEW 16:18

In September 2005, I moved from Northern California to Los
Angeles to establish a base for our Campus Church Networks ministry in Southern California. During this time, the Holy Spirit connected me with two students on the UCLA campus who were
contending for revival. Believe it or not, their names are Caleb and
Joshua—yes, just like the two heroes of faith in the Bible (see Num.
13:30–14:38; Josh. 1–3)! These two students had been waking up at
5:30 A.M. every day of the week for more than a year to pray for
revival to come to UCLA. Every Friday they would go into the middle of campus and preach publicly. Many students laughed at them
and others cursed them, but they kept on preaching. They truly
believed that revival would come. When I saw their faith, I knew
that I had to be a part of what they were doing.

When Caleb first approached me for help to plant a student-
led house church at UCLA, I asked him why. He replied, "If revival
really did come to UCLA, and 3,000 were saved in a day, what
would we do with all of them?" He didn't believe that the existing

campus ministries and local churches would be able to contain and disciple all the new souls. He said that some of his lost friends were just too different and wouldn't fit into any of the existing Christian cultures. His most logical conclusion was that they needed to start a new church, or a lot of new house churches, to prepare for the coming revival on campus.

In the book of Acts, the Christians had to plant multiple house churches in order to disciple the many souls who were daily coming to Christ. Caleb and Josh wanted to follow the New Testament example. When I heard their vision and passion, I sensed God's calling to train them in simple church planting at UCLA.

As I began to coach and train Caleb and Josh in some simple church-planting strategies before the school year started, I received a prophetic dream. In this dream, I saw Cindy Jacobs, a well-known international prophet, in front of a house across the street from UCLA. She looked at me and said, "Jaeson, back in the Jesus People movement, we prayed daily for revival to come to our college campus, but we never thought it would actually come in three days! When revival did come, this is when we met Bob Logan, but he wasn't the right person." Then I saw a big white guy walk onto the grass where Cindy was and shake her hand. Then the dream ended. After I woke up, I wrote the dream down and pondered its meaning.

A few days later, during the first week of school, the presence and power of God broke out near the grassy hill at Bruin Walk. That was the first day Caleb, Josh, a few others and I went out to pray, to prophetically worship and to preach on the UCLA campus. This was the blog story I recorded in chapter 8, when a large crowd of students gathered to hear us preach the gospel. Some were saved on the spot, and God opened the doors for us to reach pockets of unreached students right on the Bruin walkway. In the story, I didn't mention specifically that there was a big white guy who was with us that day. His name is Neil Cole.

Neil is a well-known church-planting trainer I met a few years back. He wrote a popular book called *Organic Church*, in which he tells the story of how he planted more than 600 organic, or simple, churches out of Long Beach, California. These churches met in homes, cafés, locker rooms, universities, parks, parking lots and even vampire clubs. These simple churches met anywhere, any time, with any number of people who were following Jesus. Neil heard that we were doing something similar at UCLA and decided to come with me that day to help with planting the student-led church there.

After the Holy Spirit encounter at Bruin Walk, Neil looked at me and said, "Jaeson, the Holy Spirit spoke to me today while you were preaching about the difference between the ministries of George Whitefield and John Wesley. You see, they were both great evangelists during the Great Awakening revivals in America. But at the end of George Whitefield's life, he said, 'My brother Wesley acted wisely. The souls that were awakened under his ministry he joined in class, and thus preserved the fruit of his labours. This I neglected, and my people are a rope of sand.'"[1]

Neil explained how George Whitefield preached a powerful, prophetic word in his day, and how many people were converted, but not many became disciples after the large gatherings. Whereas, John Wesley, although not as powerful a preacher as George White-field, preached to the masses, and his converts became disciples because he had systems in place that led ordinary people to do the work of the ministry.

Everywhere Wesley preached, he set up "classes," or small groups of accountability for new believers who would meet together regularly to pray and hold each other accountable to obey the Word of God. In fact, John Wesley planted more Methodist churches through this class, or method system, the years after he died than while he was alive. In other words, Wesley was wise, because he didn't think in terms of adding disciples, but in terms of multiplying disciples. He prepared wineskins for the wine. Neil went on to explain to me that God was pouring out new wine at UCLA, but that there needed to be new wineskins to contain the wine.

No one puts a piece of unshrunk cloth on an old garment; for the patch pulls away from the garment, and the tear is made worse. Nor do they put new wine into old wine skins, or else the wineskins break, the wine is spilled, and

the wineskins are ruined. But they put new wine into new
wineskins, and both are preserved (Matt. 9:16-17).

Later on, I shared with Neil the dream I had about Cindy Jacobs
and the man named Bob Logan at UCLA. When I said the name
"Bob Logan," he was stunned. He told me that Bob Logan was one
of his early mentors in church planting and that my dream was not
an accident. To Neil, in the dream, Cindy Jacobs represented the
"prophetic" or "new wine" that would be poured out soon at UCLA,
and Bob Logan represented the "apostolic" or "new wineskin" that
would be needed to contain the new wine.

In the New Testament, it was the prophetic outpouring of the
Holy Spirit that released new wine, or revival, on the day of Pentecost (see Acts 2:13). The prophetic message turned the masses to
Christ and predicted what was to come. But once the Spirit was
poured out and souls were saved, it was the apostles who brought
leadership to the Early Church and planted the first churches to
disciple the new converts: "And He Himself gave some to be apostles, some prophets" (Eph. 4:11). Likewise, that year at UCLA,
everything unfolded as the dream had indicated. First, the prophetic was released as we prayed and preached the gospel all over
campus in the power of the Holy Spirit. As souls were saved, the
apostolic or missionary spirit came into place as we gathered new
converts into simple churches that met in dorms, apartments,
homes, fraternities, student unions, on the lawn. The Church
spread all over campus; it couldn't be stopped and it had no walls.

In the dream, Cindy Jacobs had said that Bob Logan wasn't the
right person. I believed it was because Neil Cole was the right person.
He was the "big white guy" in the dream! That year, Neil came to
UCLA every week and trained staff and student leaders from different
campus ministries all over UCLA to plant organic, or simple, churches
in every pocket of unreached students on campus. It ignited a student
missionary movement at UCLA in which students saw themselves as
missionaries on campus, called to go and reach the lost.

It is not enough that we have a passion for prayer and a passion for power evangelism. We must have a passion for planting

simple churches to prepare for the coming harvest. Prayer and power evangelism can bring revival, or the outpouring of new wine. But we must first have wineskins prepared for the new wine that will be poured out on college and university campuses all over the world. These new wineskins will be simple churches or house churches like the ones we read about in the New Testament—churches without walls, simple churches that anyone can form. These churches can multiply easily to disciple the multitudes that will turn to Christ.

We must have a passion for planting simple churches on campuses. This movement will be focused on bringing in the harvest and will be led by an army of students on every campus and in every city and nation of the earth until God's kingdom comes. It is now time for the mobilization of an end-time army that will finish the Great Commission in this generation by bringing church to every sphere of society!

Note

1. George Hunter, *To Spread the Power: Church Growth in the Wesleyan Spirit* (Nashville, TN: Abingdon Press, 1987), p. 126, originally cited in Stanley Ayling, *John Wesley* (New York: William Collins Publishers, 1979), p. 210.

CHAPTER THIRTEEN

SIMPLE CHURCH PLANTING

For where two or three are gathered together in My name,
I am there in the midst of them.
MATTHEW 18:20

I have already told about how, in 1998, the Holy Spirit led me on a journey to start a ministry called Campus Church Networks at San Jose State University. God began to grant me and our campus ministry so much favor with the San Jose State student government that they actually sponsored us to put on major evangelistic rallies on campus, such as UNIVERSOUL and others. Through these major outreaches, hundreds of students were touched and saved.

As exciting as it was to see students being saved, I realized that many who had made decisions for Christ were not integrated into a healthy local church family. In fact, most of the churches around the college campus did not have college-age ministries. Many didn't have a clue about what to do with college students or young adults. Although some of the Christians on campus could attend a campus fellowship while in school, sooner or later they would graduate and find the same problem of not fitting into traditional churches or not finding a church where they could be empowered.

Through these experiences I began to pray about how I could start simple churches on campuses that would bring the church to the students instead of the students to the church. After much study in missionary church planting models, such as the underground house churches in China, I was convinced that simple relationship-based churches would meet the most practical needs of college students. In relationship-based churches, believers can encounter God personally, experience authentic community and be empowered to do God's work.

In my studies and research, I read how newly born-again 18-year-old Chinese girls were planting more than 100 house churches in China in less than a year. Many were uneducated but relied on the power of the Holy Spirit and on-the-job training from other seasoned church planters. The more I studied about this, the more excited I became. Everything I read was like reading a live account of a modern-day book of Acts. Being desperate to see real revival, God opened doors for me to visit the underground house-church movement in China before I graduated from college. The Chinese churches I visited were within networks of small churches of maybe 15 to 30 members who were meeting in homes or storefronts, sharing life together day to day under the Lordship of Christ. There was no church building, no extensive church programs and no paid professionals in these simple churches. There were only ordinary people doing the extraordinary works of God.

This kind of simple relationship-based church excited me so much that I began to wonder, *If an 18-year-old Chinese girl can plant 100 churches in one year in China, why can't a college freshman plant a few simple churches on a college campus?* It was then that I realized that a church could be planted on a college campus if the biblical concept of winning a "person of peace" could be put into action (see Luke 10:6).

A person of peace is a person of influence among a given group that is open to the gospel. If a trained student missionary could pray and win a student of peace to Christ and teach this person to win his or her circle of friends, then a simple church could be started. The missionary would teach the student of peace to share his or her testimony and start a simple evangelistic Bible study. As seeking students came to Christ through the Bible study and were baptized, a small church would be born. Once started, the missionary would model and coach the natural leaders of the group how to shepherd the church. The goal would always be that one day these students would actually become the elders or spiritual leaders themselves. Finally, the student missionary would train the students to raise up their own student leaders to start other simple churches on the campus to spark an unstoppable missionary movement.

Essentially, one church on a campus would not be enough. There are so many various kinds of student clusters on a campus that no one church could ever reach every student segment. There are sports students, engineering students, international students, fraternity and sorority students, religious students, and the list goes on. I had experienced through our evangelistic efforts that many students who became new believers did not fit into the Christian fellowships that already existed because they were culturally or socially different. But by applying missionary methods to this situation, it became important to look at each student segment as though it was an unreached people group. The best way to reach a campus would then be to plant a unique church for each of these unreached groups. Instead of just focusing on having one campus church, the goal would be to start as many simple churches as it would take to reach every kind of student in the school. We need to bring church to them, not bring them to church.

These simple churches would normally have about 15 to 20 students meeting anywhere on or near campus: a dorm, apartment, home, student union, classroom, business office, outside, or even in cafés! Once the simple church outgrew its meeting place, instead of looking for a bigger meeting place to rent, the church would train up another student leader(s) to start another church somewhere else on campus! In essence, it would multiply itself. Pretty soon, the whole college community could be saturated with churches and every student would be reached for Christ and established in healthy discipleship communities.

The power in the simple church-planting model is that students learn to do church where they are. They no longer see church as something they go to on Sundays, but rather, they see it as something they live out daily wherever they may be. They realize they have been given "permission" by Jesus to do everything the Bible says they can do! This is not to say that students don't need to go to a congregational church on Sunday, although that may be the case in certain instances; but they need to see church as a lifestyle, not an event. The congregational church should instead act as an apostolic mission base, equipping and sending students out to plant autonomous simple churches. When students graduate, they would be sent out to start simple churches in their communities, in their workplaces and all over the city. Since the churches they plant would not be restricted or confined to church buildings or to paid professionals, they would be able to do church anytime and anywhere.

Most churches outside of the Western context are in persecuted environments where the churches are forced to meet underground in homes. If students learn to do house churches or simple churches on their campuses and in the cities where they live, they would already be trained and ready to plant simple churches to reach the unreached nations with the gospel of Jesus Christ! They would already be prepared to be missionaries in every sphere of society and on every nation of the earth.

This new strategy of reaching the college campuses burned inside my heart my final year in college. During that time, I put the vision into action and started our first simple church at San Jose State University. Through a season of trial and error, the Holy Spirit began to breathe upon the vision and we started to see it become a reality. Students of peace were saved and they, in turn, reached their friends, and new churches were planted. Supernaturally, we began starting simple campus churches not only at San Jose State University but also in the city and on campuses all over the United States and in East Asia. We began to partner with major campus ministry organizations and local churches to train students as missionaries on their campuses, to plant simple churches.

In order for many parachurch organizations and local churches to buy into this radical new idea of church, we explained that simple churches are missional communities, or an extension of their ministry on campus to do whatever it takes to win the lost. In the first three years of ministry, we had equipped students and witnessed hundreds of simple churches planted across the Body of Christ. Now the campus church-planting movement is beginning to unfold. Currently, I am serving with the CCN ministry reaching out to campuses with the dream of one day seeing every campus, every city and every nation saturated with simple churches that are engaging the lost and equipping and empowering students to fulfill the Great Commandment and the Great Commission in this generation.

Why Plant Churches on Campus?

My heart is passionate about planting simple churches on campuses. The campus is one of the most important mission fields of our day. It is the greatest harvest field. The world-changers and history-makers of tomorrow are on our campuses today. These students will be the future movers and shakers of society. They are the ones who will birth new revivals and missionary movements in our time. Also, as we reach the hundreds of thousands of international students in our colleges and universities, they will in turn reach their nations for Christ. If we can change the campus, we can change entire nations. Let's do this!

But why are we to plant churches? C. Peter Wagner, church growth expert, says, "The single most effective evangelistic methodology under heaven is planting new churches."[1] If we are going to win and disciple lost students, we must plant new churches.

Fuller Seminary did a study proving that new churches provide the greatest opportunity for salvations:[2]

Age of Church	People/Salvation Ratio
10+ years old	85 to 1
4-7 years old	7 to 1
3 years and under	3 to 1

When we empower students to do church on campuses, they will begin to live a mission-minded lifestyle and do church wherever they are. Believers in this generation must have this mindset to focus on the lost. Between 3,500 and 4,000 churches close their doors each year in America. Half of all churches last year did not add a single new member through "conversion growth."[3] Approximately 98 million people are under the age of 25 in the United States, and those between the ages of 18 and 25 are the least likely to attend a church.[4] We must break out of the traditional bounds of church in order to reach the millions of young people who are not being reached with the gospel.

George Barna, the foremost church research expert, wrote a challenging book in 2005 called *Revolution* that predicted the future of the Western Church in the next generation. He wrote:

1. One million believers are leaving the North American church each year to preserve their faith.

2. Millions of believers have moved beyond the established church and chosen to be the Church instead.

3. The number of Christians attending local churches in the USA is declining rapidly.

4. Today, 70 percent of Christians attend traditional churches, but this will sink to 30 to 35 percent in 20 years.

5. The number of followers of Jesus who do not attend a local church will grow from 30 percent to 70 percent in the next 20 years.

6. Alternative forms of fellowship (including house churches/simple churches and postmodern churches) that are currently home for 5 percent of American Christians will grow to make up 30 to 35 percent; another 30 to 35 percent will live out their faith in the fields of media, arts and culture; the remaining 5 percent of Christians attending non-traditional forms of church will have a family-based spiritual life.[5]

Many in this generation are leaving the local, established church and are pursuing faith in other ways. I have a lot of friends who love God but who don't love church and have stopped going. We have to reach them and others who have never heard of Christ by taking church out of the four walls and into society—into everyday life—so that this generation can find faith where life happens. In order to do this, we must have a new understanding of church as we know it.

What Is Church?

One of the best definitions for church I have heard is "a group of believers of any size, committed to one another to obey Jesus' commands." Robert Fitts, in his book *The Church in the House*, defines church as the following:

> The Greek word for church, *ekklesia,* is composed of two words: "*ek*" meaning "out of," and "*kalleo,*" meaning "I call." The full and simple meaning of "church" according to the original word is, "I call out from."
>
> Actually, ekklesia carries two concepts: being called out and being assembled together. We cannot experience church until we come together. When two or three true born-again believers come together in His name, Jesus is in the midst. Jesus *in the midst* is church! It is a different experience than Jesus within. We cannot experience Jesus in the midst when we are alone. We can only experience Jesus in the midst when we are in company with others—at least one or two others.
>
> But is it a church in the fullest sense of the word? Yes, it is a church in the fullest sense of the word. It is the basic church. You can have more than two or three and it is still a church, but it does not become "more church" because there are more than two or three. It only becomes a bigger church.[6]

"Simple" church is a way of doing and being church that is so simple that any believer would respond by saying, "I could do that!"

Jesus said, "Where two or three are gathered together in My name, I am there in the midst of them" (Matt. 18:20). Therefore, the smallest unit of a church is two or three believers gathering together under the Lordship of Jesus. In other words, church is simple![7]

When I say, "My passion is to plant simple churches on campuses," I don't mean planting churches with buildings, budgets and bureaucracy. I mean being and doing church where I am—where you are. It is a mentality, a paradigm shift, to lower the bar of how we do church and to raise the bar of discipleship. Simple church is so simple that when we see it we know that we can do it! It is not difficult. It does not take a paid professional or years of training to make church happen. There is a place for that, but church, at its most basic level, is simply loving God and loving others.

Church is a spiritual family. Church is a missional community. Simple church is giving God's people "permission" to do everything the Bible says they can do. If we can win a few of our lost friends to Christ, gather them, and teach them to obey Jesus, we can do simple church! It only takes two or three believers to begin a simple church and start a revolution on a campus, in a workplace or anywhere for Christ.

A Paradigm Shift: From Going to Church to Being the Church

As Christ followers, we must shift our thinking from merely going to church to being the church. In order to do church "simple," this generation needs to understand three things about church:

1. *Church is not a building; it is people.* We don't *go* to church; we *are* the Church. Yes, we *be* the Church!

2. *The preacher is not a performer and the congregation is not an audience.* We don't treat church like an event, with a consumer mentality, as when we're watching a movie or eating at a restaurant. It's not about what the church can do for us; it's about what we can do for God and His

people. We don't go to church only to receive; we go to church to give (see 1 Cor. 14:26).

3. *We are called to make disciples as our priority.* The church is not a social club. The church is a spiritual family. It is also the army of God called out to change the world. In the New Testament, the early believers did simple church, or house church (see Acts 18:6-7; 20:20; 28:30-31; Rom. 16:3-4; 1 Cor. 16:19; Col. 4:15). There were no church buildings or clergy in the Early Church until A.D. 324.[8] The earliest remains of a Christian church ever uncovered by archaeological excavations was found at Dura-Europos in Syria, was dated to the third century A.D. and was an ordinary house![9]

The Early Church was unstoppable until in A.D. 324, when the movement turned into a monument once the first church building was erected. This doesn't mean that we should stop going to a church with a building. If we attend a local congregational church or campus fellowship, we can still be missionaries where we are by planting a simple church among our lost friends or a lost community on campus. It's all about our mentality!

What Typifies Simple Church?

When I say simple church, I mean a church that listens to God, follows His leading and obeys His commands. Jesus commanded us in the Great Commission to do four things: to go, to make disciples, to baptize them and to teach them to obey all He commanded (see Matt. 28:18-20). The apostle Paul did exactly these four things. In every city he went to, he listened to the Holy Spirit, intending to do evangelism, discipleship and leadership training (see Acts 14:21-24). Through following the Holy Spirit and teaching others to obey Jesus' commands, Paul started a revolutionary movement that empowered ordinary people to plant simple churches that planted other simple churches that spread the gospel all over the known world.

Like Paul, we must equip students on every campus to listen to the Holy Spirit and obey Jesus' commands. If we do, we can reproduce disciples. If we can reproduce disciples, we can reproduce leaders. If we can reproduce leaders, we can reproduce churches. If we can reproduce churches, we can reproduce movements—that is, revolutionary movements for God in our generation!

Jesus said, "If you love Me, *keep my commandments*" (John 14:15, emphasis added). If we can teach students to obey Jesus' basic commands (see Matt. 28:19-20; Acts 2:37-47) with a motive of love, not legalism, we can plant simple-church movements on campuses to reach every segment of unreached students. Jesus commanded:

- *Repent, believe and receive the Holy Spirit*—These acts go together; we can't do one without the others (see Mark 1:15; John 20:22; compare to Acts 2:38; 19:2).

- Be *baptized*—Forever live the new, holy life that baptism signifies. We are to baptize new converts immediately as they did in the book of Acts. Jesus commanded us not only to be baptized but also to be baptizers (see Matt. 28:19-20; Acts 2:38).

- *Love* God, family, fellow disciples, neighbors and even enemies; forgiveness is crucial in love (see Luke 10:25-37).

- *Celebrate* the Lord's Supper—Cultivate the communion with Christ and His people (see Luke 22:14-20).

- *Pray* daily—And feed on the Bible daily; we need to keep connected with God (see Matt. 6:5-13).

- *Give* generously (see Matt. 6:19-21).

- *Make disciples*—Witness, teach, train leaders and others to be like Jesus by obeying His commands (see Matt. 28:18-19; Luke 24:46-48).[10]

God blesses simple obedience to His Word. When we obey Jesus' commands, simple churches will be born and multiplied automatically and rapidly. Being a true disciple is not about obtaining more knowledge about God; it is about being more obedient to Him.

In order to protect us from making church so complicated that no one can do it, we must recognize the differences between divine commands, apostolic practices and human traditions. Jesus commanded us to obey His *divine commands* that are found in Scripture and that are to be obeyed in any circumstance. We do not necessarily have to obey *apostolic practices*, which are not divine commands, but customs practiced in the New Testament by the apostles, such as worshiping on Sunday, using one communion cup, and so forth. Finally, we cannot force anyone to practice *human customs* in church that are not found in the New Testament. Examples of human customs are choir, church buildings, pulpits, baptism ceremonies, any non-biblical requirement for ordination or anything that impedes obedience to God's Word.[11] Simple church is simply teaching others to obey Jesus—no more, no less.

The most basic understanding of simple church is that it puts into action the Great Commandment and the Great Commission (see Matt. 22:37-40; 28:18-20). It is about loving God with all our heart, soul, strength and mind and loving others as ourselves. It is also about going out to make disciples of all nations, baptizing them and teaching them to obey all that Jesus commanded. I will say again that a simple church is simply any number of believers committed together to love God, love each other and love the lost.

This is the spiritual *DNA* of the simple church. It is a commitment to *divine truth* (loving God), *nurturing relationships* (loving each other) and *apostolic mission* (loving the lost). Simple church is a missional community. In simple church, we are called to do the four verbs of the Great Commission. We are called to *go* to the lost, not say, "come to our church." We are called to *make disciples,* not converts. We are called to *be baptizers,* not wait to be baptized. We are called to teach others to *radically obey God's Word,* not just receive more theory and theology. Simple church is a group of believers sent out on a specific assignment to reach and disciple the lost. It is something anyone can do, anywhere they are.

Simple Church Is Family

Simple church is a spiritual family. It is about spiritual parents raising spiritual sons and daughters to establish their own families (see Mal. 4:6). My spiritual father, Pastor Ché Ahn, sent me out of my local church (Harvest Rock Church, a megachurch in Pasadena, California) to plant my own simple church or "spiritual family." That church has now multiplied and birthed other simple churches or families on different campuses, cities and nations.

I am thankful for my spiritual father, Pastor Ché, because he doesn't want to control but rather empower, come alongside and support the emerging young leaders to change history for God! I love his heart and pray that other spiritual fathers would come alongside and empower their spiritual sons and daughters to give themselves fully to the work of God in their generation. Both Pastor Ché and I know that our callings are different, but our mission is the same (see Matt. 28:18-20). We respect one another, love one another and honor each other to do God's work.

In Matthew 9:17, Jesus says, "People [do not] put new wine into old wineskins, or else the wineskins break, the wine is spilled, and the wineskins are ruined. But they put new wine into new wineskins and both are preserved." God wants revival in both generations. Although the wineskins may look different, the wine is the same and the purpose is clear: God wants revival in every generation, and we must work together, not apart, toward the common goal of preaching the gospel to the lost. In the future, I foresee many local megachurches and community churches equipping and releasing young adults to venture out and plant simple-church movements among the lost in every sphere of society as this next wave of revival is poured out in our generation. These megachurch, community church and simple church networks will work alongside one another to truly pastor and transform every part of society and not leave one stone or one soul unturned in a city for Christ!

I pray that God will turn the hearts of the fathers to the children and the children to the fathers to work together and do whatever it takes to win this new generation to Christ. I pray that it will be the passion of your heart to take the gospel out of the four walls, out of your Christian ghetto or bubble, out of your comfort zone and into the harvest field on your campus and in your city by planting simple churches among the lost. Spread the vision of simple church planting. It's simple. Anyone can do it. *You* can do it. It is for His glory!

Notes

1. C. Peter Wagner, *Church Planting for a Greater Harvest* (Ventura, CA: Regal Books, 1990), p. 11.
2. American Society for Church Growth (ASCG), "Enlarging Our Borders," report presented to the Executive Presbytery, January 1999.
3. Ibid.
4. George Barna, "Twentysomethings Struggle to Find Their Place in Christian Churches," *The Barna Update*, September 24, 2003. http://www.barna.org/Flex Page.aspx?Page=BarnaUpdate&BarnaUpdateID=149 (accessed March 2004).
5. George Barna, *Revolution* (Carol Stream, IL: Tyndale House Publishers, 2005), p. 49.
6. Robert Fitts, *The Church in the House: A Return to Simplicity* (Salem, OR: Preparing the Way Publishers, April 2001), pp. 17-18.
7. House2House, "What Do We Mean by Simple Church?" March 14, 2005. http://www.house2house.net/modules.php?name=Content&pa=showpage&pid=2 (accessed January 2007).
8. Gene Edwards, *A Plea for Church Life*; see specifically, "Where Did Church Buildings Come From?" http://www.homechurch.com/johnzens/ST_Edwards_Plea.html (accessed January 2007).
9. L. A. Dirven, *The Palmyrenes of Dura-Europos: A Study of Religious Interaction in Roman Syria* (Leiden: E. J. Brill, 1999), n.p.; Susan B. Matheson, *Dura-Europos: The Ancient City and the Yale Collection* (New Haven, CT: Yale University Press, 1982), n.p.; Simon James, "Dura-Europos, 'Pompeii of the Syrian Desert,'" The University of Leicester, September 5, 2005. http://www.le.ac.uk/ar/stj/dura.htm#destruc (accessed January 2007); "Healing of the Paralytic, Dura Europos (c. 235)," ReligionFacts, January 12, 2006, http://www.religionfacts.com/jesus/image_gallery/230_dura_europos.htm (accessed January 2007); "Early Christian Architecture," University of Pittsburgh History of Art and Architecture Department, http://www.pitt.edu/~tokerism/0040/syl/christian.html (accessed January 2007). In the 1920s archaeologists working in present-day Syria uncovered in the desert sands a Roman garrison town, Dura-Europos. The archaeologists discovered a house, dating to 256 A.D., which had been renovated for use as a Christian church. The renovated house had a special room dedicated for baptisms, with a large baptismal pool and frescoes illustrating the healing of the paralytic by Jesus in Luke 5.
10. George Patterson, *Church Planting Through Obedience Oriented Teaching: The Spontaneous Multiplication of Churches* (Pasadena, CA: William Carey Library, 1981), n.p.
11. Steve Hawthorne, *Perspectives on the World Christian Movement Study Guide* (Pasadena, CA: William Carey Library, 1999), p. 128.

CHAPTER FOURTEEN

SATURATION CHURCH PLANTING

And this continued for two years, so that all who dwelt in Asia
heard the word of the Lord Jesus, both Jews and Greeks.
ACTS 19:10

My longing to see the book of Acts in practice again, to see God do more in my generation, to see true revival, had brought me from America to a corner of Southeast Asia. The morning I walked into a small missionary office, I had a scheduled meeting with Bill (I can't say his last name to protect his identity), whom I have decided to call "Morpheus." Why? Because he held the secret to the "matrix" that many of us Christians live in. That is, the matrix of living in a Christian culture, a Christian bubble all our lives, going to church each Sunday, but wondering in the back of our minds, *Is there something more to church than this?* There is more. Bill asked me, "Jaeson, do you want to see the cutting edge of evangelism?"

I said, "What do you mean?"

"Jaeson, it's great to have big churches, see people saved and members added, but that is only addition growth. What I'm about to show you is multiplication growth." He then showed me a report of one of his strategy coordinators in China who had planted more than 1,000 churches in a few months in a specific region through the leaders in their house-church network.

"How is this possible?" I asked.

He smirked and said, "Let me show you a picture of two of my top church planters in another region. They help plant more than 100 churches every year, and they are fairly new believers." I thought he would show me a picture of apostle Paul "Chang" or the "heavenly man." Instead, he showed me a picture of two young Chinese women, one about 18 years old and the other in her early 20s. At that moment, I was both astonished and convicted. *How was this possible?*

Bill said, "These two don't plant big churches; they plant small churches. Each day they evangelize from house to house, start evangelistic Bible studies, gather new converts into house churches of 10 to 20 people, teach them to obey Christ's commands, set up simple training programs, and move on." He then shared how these small churches intentionally plant other small churches and how it continues on rapidly until an entire region of towns and cities are saturated with the gospel. He explained that this is the concept of "saturation church planting." Saturation church planting (SCP) is the vision of seeing Christ incarnate in the midst of every small unit of a population in a people group, a region, a city, a country and the world.[1] In other words, it is the goal to see church happening in every corner of every place, everywhere—yes, even on campus!

This encounter with Bill forever changed my view of what church is and how to spread the gospel. From that point on, I would not be satisfied with just winning a few souls or helping to plant one college church or campus fellowship as I had done before at San Jose State University. I was determined to empower every student, on every campus, to plant simple churches among every pocket of unreached students on that campus, until the campus was completely filled and saturated with the gospel.

The University of Texas

After a few years of starting simple church plants with students on different college and university campuses, the Holy Spirit led me to meet Jeremy Story, president of Campus Renewal Ministries.[2] Meeting Jeremy is a story in itself, but what matters is that we had the same vision and were doing the same thing: *saturation church planting on university campuses.* Our visions were so similar that Jeremy and I began a partnership in a ministry called Campus Transformation Network that currently resources staff and student leaders to *connect leaders, mobilize prayer and plant simple churches* on every college and university campus.[3]

For more than a decade, Jeremy and his team have been uniting students and staff leaders to pray daily and weekly for revival and transformation at the University of Texas (UT). They began to strategically unite in prayer when they realized the dark and desperate spiritual state of their campus. Through surveys and data research, they discovered that at UT there were nearly 50,000 students and that less than 4 percent of the population was evangelical Christian. They knew in their hearts that this was not okay, so they began to unite in prayer and hold outdoor worship and prayer rallies, gathering 500 to 1,000 Christian students on certain nights, to seek God for the transformation of University of Texas. After years of united prayer, they realized they also needed to be united in action. Together they developed four key disciplines to effectively reach a campus for Christ:

1. *Prayer Mobilization*: uniting the entire Body of Christ on campus in strategic mobilized prayer

2. *Leadership Development*: uniting campus staff and student leaders to learn from one another, share resources and work together

3. *Spiritual Mapping*: discerning what the Lord and the enemy are doing on a campus through diagnostic mapping

4. *Campus Saturation*: the identification of people groups that do not have a community of believers living among them, and the sending of believers as missionaries into those groups to plant simple churches

They realized that as a body of Christ at University of Texas, the only way they could see every student on their campus reached for Christ was if they all joined forces and resources to pray and plant a missional community, or simple church, among every pocket of people on that campus. It was about the *whole* Body of Christ, taking the *whole* gospel to the *whole* campus. This was *saturation church planting*. Through diagnostic mapping and research, they identified more than 700 unreached student/staff groups on their university campus and they were determined to reach them all.

In the last few years, I have had the privilege to work with Jeremy and his team to see more than 120 missional communities, or simple churches, planted among pockets of unreached peoples at the University of Texas. Students from different fellowships have volunteered to be campus missionaries by attending bimonthly simple church trainings and then going out two by two to different unreached student groups. Almost every year, the number of students being saved has steadily increased and the number of simple church plants has doubled. At this rate, we believe within a few years every unreached community of students/staff at University of Texas will be reached for Christ. In the near future, there will not be one place any student can go without experiencing the message and presence of Jesus on that campus!

Jeremy shared with me how they have already produced simple church plants, or what they call "authentic faith communities," at UT within the homosexual student community, ethnic and religious groups, sports teams, fraternities/sororities, international students, dorms, club organizations, and the list continues. In 2006, six ministries worked together to send 25 students into one dorm to win it for Christ!

Another major paradigm shift is that the Christians on campus no longer see themselves as spectators but as missionaries on campus. They are praying for their lost friends, caring for their practical needs and sharing the gospel by starting simple evangelistic Bible studies, resulting in simple churches. In the coming days, I pray that we may we see the whole Body of Christ bring the whole gospel to the whole campus in every city and nation of the earth. We have seen this vision reproduced on other campuses in East Asia, Los Angeles, and elsewhere. It is possible—entire campuses can be transformed. But we must act strategically to see this happen.

Saturation Church Planting on Campuses

[These were the] men who understood the times and
knew what Israel should do.
1 CHRONICLES 12:32, *NIV*

The sons of Isaachar, though small in number (200 chiefs), knew what to do in the day of battle because they understood the times. Many other regiments in King David's army had more men then Isaachar did (Ephraim had 20,800; Zubulan had more than 50,000; see 1 Chron. 12:30-37), but Isaachar had a pivotal role in David's mighty army because it had revelation and understanding from God. If we are to see every campus in every city saturated with the gospel, we must first understand the times, catch the vision and then know what strategic actions to take.

Recognize a Desperate Need

If the national average of Christians on college and university campuses is about 5 percent and most of that 5 percent come from Christian backgrounds, are we, at the end of the day, reaching the lost on our campuses?[4] No. Most of our campus ministries are only recruiting Christians to their fellowships, or Christians on campus are simply moving from ministry to ministry each year according to the best speakers, bands or programs. This is good; but it's not good enough if we are going to see the whole campus saturated with the gospel. We must not be satisfied until we see all come to repentance. For God is "not willing that any should perish but that all should come to repentance" (2 Pet. 3:9).

Take Ownership for Your Campus

The heart cry of the great reformer John Knox was, "Give me Scotland or I die." God gave him Scotland with a sweeping revival that transformed that land in the 1550s, but it came with a price. In the same way that John Knox took ownership for his country, you must take ownership for your campus! May you recognize the *lostness* on your campus and cry out to God, "Give me my campus or I die!"

I have been praying this prayer for every campus, city and nation for years. When God finds such a person on a campus, saturation church planting is made possible. Our hearts begin to burn with a passion to see every pocket of people on our campus encounter the message and the powerful presence of Jesus. We are utterly consumed with a vision for campus transformation.

Understand the Church-Planting Movement (CPM)

The term "church-planting movement" was first explained to me by a Southern Baptist missionary named David Watson. He is now a mentor of mine who has planted more than 30,000 house churches in Northern India with more than one million new believers in less than 12 years. The movement was completely indigenous (led by locals) and started with six house churches that exponentially multiplied, almost out of control. This CPM is one of many that are happening all around the world at this hour.[5]

The Southern Baptist International Mission Board has given the movement this definition: "A simple, concise definition of a Church Planting Movement (CPM) is a rapid and exponential increase of indigenous churches planting churches within a given people group or population segment."[6] David Watson witnessed a CPM that was focused on an unreached people group. We will witness a CPM that is focused on unreached student groups on our campuses and, ultimately, in our cities. This will not happen by chance; in every church-planting movement, someone has to implement a strategy of deliberate church planting.

As we go to an unreached student population, our goal is an indigenous movement of spontaneously multiplying simple churches. Let's define these terms:

- *Indigenous:* well adapted to the local situation/community; fits in with the heart language and the heart culture of the campus

- *Movement:* action, self-propelled (alive, as in not still or dead)

- *Spontaneously multiplying:* has "babies" on its own (growth is not incremental [adding a few churches every few years]; it is multiplicative. Like population, it compounds and explodes)

- *Simple:* consisting of few parts, without any or much ornamentation, sophistication or complexity

- *Churches:* a group of believers of any size, committed to one another and to obeying Jesus' commands

In order to see an indigenous movement of spontaneously multiplying churches, we must go small in order to impact big. I had the privilege in 2005 to join the Bill Bright Church Planting Congress in Dallas, Texas. In a video, the late Bill Bright challenged the Body of Christ with a vision of planting 5 million new house churches for a billion-soul harvest in the next decade. Dr. Bright knew that in order to multiply rapidly, to reach 5 million churches, it would not be possible to do church planting the traditional way we do it in the West. How would it be possible?

It is possible primarily through house churches, or what Wolfgang Simson, author of *Houses That Change the World*, would call a "spiritual rabbit plague."[7] Simson says that in order to see rapid reproduction of churches, we must differentiate between elephant- and rabbit-type churches.

Let's look at some fundamental distinctions between the elephant and the rabbit:

Elephants	Rabbits
Fertile 4 times a year	Practically continuously fertile
1 baby per pregnancy	Average of 7 babies per pregnancy
22-month gestation period	1-month gestation period
Sexual maturity: 18 years	Sexual maturity: 4 months
Grow in 3 years from 2 to 3	Grow in 3 years from 2 to 476 million

To see a CPM happen, we cannot merely plant elephant-type churches (congregational churches with buildings), because their offspring reproduce too slowly. Instead, we must plant rabbit-type churches (simple churches) that reproduce rapidly, because leaders are raised up quickly and because simple churches are not dependent upon buildings or professional staff.

We need both elephant and rabbit churches to be planted in order to see campuses, cities and nations completely discipled. But it is not enough for one or even a few elephant campus ministries to reach an entire campus. We need a "spiritual rabbit plague" of simple rabbit churches planted all over, on every campus and throughout the city!

The ultimate goal of Campus Church Network, the ministry I help lead, is to have at least one evangelical congregation sharing Christ within easy access of every unreached student group on a campus. As mentioned earlier, there are eight kinds of student groupings to target: *pragmatics, athletics, ethnics, intellectuals, socials, creatives, activists* and *religious*. Every club, organization, student group or community will fall under one of these eight areas.

At UCLA we have identified and are now targeting more than 1,000 of these unreached student and staff communities to be reached for Christ. Jim Montgomery, the founder of DAWN ministries (Discipling A Whole Nation), once asked the Master some years ago how the Great Commission was to be fulfilled. The Master's answer to him was, "See to it that I, the Lord, truly become incarnate in every small group of people on the earth."[8]

Our aim is to identify and support the John Knoxes, or what we call "strategy coordinators" (SCs). These can be students or staff leaders, volunteers, professionals or anyone who has a vision not only to plant a network of simple churches within specific student groups on their campuses but also to release a campus-wide church-planting movement (CPM) that will extend into the surrounding region and affect every level of society. These strategy coordinators will have a long-term calling and vision for a region and will need to understand the core elements necessary to release a CPM.

Peter Gent is our strategy coordinator at UC San Diego. He was a Ph.D. student who started a network of simple churches while at UCSD and who now has the vision not only to plant simple churches on campus but also to plant them in the city of San Diego to bring revival.

If you are the John Knox for your campus, let us know. Our ministry's passion is to connect you with other strategy coordinators to help coach, mentor, equip and encourage you in this process. It's time to start a simple-church revolution![9]

Eight Keys of a Campus Church-Planting Movement

We believe that the following eight keys are foundational for a campus church-planting movement to be healthy, effective and growing. These elements are not intended to give the impression of an organized program, but rather they serve as descriptive analyses of what church-planting movements often look like. Campus Church Networks believes that only a total dependence on the Holy Spirit will allow these elements to be fully incorporated into the DNA of a movement:

1. Prayer (24/7 Prayer)
2. Scripture Authority
3. Evangelism (Abundant Gospel Sowing)
4. Churches Planting Churches
5. Discipleship (On-the-Job Leadership Training)
6. Marketplace Ministry and Missions
7. Student Leadership
8. Simple Churches

1. Prayer (24/7 Prayer)

Prayer always precedes revival, and it also sustains revival. Starting and developing a successful campus church network requires much prayer. In a CPM, prayer is foundational at an individual, corporate and regional level. Individually, believers on campus must live a lifestyle of prayer. Corporately, campus churches or simple churches must regularly meet to engage in spiritual warfare and intercession for the lost. And regionally, campus churches must make it a goal for network intercessors to sustain 24/7 prayer over their campus and city. Prayer is the first priority of those called to start simple campus church planting movements. It is your lifestyle of prayer that will shape the movement, from the beginning, as one of total dependence on God (see Luke 18:7; Isa. 62:6-7).

2. Scriptural Authority

Studying the Word and obedience to Scripture must be embedded in the core of every campus church. The Bible must be the guiding source for doctrine and church polity; accepting its authority and living in radical obedience to the Word of God is essential to the success of any campus church movement.

The teaching of Scripture is not knowledge-based but rather obedience-based. Therefore, instead of one pastor or teacher carrying the load of preaching a weekly sermon, the Bible is learned in a way in which all members can participate, interact, learn and be held accountable to each other to immediately obey what has been studied. Each time you gather, you hold each other accountable regarding whether you obeyed the Word from the last study and whether or not you taught it to others.

3. Evangelism (Abundant Gospel Sowing)

There must be abundant sowing of the gospel in any campus church movement. There are many methods, but the key is the continual presentation of the gospel to as many students as possible. In a simple-church movement, the harvest is the focus! Luke 10 serves as our model for evangelism. We believe that the harvest is plentiful and the workers are few. So we pray for God to send out workers two by two to go out into the harvest to specific unreached areas or groups on campus to *pray* for them, *care* for them and *share* with them the Good News.

4. Churches Planting Churches

Mass evangelism on a campus is great, but it is not effective unless it results in a church being planted that will plant more churches. For a church-planting movement to occur, new believers must be discipled, brought into a healthy spiritual family and must immediately be given the vision to win their friends and loved ones in their community for Christ. Evangelism that results in churches that plant other churches does not occur randomly; it must be intentional and deliberate from the beginning. The missionary may start the first church, but afterward, it is the indigenous student leaders who take leadership and plant the next generation of churches.

5. Discipleship (On-the-Job Leadership Training)

In a true church-planting movement, with its rapid multiplication of churches, there is not enough time for new simple-church leaders to leave their campuses for extended periods of theological training or to go through years of discipleship training before leading or planting a church, let alone a multiplying movement. Doing so would hinder the rapid spread of the gospel.

We believe in bringing training as close to the action as possible. The forms of this on-the-job training vary from mission field to mission field, but typically include a series of short-term training modules that do not impede the primary tasks of evangelism, church planting and pastoral leadership. We envision apostolic mission centers near every major university population with a permanent 24/7 prayer room and modules to equip student missionaries on campus with just-in-time training.

6. Marketplace Ministry and Missions

A church-planting movement on campus should not end with the campus or with graduation. Marketplace ministry means infiltrating and changing society at all levels: government, business, education, media, arts and community. Students must be trained and empowered from the get-go in any campus church network to bring the Kingdom and start simple churches in every sphere of society, especially among the poor and into the unreached "10/40 window" (the demographic region in the world with the most unreached people groups).

7. Student Leaders

The campus church-planting movement needs to be driven by student leaders. This is because student leaders take on the general profile of those they are trying to reach with the gospel and identify best with their peers. As a campus church network develops, a student graduate can become paid staff. However, the majority and growth edge of the movement will continue to be led by lay or bivocational student/alumni leaders who work near campus and continue to mentor students on campus to do the work of ministry (see Eph. 4:11). This reliance upon student lay leadership ensures the largest possible pool of potential church planters and simple-church leaders. Dependence upon seminary-trained, or even educated, campus staff/pastoral leaders means that the work will always face a leadership deficit.[10]

8. Simple Churches

Campus churches must not be dependent on outside funding or owning a building in which to meet. This only stifles campus church planting and slows down the growth process. Instead, because a simple church can meet anywhere (apartment, home, storefront, park, and so on), the cost of a building becomes obsolete, and giving can be used for more ministry opportunities (such as churches planting churches, social justice efforts and overseas missions). In this way, the burden to finance a building never inhibits the reproduction and growth of a simple church. Furthermore, since these simple churches have decentralized leadership, they will form networks of alliances and relationships in a campus region for united citywide church efforts to win the lost. The more that simple churches saturate a campus, the more potential there is to reach the many different segments of students that exist on the campus.

It is the passion of my heart to see students rise up on every campus to catch the vision of saturation church planting and CPM on campuses, with the goal of reaching cities and nations. It is not enough to reach only a few on our campuses; we must go for the all.

Father, raise up workers on every campus to be the
John Knoxes in our generation!

Notes

1. Steve Hawthorne, *Perspectives on the World Christian Movement Study Guide* (Pasadena, CA: William Carey Library, 1999), pp. 606-612.
2. For more information about Campus Renewal Ministries, visit the website at www.campusrenewal.org.
3. For more information about Campus Transformation Network, visit the website at www.campustransformation.com.
4. "College Students: The Powerful Percent," Campus Renewal Ministries. http://campusrenewal.org/about/need.html (accessed January 2007).
5. For more information on current church-planting movements, check out David Garrison, *Church Planting Movements* (Bangalore, India: WIGTake Resources, 2004).
6. David Garrison, *Church Planting Movements* (Richmond, VA: International Mission Board of the Southern Baptist Convention, 1999), p. 8.
7. Wolfgang Simson, *Houses that Change the World* (Hyderabad, India: OM Publishing, 2001), p. 106.
8. Jim Montgomery, *DAWN 2000* (Pasadena, CA: William Carrey Library, 1989), pp. 31-32.
9. For more information about Campus Church Network (CCN), go to www.campuschurch.net or e-mail coach@campuschurch.net
10. Garrison, Church Planting Movements, p. 35.

CHAPTER FIFTEEN

STRATEGIC AND STUDENT-LED
CHURCH PLANTING

*The harvest truly is great, but the laborers are few; therefore pray
the Lord of the harvest to send out laborers into His harvest.*
LUKE 10:2

Beep, beep, beep . . .
*Father, the harvest is truly great at UCLA, but the laborers
are few. Therefore I pray to the Lord of the harvest to send out
laborers. Lord, send out workers into the harvest field of UCLA,
into the harvest fields of every campus, every city and every
nation. Lord, send out workers today—thousands of them—
and let the believers and nonbelievers find me, before I find them.
Put it in the hearts of students everywhere to go into the harvest
fields on campuses to preach the gospel and reap a great harvest.
Lord, stretch out Your mighty right hand and perform signs,
wonders and miracles in the name of Your Holy Servant, Jesus,
through the hands of Your servants, Your workers on the campus.
Thank You, Lord, that this is Your will. The harvest is plentiful
on campuses everywhere; therefore, send out more workers!*
In Jesus' mighty name,
Amen.

Every morning at 10:02 A.M., the alarm on my cell phone goes off.
Beep, beep, beep . . . It's time to call my church-planting partner, Sam
Lee, in Northern California to pray for more workers to be sent
out into the campus harvest fields. We call this prayer the "Luke

10:2b virus." Church planters all around the world have caught this virus, committing to pray every day at 10:02 A.M. for the Lord of the Harvest to send out more workers. It was started by two church planters in Colorado who committed to pray this prayer daily until Jesus comes.[1] From them, I caught the virus and committed with Sam to pray this prayer daily. If Sam doesn't pick up, I pray Luke 10:2b into his voicemail and vice versa.

Ever since the day Sam and I started praying the Luke 10:2b prayer, God has answered. I kid you not. Nearly every week a random student or person will contact me to ask about starting a simple-church movement on his or her campus. Many new simple churches have been started on different campuses and cities by praying this simple prayer. God answers this prayer, because it is His command, His will and His prayer. The harvest is plentiful; we just have to pray, go and reap the harvest. Catch the virus; pray Luke 10:2b and watch God do miracles on your campus.

The Luke 10:2b prayer comes from the passage in Luke 10 where Jesus sends out the 70 disciples into the towns and villages to strategically preach the gospel. He sent them out two by two, equipping them to start churches that resulted in a worldwide church-planting-movement epidemic. When we understand that church is simple and that a book-of-Acts church-planting movement is possible, we then need a practical strategy on how to do it.

Five Steps to Multiply Simple Churches on Campus

In 2006, our simple-church network at UCLA began to adapt the missionary principles found in Luke 10 with mentoring help from Neil Cole, the seasoned simple-church planter I mentioned in the beginning of this section. Every week, Neil came to UCLA and trained our simple-church leaders and two dozen other campus staff and student leaders in the principles of church multiplication. Leaders from different campus ministries and local churches were trained weekly for one-quarter of the school year to start a simple-church movement among the unreached pockets of people on campus. The results were amazing and are still multiplying today as the simple-church network at UCLA and other campuses continues to bear fruit and grow. Many new simple churches were started and many souls were saved.

I have included some of the powerful student stories below. The following strategy was developed through an in-depth study of Jesus' missionary tactics in Matthew 9–10 and Luke 10, and it was adapted from Neil's book *Organic Church* and Greenhouse Church Planting training.

1. The Practice of Prayer

The first step to planting a campus church or simple church is to start on our knees. Jesus said in Luke 10:2 that, "the harvest truly is great, but the laborers are few; *therefore pray* the Lord of the harvest to send out workers into His harvest" (emphasis added). We must see what the Father is doing and simply join Him. Before we send out any student church planter, that person needs to seek the Lord in prayer and fast for God's direction. Prayer must precede planning.

Practically, pray for God to bring you a team. Jesus sent out the disciples two by two to proclaim the kingdom of God, and, likewise, it is essential that you have a partner to team up with to reach the campus harvest. You can begin by talking to other believers you know who can join you on or near campus. Or simply pray Luke 10:2 and watch how God will provide the workers (nonbelievers) from the harvest for you to win and empower. Don't look outside the campus for workers. Remember, the workers are in the harvest!

Shortly after gathering a team, start a prayer cell or prayer chain or begin taking prayer walks in the area of students where the Lord is leading your team to start a campus church. Begin to ask the Lord for the harvest; ask Him to raise up student workers from within it. Ask the Lord what the spiritual strongholds are, both of and in the different areas of the campus. Then pray for God to destroy the strongholds: "For we do not wrestle against flesh and blood, but against principalities, against powers, against the rulers of the darkness of this age, against spiritual hosts of wickedness in the heavenly places" (Eph. 6:12). We must pray it out before we walk it out!

Timothy's Story—Prayer Breaks Open Fraternity!

Timothy and Dave were radically saved out of one of the most notorious fraternity communities at UCLA through an evangelistic Bible study in the third quarter of 2006. After being born again for less than three months, our team gave them the vision to start a simple-church network among their fraternity. I explained to Timothy, "Without prayer and fasting, nothing will happen. Seek God's face for your fraternity and watch Him do it!" Timothy and Sharon (a sorority sister) decided to go on a 40-day fast through the summer. Being new believers, they had never done this, but they sensed the Holy Spirit's leading them to do so. They fasted from meals, meats, sweets and, some days, they only drank water. Every night for 40 days, Timothy, Sharon and, sometimes, Dave, would come together and pray for one to two hours for the fraternities and sororities for which they were targeting a simple-church plant. Interesting things began to happen.

During the first week of school, a random fraternity brother walked up to Timothy and said, "I heard you were starting a church. Can you baptize me as soon as possible?" Timothy was shocked because he had never witnessed to this frat brother, but word had spread and God was already answering their prayers. Many since have been baptized in water, some in the fraternity-house bathtub, others elsewhere. A simple-church movement has been started and nearly half the fraternity has already shown up, many converting to Christ. All this was a result of strategic, focused, radical prayer.

2. Pockets of People

"But whatever house you enter, first say, 'Peace to this house'" (Luke 10:5). The second step is to look for pockets of people who are unreached with the gospel. In Luke 10, Jesus sent out the 70 to towns and villages (specifically to the lost sheep of Israel). We are to look for the lost sheep—not those who are well but those who are in need of a physician. Jesus came to call not the righteous but the sinners to repentance. Jesus also commanded the 70 to specifically target the house or households.

The Greek word for "household" is *oikos*,[2] which refers to family, household, relatives, friends and even neighbors. As we venture out to plant, we are to focus upon an *oikos*, or a specific *student group* or community of friends who are in close relationship. It is most effective to target *one specific* unreached student group per team. The gospel will spread with the least barriers within a student group with common affinity to one another (see Acts 10).

As a campus church-planting movement, we are specifically targeting pockets of students (*oikos*) normally untouched by other fellowships on campus. Don't try to recruit and win believers, but always focus and start with unbelievers. Go to the campus hangouts, cafés, the center of campus, fraternities, sororities, sports teams, campus clubs/organizations, student events, downtown—places where students congregate. It is crucial to remember that our goal is not to bring the students to the church, but the church to the students.

Work with your team to spiritually map out the campus in order to understand and identify all the different student cultures and social groupings that are represented. Seek the Lord to find out what God is doing, what Satan is doing and what the Holy Spirit is leading your team to do to engage in spiritual warfare to take the campus one prayer and one unreached student group at a time (see Num. 13). Ask the Holy Spirit which unreached student group He has burdened in your heart to reach, adopt them in prayer, and then begin to strategize how you will reach them. If there are other receptive student groups in the area, organize more strategic mission teams to reach them. The aim is a *simple church for every student group*. We want to reach every unreached student population group *whole* (not just a few individuals) by planting a simple church among every population. Avoid one-by-one extraction, or taking the new convert out of their *oikos* and into your Christian culture. Keep them in their *oikos*, disciple them, keep them accountable and give them the vision to reach their natural community for Christ.

Richard's Story—Targeting the Runners!

At the University of Tennessee, one student named Richard had a burden for a particular oikos on campus—the track and field team. As he began to pray for them, the Holy Spirit told him to join the elite track team. He knew this commitment would be a sacrifice. Richard was already a track runner, but in order to join the elite team, he would have to commit to running more miles each day than he was used to. He also would have to move out of his Christian apartment (with Christian guys) into the house where the top track runners lived. Richard took a step of faith, became a missionary and moved into the track house and joined the team.

After weeks of praying, and running mile after mile, God started to move. Richard was able to develop meaningful relationships with his teammates. As God opened doors, many of the star track team members began to open up to Richard about spiritual matters. Pretty soon, Richard invited them to study the Bible daily with him. Many committed, some were radically saved and one teammate said, "Richard, I would never step foot into a church building, but I really enjoy this kind of church!" Richard started a simple church because he not only prayed but he also focused his prayer on a target oikos that God had put on his heart, and he brought church to them.

3. The Power of Presence

"And as you go, preach, saying, 'The kingdom of heaven is at hand.' Heal the sick, cleanse the lepers, raise the dead, cast out demons" (Matt. 10:7-8). The third step in multiplying simple churches is to simply show up. Jesus commanded His disciples to go and make disciples, not to wait for disciples to come to a church building.

We are to live not a "come" gospel, but a "go" gospel. Jesus has commanded us to shine our light in the darkness (see Matt. 5:14-17), knowing that if we show up, the Holy Spirit will show up with us. Light always outshines the darkness, and we are called to be the light of the world. We are called to shine our light, not hide it. As we pray and are led by the Holy Spirit to pockets of unreached students, we are to show up and befriend those lost groups of students.

The most effective way of befriending a lost group of students is by serving and caring for their needs. Find out their needs and meet them before you share the gospel. For example, college students are hungry for a good meal, so hold free dinners. If the international students want to practice their English, hang out and speak English with them. Find out what their spiritual needs are and practice prayer evangelism. Simply ask them if you can pray with them, because there is no prayer too big or too small that God can't answer. Whatever it may be, meet the students' felt needs. If they open their hearts to you, ask if you can pray for them and release prophetic words of knowledge. If they are sick, pray for their divine healing. If they are oppressed, pray for demonic deliverance. So, we *pray* for them, we *care* for them and, when the door of opportunity opens, we *share* with them the good news of Jesus Christ!

To recap: Whatever it may be, meet the students' felt needs by (1) *praying* for them, (2) *caring* for them, and, when the door of opportunity opens, (3) *sharing* with them the good news of Jesus Christ! Prayer evangelism is simply prayer, care and share.

Ada's Story—Prayer, Hot Pot, Karaoke and Simple Church

At UCLA we called her "Apostle Ada"[3] because in only two quarters she planted more than three simple churches in one pocket of unreached students. When Ada first approached our simple-church network (Passion Church) at UCLA, she told me in an e-mail, "Hi, my name is Ada, and I believe God has called me to plant a campus church network among the Hong Kong students at UCLA." We ended up meeting with Ada and gave her some basic training. Then we prayed for her and sent her out to be a missionary to reach the Hong Kong students on campus.

During the first weeks of school, she committed to praying daily for God to save the Hong Kong students at UCLA. She then started calling up a few of her UCLA friends who were believers from Hong Kong to join her in the simple-church plant. After sharing the vision with them, about 10 believers joined the mission. As they prayed every morning together, they were suddenly inspired by the Holy Spirit to take strategic action. Ada and others said, "Hey, we should all join the Hong Kong student society group on campus!" With this inspiration, they all went to the first orientation meeting.

There were more than 200 Hong Kong students in the society. That night, the president announced that the group was too large and decided to divide the society into 10 subdivisions. At that moment, Ada and the others all received a divine strategy from heaven. Ada gathered her team and they agreed that since there were about 10 of them, each would join one of the subdivisions to be a missionary for Jesus.

The rest is history. In the following weeks, Ada and her teammates spent time hanging out with the Hong Kong students, eating hot pot and singing karaoke, while praying for them daily and asking God to open up doors of opportunity. One day, a random Hong Kong student walked up to Ada and said, "Ada, do you read the Bible? I heard you read the Bible and I want to read it too!" Ada was stunned because she had never shared Christ with this student. That night Ada called me, totally panicked, asking me what she should do. I encouraged her to start a simple evangelistic Bible Study. The next day, the Hong Kong student showed up for Bible study promptly, but not alone. He showed up with his friends! They were all unbelievers. By the third Bible study, nearly a dozen seeking Hong Kong students came. And by the fourth Bible study, nearly half had given their lives to Jesus Christ!

Ada began to teach the new simple church how to pray, worship and obey Jesus' commands. In a short while, two separate evangelistic Bible studies were started out of the first simple church to reach other groups of Hong Kong students who were spiritually hungry. By the second quarter, students were baptized in water, filled with the Holy Spirit, and more than 40 Hong Kong students were coming out to the weekly gatherings. Ada raised up spiritual leaders for each of the simple churches, met with them weekly and appointed them to continue the work. That's what apostles do—they establish foundations for others to build upon. Through Ada's faith and obedience, the unreached Hong Kong student population was being transformed with the gospel. Like Richard, she didn't wait for them to come to church, but she brought simple church to them!

4. A Person of Peace

"And if a son of peace is there, your peace will rest on it; if not, it will return to you" (Luke 10:6). The fourth step is to find the "person of peace," or the "student of peace," within the pocket of students. Jesus told His disciples to go into the towns and villages, looking for the person of peace who would welcome the gospel and open up his or her home. Students of peace are critical because they will be the indigenous leaders who win that community of lost students. They become the conduit for passing the Kingdom message to the entire community of friends. Can you imagine if you won the leader of a fraternity to Christ? The whole frat would follow and come to Christ! Yet, the leader of a fraternity may not necessarily be the president or positional leader; he is simply the person who holds the influence over the others in that community.

A student of peace is (1) *receptive:* he or she is open to the message of the person and peace of Christ; (2) *relationally connected:* he or she knows lots of students on campus and in the community; (3) *reputable:* he or she is a person of reputation, good or bad (like Cornelius in Acts 10 or the Samaritan Women in John 4); and

(4) *reborn:* he or she is normally a seeker won to the Lord and who is born again.

Dragon's Story—I Want What Dragon Has!

At UCLA, during one of our ministry's open-air preaching outreaches, the president of one of the most well-known Asian fraternities was won back to Christ. A week later, through another open-air preaching event, the former vice president of the same fraternity was won to Christ. Their names were Ed and Dragon. These two fraternity brothers began to study the Bible weekly. Their lives were soon transformed and they began to reach out to the rest of their fraternity brothers and sorority sisters.

Dragon, in particular, started studying the Bible daily and witnessing to his fraternity and sorority friends. During the third quarter, he started inviting friend after friend to an evangelistic Bible study. In a few weeks, it grew too large for the room where it met. Many of the frat brothers told us, "The reason I wanted to find out what this Bible study was all about was because I saw Dragon's life change so dramatically; I want what he has!"

Today a simple church has been planted among that fraternity and nearly a dozen new believers have come to Christ. They meet regularly for simple "fraternity church" and are planting simple churches among other similar groups on campus! This would not have been possible without the man or student of peace, my man, Dragon.

5. A People of Purpose

"Now whatever city or town you enter, inquire who in it is worthy, and stay there till you go out. And when you go into a household, greet it. If the household [*oikos*] is worthy, let your peace come upon it. But if it is not worthy, let your peace return to you" (Matt. 10:11-13). When the student of peace brings his or her friends and family to Christ, a simple church is born. The uniqueness of this birth is that the church is born out of the harvest, is found among the harvest and is bent on a mission to continue to reach the lost. The student of peace could have the new church meet in his or her home, apartment, dorm or wherever it is convenient on or near campus, and may even become the new leader of the emerging church.

The fifth step, then, is the following: The key is that once the new church is born on campus, it is imperative for the simple-church planter to work his or her way out of the new church plant by modeling and training the emerging student leader(s) to lead and shepherd the new simple church. In this way, the new simple church will not be dependent on the church planter to shepherd them, but they will indigenously take responsibility to lead themselves and will naturally reproduce leaders of their own kind. This way, as a church, their focus from day one will not be inward; rather, their focus will be outward to win their friends, families and the world to Christ. The basic strategy to ensure that the new simple church remains missional and becomes a church-planting church is described by a process called *MAWL*.

M = Model

The campus church planter's goal is to work his or her way out of a simple-church plant. The first aim is for the church planter to identify the person of peace (see the Luke 10 model), and win that person's household (*oikos*) to Christ, starting a simple church. When the church is born, the campus church planter *models* for the potential student leader how to do church in a simple, reproducible way, and teaches the student leader to win his or her friends to Christ and start additional campus or simple churches.

A = Assist

After the campus church planter has worked alongside the natural student leaders (elders) of the simple church, and after the church planter has modeled to these student leaders how to do church, the church planter then takes a step back and *assists* the new student leaders by empowering them to shepherd the simple church. At this point, the church planter would be working with the new student pastors to lead the congregation.

W = Watch

After a time of modeling and assisting, the campus church planter will empower the student leaders to organize, oversee and pastor the congregation completely by themselves so that they will not be dependent on the campus missionary. The campus church planter at this stage will only watch but not assist the student leaders. At this stage, the campus missionary will be able to give input to the leaders but will take a backseat role.

L = Leave

When the local students on campus are able to independently lead the simple church, the campus church planter's role has been accomplished. The church planter will then *leave* the church to start another one. The campus missionary will still be available to the leadership of the simple church for continual coaching and needed resources. Also, the campus church planter must make certain before he or she leaves that the local student leadership is equipped and trained with a vision to raise up leadership from among their congregation to reproduce and plant another simple church on campus. As this cycle repeats itself, a campus church-planting movement is well underway.

"PC 2": MAWL Story

In the third quarter of 2006 at UCLA, we sent out two juniors, "Anita" and "Amy," to plant an evangelistic Bible study for their lost friends in one of the apartment areas of campus. They began to pray early morning, three times a week for this new outreach. By faith, they dreamed up and wrote on paper what they wanted to see the Holy Spirit do. Their goal was to win souls, make new disciples and to multiply simple churches out of this one apartment church plant.

In order to outreach to their lost friends, Anita and Amy hung out with them and invited them to a free dinner every Tuesday night at their apartment. The Holy Spirit began to move through their prayers and action. A few lost students came to the first dinner and began to discuss spiritual things. At the second dinner, Anita and Amy held a Bible study, and more students came out. By the middle of the third quarter, 10 and sometimes even 20 or more students were coming to the Bible study to seek God.

Near the end of the quarter, a few students were saved and baptized, and others had recommitted their faith in Christ. Anita and Amy, both having a vision to make disciples and multiply the new simple church, began to coach the new believers to lead the Bible studies and slowly phased out of their leadership roles into coaching roles. Today, PC 2 (Passion Church 2) continues on and has sent out students to plant other simple-church plants. Anita is no longer the leader at the church but is now starting new simple churches among international students and is coaching other student missionaries to reach more pockets of students. Anita and Amy were a perfect example of MAWL, living the life of a true campus missionary.[4]

As you step out in faith to go win souls, make disciples and plant simple churches on your campus, remember that it is a work of the Holy Spirit. Be led by the Holy Spirit. Obey the Holy Spirit and you will see God do wonders. You can create your own simple-church-planting stories like the UCLA simple-church network blog (check out: www.pcla.wordpress.com) to share and inspire other students on different campuses.

Lord of the Harvest, I pray that many who read this will be envisioned and inspired by Your Spirit to go out into the campus harvest fields and preach the gospel of Your kingdom. Fill them up and send them out in Jesus' name!

Notes
1. The two guys from Colorado who started the prayer movement are Jim Montgomery and John White. Check out what is going on with the movement now at their website, www.greatcommissionupdate.org, or e-mail them at DenverWH@aol.com.

2. Bauer, Arndt, Gingrich and Danker, *A Greek-English Lexicon of the New Testament and Other Early Christian Literature* (Chicago: University of Chicago Press, 1979), p. 560; James Strong, *The New Strong's Exhaustive Concordance* (Nashville, TN: Thomas Nelson, 1984), Greek #3624.

3. St. John Chrysostom and Phillip Scaff, eds., *Saint Chrysostom's Homilies on the Acts of the Apostles and the Epistle to the Romans: Nicene and Post-Nicene Fathers of the Christian Church* (Grand Rapids, MI: Eerdmans, 1971-1980), series 1, vol. 9, and part 11; Dr. Peter Lampe', *Anchor Bible Dictionary* (New York: Doubleday Broadway Publishing, 1992), vol. 3, p. 1127, "Junias." See also Romans 16:7 where Junia, a female apostle, is mentioned alongside Andronicus, a male apostle. The Church father, John Chrysostom (died a.d. 407), who had a negative view of women in many cases, marveled that Junia could be called an apostle.

4. Neil Cole, Organic Church (San Francisco: Jossey Bass, 2005).

CHAPTER SIXTEEN

Start-up Church Planting

Unless the Lord builds the house, they labor in vain who build it.
PSALM 127:1

Jesus said to Peter, "And on this rock I will build My church" (Matt. 16:18). It's important to know that Jesus is the one who builds the church and not us. It is His Church, His Bride, and we have the privilege of being a part of His building project. Any good architect will know that if he wants to build a good house, he must have the proper tools to lay down the right foundation. In the same way, as we go out to plant simple-church movements on our campuses and in our cities, we will need some practical tools to lay strong foundations for the movement to bear fruit, multiply and grow.

Many people ask me questions such as, "How do you start an evangelistic Bible study? What do you do immediately with new converts? What do you do in a simple-church gathering? What does a simple-church network look like? How can I plant simple churches while still being a part of my local congregational church?" These questions will be answered in this chapter to help us get started!

Question #1: How Do You Start an Evangelistic Bible Study?

As you follow the Luke 10 strategy, you will begin with prayer, then identify a pocket of people on campus and begin to spend time with them. My friend Brad Fieldhouse, an experienced simple-church planter in Long Beach, California, always says, "If you want to be a good church planter, spend 75 percent of your time with the lost." It is really that simple. The harvest is plentiful, but the workers are few. You just need to pray, go and spend time with lost people doing things you would normally do (watching movies, drinking coffee, playing sports, studying, and so on), but doing those things with the lost.

As you intentionally spend time with those seeking, ask the Holy Spirit to open doors for spiritual conversation. Ask those you are reaching out to about their spiritual journey. Be a good listener. Being a good listener is one of the most effective forms of evangelism. People don't want to be preached at; they want to be listened to.

If you have the opportunity, always share your spiritual journey or personal testimony of how you came to Christ. Your personal testimony is the most effective and powerful way to share the gospel. (A great way to prepare your testimony is to write the story of your life—before Christ, how you met Christ and after you met Christ—on one page of paper and practice sharing it with a friend.)

In my experience, when this kind of spiritual conversation springs forth, I take a step of faith and ask nonbelievers if they would like to simply study the Bible with me. As I gauge their interest, I may ask them to commit to studying the Bible with me once a week or even a few times a week on a certain day at a specific time. Through this simple process, I have started multiple evangelistic Bible studies that have resulted in souls saved and simple churches planted. Here are a few evangelistic Bible study methods I use:

The Seven Signs of Jesus

The "Seven Signs of Jesus" is one of the simplest, yet most powerful, evangelistic Bible studies to win souls. In the book of John there are seven miracles or signs Jesus performed:

1. Changing water into wine (see John 2:1-11)
2. Healing the royal official's son (see John 4:46-54)
3. Healing the paralytic at the pool (see John 5:1-18)
4. Feeding more than 5,000 people with fishes and loaves (see John 6:1-14)

5. Walking on the water (see John 6:15-25)
6. Healing a man born blind (see John 9:1-41)
7. Raising Lazarus from the dead (see John 11:1-46)

The purpose of these miracles, or signs, is for those who read them to believe that Jesus is the Christ: "But these are written that you may believe that Jesus is the Christ, the Son of God, and that believing you may have life in His name" (John 20:31). Each time I meet with a seeking student or a group of seeking students, we read one of the passages in John where Jesus performs a miracle, and then I ask four simple questions:

1. What does this tell us about the way people are?
2. What does this tell us about what people need?
3. What does this tell us about the person of Jesus?
4. How can we apply this to our lives?

So far, every time I have used the Seven Signs in an evangelistic Bible Study, I have led someone to Jesus before we studied the fourth sign. It is that simple. We pray and ask the questions and let those to whom we are ministering read and see the wonderful person of Jesus.

Discovery Questions

Another Bible study method useful for evangelism is "Discovery Questions." My mission strategist friend Carol Davis shared with me these six simple questions you can ask with any passage of the Bible to get a powerful spiritual conversation going with anyone. Discovery Questions help guide discussions through a passage of Scripture. They allow everyone in the group to participate. Furthermore, they help set a relational dynamic for the group, removing the need for one person to teach while others sit and listen. Take a passage, section or any chapter of the Bible, read it and ask these six questions with your evangelistic Bible study group.

1. What did you like about what you read?
2. What didn't you like?

3. What did you not understand?
4. What new thing did you learn about God?
5. What idea or phrase do you want to take with you this week?
6. What are you going to do about it?

You will be amazed at how much insight, knowledge and revelation nonbelievers will come up with in these studies. It is simple yet powerful and life-transforming, and anyone can do it. One key we teach those in the Bible study is that the best way to learn what has been studied is to immediately teach it to someone else. I always challenge those in the group who have come to Christ to start their own Bible studies with their lost friends immediately, teaching them what they learned with me that week. This instills in them immediate obedience, as well as the value of multiplication from the very beginning. Every time we meet together, I ask them, "Did you obey the teaching and teach what you learned in the last Bible study to others?" Then I will have them practice teaching each other the new study to prepare them to teach it to their friends (see 2 Tim. 2:2). This keeps them on the evangelistic edge and makes them disciple-makers from day one.

Question #2: What Do You Do with New Coverts?

I always tell students in our training sessions, "If you catch the fish, you clean the fish!" If you lead a person to Christ, it is not someone else's job to disciple the new convert; it is your job. The first 48 hours of a new believer's life are the most crucial. If a mother gives birth to a baby, she doesn't leave the baby unwashed or uncared for. In the same way, when someone is saved through your evangelistic Bible study, or in any other way, it is your responsibility to follow up thoroughly. If our new converts are birthed weak (i.e., there is no thorough follow-up), then they will stay weak. If our new converts are birthed strong, (i.e., there is thorough follow-up), then they will stay strong.

"Then those who gladly received his word were baptized; and that day about three thousand souls were added to them" (Acts 2:41). On the day of Pentecost, 3,000 were convicted of their sin, baptized in water, filled with the Holy Spirit and added to the Church. This is the New Testament standard, and we can't settle for anything less. Repentance, water baptism and the infilling of the Holy Spirit must be immediate. Every new believer in the book of Acts repented and was baptized in water on the same day. You just can't find any instance in the book of Acts in which someone repented and was baptized in water days later or weeks later. It is not there. We must baptize new converts as quickly as possible. Baptism proves their repentance, for it is a powerful spiritual act of obedience to Christ's command (see Matt. 28:18-29).

The following is a simple but radical 14-step process on how to follow up with a new convert. Our student leaders on different campuses practice this process and, because of it, have witnessed not just salvations but also true conversions. The steps below are not the only follow-up methods; they can be modified and changed to fit into your context. I learned, practiced and adapted them from Pastor Bob Weiner, who pioneered some of the first university churches in the 1970s and 1980s.

1. *Conviction of sin* (see Rom. 7:7; 1 Tim. 1:8). Make sure they are convicted of their sin by sharing with them the 10 Commandments.

2. *Repentance* (see Acts 2:38). Lead them in a prayer of repentance in which they not only ask for forgiveness but also turn radically from sin. (You can use the Four Spiritual Laws, Four Passions of Christ, and so forth.)[1]

3. *Water baptism* (see Acts 2:38). Baptize them in water immediately. You have been given authority by Christ to do so (see Matt. 28:18-19). Find a bathtub in a student's apartment or dorm, use a swimming pool, baptize them in a lake or ocean, and so forth.

4. *Holy Spirit baptism* (see Acts 2:38). Pray with them to receive the baptism and infilling of the Holy Spirit.

5. *Break the generational curses* (see Gal. 3:13). Identify curses and strongholds in their life and break them through prayer in Jesus' name.

6. *Cast out the demons* (see Mark 16:17). Once you have broken the curses, command any demons to be cast out in Jesus' name.

7. *Command the blessings of Abraham* (see Deut. 28:1-3). Pray God's blessings over the new convert's life and have others release any prophetic words of destiny, strength and encouragement.

8. *Get into a simple church* (see Acts 2:46). Make sure they continue in the Bible study group that now becomes their church.

9. *Connect with a personal coach* (see 2 Tim. 2:2). This is usually the person who led them to the Lord.

10. *Get them a Bible* (see 2 Tim. 3:16-17).

11. *Plug them into a Life Transformation Group* (see Ps. 11:3). An LTG is a simple group of two to three same-gender people meeting once a week for one hour. (See the next section titled "Life Transformation Groups.") They hold each other accountable to reading 35 chapters of Scripture weekly, confessing known sin and praying for the lost each time they meet.

12. *Immediately begin a 14-day follow-up plan* (see Acts 2:42). The first 14 days are crucial. Challenge them to meet every day with you for the next 14 days to pray, read the

Word and study Matthew 5–7. There are 21 sections in Matthew 5–7 that teach the Christian basics.

13. *Coach them to give their testimony* (see Rev. 12:11). Immediately teach new converts to give their testimony—before, how and after they came to Christ. Ask converts to visit and share the gospel with 10 of their friends, have the coach pray with them for support, and then have the new converts share their testimony to win their friends to Christ. The converts will then repeat steps 1 through 13 with them.

14. *Start a simple church* (see Acts 2:46)! New believers start brand-new evangelistic Bible studies that will ultimately mature into simple churches with the new believers' networks of friends.

Life Transformation Groups

A simple tool we use to disciple new converts, which was mentioned in the eleventh step, is called Life Transformation Groups, or LTG. This is a very simple discipleship method that Neil Cole developed to release the most essential elements of a vital spiritual walk. It is unique because it does not require any leader or any discipleship teaching material, only the Bible. LTGs are simple, reproducible and anyone can do them. I always say, "If it's not reproducible, don't do it." An LTG is a separate discipleship group outside of the regular simple-church gathering. You can start one and print the LTG Character Conversation Questions below on paper to create a simple card or sheet that you and your LTG can use when you meet.

Life Transformation Groups typically work as follows:

- They meet once a week for approximately one hour.
- They comprise groups of two or three people.
- The groups are not coed but gender-specific (all males or all females).

• There is no curriculum, workbook or training involved.
• There is no leader needed in the group.

There are only three tasks:

1. Sin is confessed for mutual accountability, using the LTG character conversation questions (see below).
2. Scripture is read repetitively in context and in community.
3. Souls are prayed for strategically, specifically and continuously.

LTG Character Conversation Questions

These questions are to be asked of one another in a weekly meeting of accountability (see Prov. 27:17). They are to stimulate conversations about character and confession of sin in a safe environment that values honesty, vulnerability, confidentiality and grace.

1. Have you been a testimony this week to the greatness of Jesus Christ with your words and actions?
2. Have you been exposed to sexually alluring material or allowed your mind to entertain inappropriate sexual thoughts about another this week?
3. Have you lacked integrity in your financial dealings or coveted something that does not belong to you?
4. Have you been honoring, understanding and generous in your important relationships this week?
5. Have you damaged another person by your words, either behind their back or face to face?
6. Have you given in to an addictive behavior this past week?
7. Have you continued to remain angry toward another?
8. Have you secretly wished for another's misfortune?
9. Your personalized accountability question. (This is specific to each person.)
10. Did you finish the reading and hear from God? What are you going to do about it?
11. Have you been completely honest with me?[2]

Question #3: What Does a Simple-Church Gathering Look Like?

You may be wondering, *So what do you actually do in a campus church gathering?* It is very simple: We do what the Early Church did:

And they continued steadfastly in the apostles' doctrine and fellowship, in the breaking of bread, and in prayers (Acts 2:42).

How is it then, brethren? Whenever you come together, each of you has a psalm, has a teaching, has a tongue, has a revelation, has an interpretation. Let all things be done for edification (1 Cor. 14:26).

And let us consider one another in order to stir up love and good works, not forsaking the assembling of ourselves together, as is the manner of some, but exhorting one another, as so much the more as you see the Day approaching (Heb. 10:24-25).

As seeking students become Christians in your evangelistic Bible study and are baptized, the study naturally becomes a new church. As the new church matures and grows, it follows the biblical New Testament model of a house church. On some campuses, mature believers will first start a simple church with other believers who have a vision for planting simple churches among the lost. As they experience simple church together, each member goes out to share the gospel and start an evangelistic Bible study among a pocket of unreached students. As these new evangelistic Bible studies begin and become new churches themselves, the process naturally repeats itself. Everyone is in a simple church. Everyone starts a simple church among the lost!

Now, what do simple-church gatherings look like? Simple-church meetings are about coming together with brothers and sisters in Christ to love God, love one another and love the lost. This can happen in a variety of ways. Below is just one example that we use in simple churches to facilitate our gatherings on different campuses. Remember, the key is not the method or format; rather, it is following the biblical pattern, adapting it to your own context and, most of all, listening to and following the leading of the Holy Spirit in each gathering.

The Five Ws

The five Ws is a simple format for spending your time together as a simple church.

1. *Welcome*

You can start the meeting with some food. In the Early Church, they called this the "breaking of bread." Eating together produces an informal atmosphere, making it easy for people to share their lives together. (Remember, students love food!) Also, a simple ice-breaker is a great way to foster a welcoming environment. For example, have each person talk about a funny or interesting thing that happened to him or her that day or during the week, and then have him or her introduce himself or herself. Regularly in simple-church gatherings, during our times of eating, we will also take communion to remember the reason of our coming together: It's all about Jesus!

2. *Worship*

Worship is expressing our love and appreciation to God for who He is and what He has done. One way we do this is by singing love songs to God or expressing our love in other creative ways, such as drawing, dancing or giving testimony, to give Him praise.

Not having a worship leader doesn't mean you can't worship. Think creatively. Go around the group and let those who want to give thanks to God sing praises *a cappella* or sing together accompanied by a worship CD. In a new simple church, you may sing only a few songs, whereas in a more mature simple church, this time for praise and worshiping the Lord may go on for an extended time of spontaneous worship.

Also, worship is expressed in our giving. It is appropriate to have a time of taking tithes and offerings, since giving is also an essential expression of our love for God and a way to support His Church. Many simple churches on campus use the tithe to give to causes of compassion or justice. At UCLA, one simple church gives 50 percent of their tithe to Blood Water Ministries, an organization that digs and builds water wells in Africa for those without water. Other simple churches in the network give 50 percent of their tithe to the Skid Row Fund, our homeless ministry in downtown Los Angeles. Also, we use the tithe to bless those in the group who are in need. This is our duty.

3. *Waiting*
In our busy lives we rarely get the chance to wait on God or be silent. In simple churches, we practice times of silence in order to quiet our souls and grow in intimacy with God. This may be difficult the first few times, or even for a long time, but through practice, waiting on God becomes easier. Silence allows God to speak to us and it allows us to hear His voice together.

If you are facilitating the gathering, explain how to wait on God and hear His voice each time so that people will know what to expect and how to respond. Sometimes someone will get a word, a prophecy, see a picture, receive a vision or be inspired with a Scripture and share it with the group or an individual for encouragement and interpretation. Sometimes no one will get anything at all. That's okay! God speaks to different people in different ways. In a gathering, you can wait on God in silence for a few minutes or as long as you want; the key is to be aware of the Holy Spirit's presence during your meeting time and to let the Holy Spirit direct the flow of the meeting.

The waiting time usually comes after the time of worship. Once you are finished waiting in silence and hearing God's voice, the facilitator can simply ask, "Does anyone have a praise report, a prayer request, a word from the Lord or a sin to confess?" Thus, at each simple-church gathering, each person is expected to hear from the Lord and share with the group what God has put on his

or her heart, whether it is a biblical teaching, a new song, a prophecy, a word of knowledge, a testimony, a prayer or something else.
This way, everyone is exercising his or her spiritual gifts and all are
edified (see 1 Cor. 14:26).

Sometimes the Holy Spirit moves so dynamically during this
waiting and sharing time that it is best to just continue waiting on
the Lord, sharing and moving with the Holy Spirit. Be open to the
Holy Spirit to speak and lead each meeting. Don't be too set on a
formula or meeting structure. Anticipate the unexpected!

4. *Word*

We hear and learn God's word in many ways, but God speaks
mainly through the written Word (Scripture). In my experience, at
each simple-church gathering, we set aside a time after welcome,
worship and waiting to get into the Word. This is done in a participative style, rather than a preaching style. Instead of one pastor or
teacher carrying the load of preaching a weekly sermon, the Bible
is learned in a way in which all members can participate, interact,
learn and be held accountable to each other to immediately obey
what has been studied. In this way, the one leading the Bible study
plays more the role of a coach or facilitator rather than the role of
a preacher. The responsibility of the facilitator is to make sure the
study keeps moving, that everyone is taking part, that no one
dominates and that everyone is held accountable for what is
learned. In a community that values obedience to the Word, new
believers will often mature rapidly.

A simple example of this would be a small group of students
gathering together, jointly reading a story or passage of the Bible
and then discussing the truth they find in that story or Bible passage. One simple, participative Bible study method is asking,
"What does it say? (Who/what/when/where/why was it said?)"
"What does it mean? (What did it mean then, and what does it
mean now?)" "How do we apply this to our lives immediately?"
And finally, "Who will I tell?"

It is crucial that in the DNA of every simple-church member is
an obedience to train others in what he or she has just learned,

resulting in new simple churches being planted. As they study the Word together (they can break up into pairs for each question), members of the group are asked how they can apply the Scripture in their lives during the upcoming week. The next time they meet, each member reports to the group his or her experience with this application and whether or not he or she has taught it to others. Below is a further explanation of these three simple Bible discussion questions that you can use in any simple-church gathering.

1. *Observation: What does it say?* Who was involved? What happened? What ideas are expressed? What are the results? What is the purpose? Where did this take place? When did it take place? Why did it happen? How are things accomplished?

2. *Interpretation—What does it mean?* What did it mean to the original audience? What does it mean now? What is the main idea? How does this passage relate to the rest of the chapter/book? What other Scripture passages might shed light on this one?

3. *Application—What should I do?* S.P.E.C.K. (see Matt. 7:3-5):
   · Is there a *Sin* for me to avoid?
   · Is there a *Promise* to claim, or *Praise* to give or *Prayer* to pray?
   · Is there an *Example* for me to follow?
   · Is there a *Command* for me to obey?
   · Is there *Knowledge* for me to learn?[3]

Another Bible study method that my home church uses is "Question mark, light bulb and arrow." This is a modified method from The Navigators. A couple of verses are read, and we look for things that correspond to three different symbols. The first is a question mark that obviously symbolizes something a person does not understand. The second symbol is a candlestick and is used to represent something that sheds light either on another passage of

Scripture or on something that is going on in a person's life. The third symbol is an arrow, which represents personal application and stands for where God is piercing a person's heart—the person has heard from God and needs to do something about it. So a person might say, "I have a candlestick on this verse." (This could describe a situation that happened on campus last week.) The main point is that we must be held accountable to being radically obedient to God's Word. God is raising up a generation who will hear, obey and tell others the Truth.

5. Works

During this time of works, we remind the gathering that our vision as a campus church is to obey the Great Commandment and Great Commission—to love God, love each other and love the lost. The goal is for everyone to be in a simple church and for everyone to start a simple church. We close our meetings by praying for renewed passion with God, praying for one another and praying for our lost friends on campus.

The works time is very important because this is when we ask the Holy Spirit to minister to each individual. We encourage those attending to break up into groups, pray and prophesy over one another, ministering in the power of the Holy Spirit. In this time we also pray for those who are sick, need deliverance or need a fresh infilling of the Holy Spirit, and we challenge those seeking to give their lives to Christ. We never know what might happen. We are just open to the leading of the Holy Spirit! It is also after this time that we make any important announcements of upcoming events or news. After this, we can close our gathering and spend more time in fellowship.

Social Justice

An important part of our works is the work of justice. At UCLA and other campuses, many simple churches have made it their passion to reach out to the outcasts of society. At Passion Church, our simple-church network at UCLA, each week students spend their time on the streets of Skid Row. It is an area in downtown L.A.

with the highest population of homeless people. They don't just go there to pass out food; they go to spend time with the people, honor them, befriend them and do simple church with them.

There are many different causes for justice, but let's do what Jesus told us to do— to give the least of these a cup of water, to feed the hungry, clothe the poor and to visit those in prison (see Matt. 25:35-40). These are God's children, our people. *Lord, fill us up; send us out!* Let's step it up for the causes of justice.

One Last Distinction

These simple-church gatherings are very different from a regular small group or even a cell group. The simple church is not just a Bible study—a supplement to a Sunday service—nor is it centered on a set teaching. Simple church is a family. It is a real church that empowers all its members to take responsibility and support one another. Most simple-church or house-church gatherings are at least three hours long, if not longer. The focus is on worshiping God, welcoming the Holy Spirit, building relationships and sharing life together as a 24/7 community. Simple church is a fellowship of the heart where everyone depends on God and one another, and where everyone gets to really know each other—the good, the bad and everything in between.

A simple distinction between a cell church and a simple-church network can be found in the illustration of the differences between an octopus and a starfish. An octopus is like a cell church; it has tentacles (that represent cells), and if we cut off one tentacle or leg, it can grow back another, but if we cut off the head (the central church the cells are a part of), the octopus dies. This is an illustration of a cell church with a centralized structure and leadership. A starfish, in contrast, is self-sufficient. If we cut the starfish in half, it becomes two starfish. If we cut the starfish into 100 pieces, each piece grows back and it becomes 100 starfish! This starfish is an illustration of a simple church with a decentralized structure and leadership. Both kinds of churches are good, but like in the illustration of the elephant and rabbit, one is quicker to multiply and reproduce.

Bigger is not necessarily better. Simple church is a small church, but it is still a real church. It is as real as a big church with a building and 1,000 people. Small things can make a big difference!

Question #4: How Does a Simple-Church Network Function?

Many people ask me how a simple-church network functions. Can it be part of a traditional or megachurch or does it have to be its own church network? The answer is yes and yes! Our ministry has worked with local churches (megachurches, community churches, traditional churches) as well as parachurch campus ministry organizations to help them plant simple churches, or missional communities, with their students on campus. We have also trained these local churches and organizations in the principles of simple church to adapt into their own ministry context.

Some students plant simple churches on campuses while still attending their local home churches that meet in a church building. At the same time, we have helped start from scratch many simple-church or house-church networks all over the world on different campuses and in different cities and nations. These simple churches are completely autonomous as an independent network of small churches that multiply rapidly and operate under apostolic leadership.

So what does an autonomous network look like and how does it function? The following definition, based on and adapted from Larry Kreider's book *House Church Networks,* illustrates what a campus church network might look like on many campuses and cities in our ministry network.

Simple churches are quite different from traditional community and megachurches. There is no need for a large church building, because each simple church is a fully functioning church itself, meeting as a small community of 10 to 20 believers.

Students can meet in a variety of places including dorms, apartments, homes, student unions, classrooms, places of business, cafeterias, skate parks, shopping malls, parks, cafés, anywhere that students meet.

A team of student leaders (elders) leads each campus church while first being mentored by a spiritual father or mother who holds them each accountable in a coaching relationship. Their responsibility is to pastor the simple church. Each simple church is committed to network together with other simple churches on their campus and in the city or region to keep them from pride, exclusiveness and heresy. These new simple churches in their area can meet together once every month or so for corporate celebration, prayer or outreach. But this monthly celebration is not the main focus. The simple churches are true churches, not just Bible studies or even cell groups. They have elders, they collect tithes and offerings, and the leadership is responsible before the Lord for the souls of the people in the church (see Heb. 13:17).

Additionally, these young leaders are intent on the rapid reproduction of these simple churches. These simple churches will have small cells for training new leaders and give every believer the opportunity to minister. Each time a student leader is sent out to plant a new simple church, he or she will stay connected by joining a leadership cell or by being coached one on one by the leader(s) who sent him or her out from his or her original simple church for ongoing mentoring. These mentoring relationships (between mentor and mentored) will meet as often as needed (e.g., once a week or bi-weekly) to discuss how they are doing in their inward life and outward ministry. As the network grows, they will have regular "retreats" for all the simple churches to come together and encounter God in foundational truths, inner healing and deliverance. Also, instead of constructing a church building, when the simple church or place where they are meeting is outgrown, a new simple church is planted. These networks of simple churches will be governed by teams of apostles, prophets, evangelists, pastors and teachers in the region who will spiritually parent and train the elders of each simple church to shepherd the churches and do the work of the ministry (see Eph. 4:11). There will be Ephesians 4:11 teams that operate at the international, national, regional and campus levels for each church-planting movement. Equipping centers and 24/7 prayer houses will be set up in each region to train leaders with just-in-time training. The 411 teams may hold once-a-month (or more) intensive leadership-development training on the weekends for all their elders in the network. Also, as these simple-church networks grow, they multiply from the campus and into the city. Graduated students will start simple-church networks in workplaces, homes, neighborhoods, among the poor and into every area of society, creating multigenerational networks of simple churches from the campus to the cities and to the nations![4]

Question #5: What Is the Leadership in a Simple-Church Network?

Leadership in a simple-church network is based on the model set forth found in Ephesians 4:11 (the "411 team"). In Ephesians 4:11, we find that God has placed apostles, prophets, evangelists, shepherds and teachers, not to lord it over the saints, but in order to equip the saints for the work of the ministry. Each office of ministry functions differently than the rest.

- The *apostle's* primary function is to build a sense of mission in God's people (expansion).

- The *prophet's* primary function is to equip the Body to hear and respond to God's voice (experience).

- The *evangelist's* primary function is to foster a sense of urgency to reach the lost, grow the church and train people how to do it (evangelism).

- The *shepherd's* primary function is to make sure people are caring for one another and growing strong together (edification).

- The *teacher's* primary function is to make sure people are feeding on God's Word and living according to it (education).

Each team member can have multiple functions, and multiple people can fulfill each role. That is, there is no set limit of how many shepherds one team may have or how many apostles or prophets another team may have. However, the team is based on proven results, not potential. People who are appointed to oversee each function are only appointed because their gift and anointing has been proven. Each 411 team generally consists of about five to seven people who share the gifts and work together to oversee a network of churches.

Of course, not everyone in the Church has to fall under one of these five gifts. However, a healthy 411 team will have all of these functions represented in their group. Furthermore, a single person may be gifted in more than one of the 411 gifts. For example, Paul described himself as an apostle and also functioned as an evangelist and a teacher (see Rom. 1:1; 1 Cor. 15:1; Acts 18:11).

The 411 team is not put in place to make all the decisions or do all the work. Rather, the team is simply there to serve the saints and help equip them as they do the work themselves. The 411 teams meet regularly on a normal basis to discuss the health and needs of the growing simple-church network on a campus. They set up regular intensive trainings, retreats and access ministries for the leadership communities within the networks of simple churches. Furthermore, additional 411 teams will arise as the number of simple churches increase in a particular region, and new networks are birthed on other campuses, in the city and into nations.

The following quick reference on how the leadership system works on a campus church was adapted from Wolfgang Simson's book *Houses that Change the World*:

- *Elders.* Simple churches are led by elders (student leaders), whose function is to spiritually father or mother the church. They bring redeemed wisdom to the church and oversee the flock (students) like a father oversees his children. They demonstrate how to live the Christian life because they have lived it and proved it.

- *Fivefold ministers.* The elders are equipped and trained by people who have been called by God for one of the fivefold ministries: apostles, prophets, evangelists, pastors and teachers. These ministers move from campus church to campus church, functioning as a spiritual circulation system that nurtures all campus churches with the necessary elements to become or remain healthy and to multiply. These ministries are like sinews and joints, linking the various campus churches together to be a whole system. The ministry of these elders transcends the individual campus church and serves the Body of Christ like a spiritual gene pool from which the simple or campus churches of a particular campus or a region can draw.

- *Apostolic fathers.* The spiritual equippers of the fivefold ministry are related to a third group of people that might be called "apostolic fathers." These are individuals with an apostolic and prophetic gifting in addition to a special calling and charisma from God for a particular campus, city region or nation. These apostolic fathers are usually recognized by the almost-unbearable agony and spiritual pain they bear for a campus, city, nation or people group (see Gal. 2:7-9). They become the local backbone—the regional or national pillars of faith—that anchors the whole movement of simple churches locally and are responsible for celebrations and the city-church that will emerge. Because they usually have a true Kingdom mentality and a broken spirit due to the spiritual burden they carry, they are least likely to build a massive movement and Kingdom around themselves but will truly function as serving all—and therefore leading all. They do this not top-down from the lofty heights of a hierarchical power-pyramid but down on Earth alongside other equippers (see Mark 9:35).

- *Deacons.* Individuals in this role can be seen as functioning together with the elders (see Phil. 1:1) but also as the secretaries and assistants of those apostolic fathers. Deacons take care of administrative needs and social aspects and keep the apostles' hands free to do their work (see Acts 6).

A Vision for the Student-Led Church-Planting Movement

Neil Cole wrote and released this powerful prophetic vision that he received from God at one of our national leadership gatherings about what God intends to do with the student-led campus church-planting movement:

- New songs will be written that express the heart and voice unique to this movement. A book of songs will be published in the next year and a half. Prophets and teachers will write the bulk of the songs. Songs will be free to the masses and passed electronically, spreading the heart and voice of this unique movement without boundaries . . . freely you received and freely you will give.

- A magazine (printed, electronic, or both) will be published and it will carry the stories of what God is doing and also the apostolic/prophetic voice of the movement.

- A national conference will meet every year and double each time in size for the next 10 years. It will meet on different campuses around the country. Each campus

where they meet will see breakthroughs, so the conference will be sought by many. The Spirit will tell you each
year where you are to meet.

- All these works will be easy, because the Spirit will hand-
select those who are to do the work, and those people will
have been waiting their whole life for the opportunity.

- This movement will not form a single organization or
denomination, but many—all carrying the same DNA
and all working together in interdependence . . . blessing
one another, never in competition, always in unity.

- Old wineskin ministries will be blessed by this movement but will not carry the movement.

- This movement will be marked by transformed lives and
will grow from new life coming from the harvest.

- Prayer will continue before the throne of God 24/7 in the
same spirit of the Moravians.

- A new missionary movement will be birthed that will
send many missionaries out, but this will be a true
Student "Volunteer" Movement in that these missionaries will be sent into the various domains of society
to work there and be the Daniels, Shadrachs, Meshachs
and Abednegos of our world. They will work for the Lord
of the harvest and they will get their support from Him
through their work . . . a laborer is worthy of his wage.
These missionaries will not do their work for money, but
for Jesus.

- This movement is not about the campuses; it will start
there, but it will not stop there. This move of God will
not just touch the campuses of our world but will also

bring the blessing of God's kingdom and His command to all the domains of society. New creative arts will emerge glorifying God; new discoveries in technology and medicine will come from the people of God. There will be a rise not just in spirituality but also in understanding and in wisdom of our entire society because of what God is birthing here.

- Millions of lives will be saved in seen and unseen ways by the people of this movement. Terrorists will be saved before destruction is afflicted, diseases will be healed and also cured, wars will be ended, abortion will eventually end because the hearts of fathers and mothers will return to their children . . . this is a movement of doves and peacemakers.

- The first breakouts besides UCLA, USC, UT and Yale will be seen at CSULB, UCSD, ASU, OSU, Florida State, Princeton, CAL . . . and Harvard. Within a few years every campus will be affected by this movement.

- The enemy will not know what to do with you. Your only head will be Jesus; your only desire will be Jesus; your only provider will be Jesus. When the enemy strikes it will multiply the advance for the Kingdom. This new generation of Kingdom agents will show the Church and the world what it means to be willing to die for Christ. Satan, out of sheer frustration over what to do and just because of his own nature, will start killing students, and this will only fan the flame to greater heights.

This chapter was not written to answer all the questions about simple church. But my prayer is that it has given you enough basic tools and understanding in how to start a simple-church movement on your campus. *Let it burn!*

Father, spark a fire, a vision, a strategy and a passion in every
person who reads this book for planting simple churches. Use
them to transform every campus, every city and every nation of
the earth for Your glory.
Amen.

How to Start a Simple-Church Movement on Your Campus

1. Make a list of at least 10 lost friends.
2. Start a prayer cell (invite other student missionaries who are committed to the vision of planting simple churches among the lost to join with you in revival prayer and fellowship).
3. Identify unreached student groups and have each person go to those groups.
4. Ask God for divine appointments and to open up doors for spiritual discussion and power encounters.
5. Start an evangelistic Bible study.
6. Follow up new converts with the 14-Step process.
7. Start a simple church.
8. Raise up new leaders to multiply the movement.

For more insight on this growing movement of simple-church planting, check out the following books:

- Graham Cooke and Gary Goodell, *Permission Granted to Do Church Differently in the 21st Century* (Shippensburg, PA: Destiny Image Publishers, 2006).
- Neil Cole, *Organic Church* (San Francisco, CA: Jossey Bass, 2005).
- Neil Cole, *Cultivating a Life for God* (Saint Charles, IL: ChurchSmart Resources, 1999).
- Felicity Dale, *An Army of Ordinary People* (Austin, TX: Karis Publications, 2005).

- Felicity Dale, *Getting Started* (Austin, TX: Karis Publications, 2003).
- David Garrison, *Church Planting Movements* (Richmond, VA: International Mission Board of the Southern Baptist Convention, 1999).
- Alan Hirsch, *The Shaping of Things to Come* (Peabody, MA: Hendrickson Publishers Inc., 2003).
- Alan Hirsch, *The Forgotten Ways* (Grand Rapids, MI: Brazos Press, 2006).
- Larry Kreider, *House Church Networks* (Ephrata, PA: House to House Publications, 2001).
- Larry Kreider, *The Cry for Spiritual Fathers and Mothers* (Ephrata, PA: House to House Publications, 2000).
- Larry Kreider and Floyd McClung, *How to Start a House Church* (Ventura, CA: Regal Books, 2007).
- James Rutz, *Megashift* (Colorado Springs, CO: Empowerment Press, 2005).
- Wolfgang Simson, *Houses that Change the World* (Waynesboro, GA: Paternoster Publishing, 2001).

You can also visit the websites for Campus Church Network (www.campuschurch.net), Church Multiplication Associates (www.cmaresources.org) and Dawn Ministries (www.dawnministries.org).

Notes

1. To learn more about Bill Bright's "Four Spiritual Laws," go online to http://www.campuscrusade.com/four_laws_online.htm or see the "Four Passions of Christ" as stated in chapter one.
2. For more information on purchasing LTG materials, go to www.cmaresources.org.
3. David Watson, "Church Planting Workshop: How to Lead a Bible Study," church planting workshop materials.
4. Larry Kreider, *House Church Networks* (Dallas, OR: House2House Publications, 2001), p. 11.

CHAPTER SEVENTEEN

EVERY CAMPUS, EVERY CITY, EVERY NATION-BACK TO JERUSALEM

And this gospel of the kingdom will be preached in all the world
as a witness to all the nations, and then the end will come.
MATTHEW 24:14

When I was 18 years old, I went on my first mission trip to China. Each morning before anyone would wake up, I would go to the roof of the Bible college where we were staying in Hong Kong, get on my knees and pray one thing: "Lord, give me the youth of China! Give me the youth of China!" I had read in Psalm 2:8: "Ask of Me, and I will give You the nations for Your inheritance, and the ends of the earth for Your possession." I believed the promise and I cried out to God for my inheritance—my Chinese people.

While in China for the mission, we went to a university in Beijing. The first day, I witnessed five young men give their lives to Jesus Christ. I shared my testimony with one, and he wept as he prayed the sinner's prayer with me. Then he told me to wait because he wanted to bring his three friends to hear the gospel. I shared with them, and they immediately began to weep and also received Christ. Again, they told me to wait, to not go, because they had another friend with whom they wanted me to share the gospel. This last university student also received Christ and began to weep. He then held my hand and said, "You promise me you will learn my language, come back to my country and preach this gospel to my people." I promised him. God birthed in my heart a supernatural passion for China at that moment—one I couldn't fully understand.

One year later, when I was 19, I received a prophetic word from a prophet named Cindy Jacobs, who is mentioned earlier in this book. I didn't know her at the time and she didn't know me, but she pointed me out of the crowd one night and began to release a long and specific prophetic word to me. In part of this prophecy, she said:

And the Lord says, "You are a bridge between the generations. I chose the year you were born. I chose the day you were born." And the Lord says to you, son, "From your loins will come a great missionary movement." And the Lord says, "I'm going to cause you to put a heart for the nations back in the youth of this nation and they're going to put their feet in the nations."

"And as I open the Middle East," says God, "you're going to go and I see you taking teams into Iraq, Iran, Saudi Arabia." God says, "I'm going to give you a harvest of Arabs. I'm going to give you a harvest of Muslims. I'm going to use you in a great way to turn this tide." The Lord says, "I will use you with the Jews. I will use you in Israel. I will use you in Palestine." And the Lord says to you, son, "The beginning is now. I am turning the page in the history of your life at this moment. I am connecting you in the ways you need to be connected."

And the Lord says, "I'm going to give you an army. There is going to be an army that stands beside you. They are going to have generals and captains and sergeants. I'm going to literally give you an army that will march across the face of the earth even into Africa, into Northern Africa, to the unreached peoples," says God, "for I am going to get you into the inaccessible places." And the Lord says, "I am going to raise up an indestructible army that marches with great wisdom."

And so the Lord says, "Write the vision and make it plain, for I'm going to give you the ability to write and you are going to write my words. And these words are going to challenge your generation in a new and startling way!"

When she spoke this word over me, I didn't receive it well. My heart was for China, but she did not mention China. I thought the prophecy may have been for someone else, because I did not have a heart for the Muslim world at that moment. For years, I tucked this prophecy away and gave it to the Lord. I continued asking God to use my life to bring revival to Chinese young people around the world.

God answered my prayers.

In 2004, God opened the doors to Hong Kong, Taiwan and Chinese communities all around North America and other countries. God gave me the opportunity to equip and train young Chinese students to bring revival to their campuses. I knew it was for some great purpose, but I didn't know exactly what. It wasn't until the end of 2004, when someone gave me a book called *Back to Jerusalem,* that I understood. This book put everything into perspective.

This book put forth the vision of the Chinese house-church leaders raising up 100,000 Chinese missionaries to preach the gospel along the Silk Road and bring the gospel back to Jerusalem. This vision was first birthed in a Bible school in 1946, when a vice principal named Mark Ma read the verse, "And this gospel of the kingdom will be preached in all the world as a witness to all the nations, and then the end will come" (Matt. 24:14). God had spoken to him that it would be Chinese missionaries who would go and mobilize others to go along the Silk Road route to preach to the unreached Muslim, Buddhist and Hindu worlds. After the Cultural Revolution, this vision was forgotten, but it was in the 1990s that the Chinese house-church leaders remembered this powerful vision of Mark Ma and decided to receive it as China's destiny to take up the challenge to finish the Great Commission.

The Silk Road was a series of ancient trade routes dating back to the time of Marco Polo that were used for selling different goods (mainly silk) from China to the known world. The main route of the Silk Road began in Xian, China's ancient capital city; a second route began in the southwest area of China and stretched into Southeast Asia; and a third route began at the city of Chengdu, in China's Sichuan province, and passed through India and Nepal into the nation of Bhutan. Each of these Silk Roads ultimately connected to the main Silk Road linking China, Central Asia, the Middle East and back to Jerusalem.

Specifically targeted along this ancient trade route were the seven areas of Iraq, Iran, Palestine, Arabia, Afghanistan, Syria and Turkey. It is in these and in surrounding areas that the largest populations and strongholds of Islam, Buddhism and Hinduism remain. More than 90 percent of the unreached people groups in the world who have never heard the gospel remain in darkness in these lands.[1] The Chinese Church fully believes it is their destiny to preach the gospel along the Silk Road, in every unreached nation, in order to tear down the last three demonic strongholds of Islam, Buddhism and Hinduism to finish the Great Commission in our lifetime and to bring the gospel back to Jerusalem, once and for all. Amen.

When I read about this vision of "Back to Jerusalem," everything began to click. The prophecy I had received years ago from Cindy Jacobs specifically named the unreached Muslim areas targeted along the Silk Road. And these unreached nations would be reached mainly through the Chinese Church mobilizing themselves and others, which was always my heart. It was God's divine hand that He would use me to rally not only Chinese students but also students around the world to preach the gospel from China, through the Silk Road and back to Jerusalem to finish the Great Commission.

Having received this revelation, I have been challenging Chinese and non-Chinese students alike to give up two years of their lives to study at East Asian universities and/or work in East Asian companies to win souls, make disciples and plant simple churches in those nations. It is from these nations of East Asia that God will raise up a mighty end-time missionary army to bring the gospel through the Silk Road, evangelize the remaining unreached nations and bring the gospel back to Jerusalem, in order for King Jesus to return.

I am believing God for 10,000 students in the next 10 years to win at least 10 million East Asian university students for Christ so that they may transform their nations and bring the gospel back to Jerusalem. These next 10 years in East Asia are crucial, as the people groups of that area will turn either toward capitalism or toward Christ. I believe we will decide history with our decision. I know this vision is from God. Already 1,500 students have volunteered all across North America, Hong Kong, Taiwan and Southeast Asia to the call. Many who volunteer may give up everything and lose everything; but because of their sacrifice, the unreached nations will be saved.

Students may go into East Asia and be tent-maker missionaries, studying at the universities as foreign exchange students for one or two years, learning the language and sharing the gospel to the emerging generation. Some may go immediately after graduating from college to work in East Asian companies—not for a career but to preach the gospel, bless the nation and reform the society. Others may be called directly to do missions in Central Asia, the Middle East or Northern Africa. Whatever the call, we must go. It is not an option; it is our destiny. I pray that our prayer will be, "Lord, I am willing to go anywhere, at anytime, to do anything for Jesus."[2]

The Blueprint Revolution

Father, give me every campus, every city, every nation back to Jerusalem, I pray. Lord, raise up young apostles, prophets, evangelists, pastors, teachers out of every corner of the earth, to equip a new generation to fulfill the Great Commandment and finish the Great Commission in this hour. Release a mighty wave of Your Spirit, Your holy fire and presence across the earth into the hearts of students far and wide. Ignite another student volunteer missionary movement and send out thousands upon thousands of student missionaries to preach this gospel to every nation, tribe and tongue with apostolic passion in their hearts. Where water once flowed, let it flow again! More than anything else, Father, let this generation know how much You love them. Oh, that we would understand what it truly means to be beloved sons and daughters of God. Let the Spirit and the Bride say, "Come, Lord Jesus, come!" Now is the time; now is the hour. Let Your kingdom come on Earth as it is in heaven. Blow the trumpet, sound the alarm, release the end-time army, Lord!

Every morning I pray a prayer like this. My prayer for this book is that it will be put into the hands of that young man or woman who is willing to go anywhere, at anytime, to do anything for Jesus Christ. The vision in my heart is to see every campus, every city and every nation won for Christ. All that is written in this book is for this one purpose: "To know Him and to make Him known."

I pray that we will have a passion for prayer, because it is prayer that brings us into intimacy with the Father. At the end of the day, it's simply about knowing Him. If there is one thing I could give anyone in the world, it would be simply this: intimacy with Jesus. If we lose this, we lose everything. Intimacy with Jesus is the most precious gift I have in the world, and it is the best thing I could ever give to anyone. I love prayer because it helps me to know God better.

And knowing God and knowing Jesus intimately is life (see John 17:3). Without this, life is not worth living.

I pray also that you will have a passion for power evangelism and be a conduit for the Holy Spirit to release His power into every campus and every sphere of society. I pray that you will have a passion for planting simple churches, because I truly believe that God is preparing this generation for a great end-time missions movement. Simple churches will be a flexible enough wineskin to penetrate into closed countries that persecute Christianity.

There is a specific reason why I pray for every campus, every city and every nation. I pray for every campus because this is where the future leaders are; I pray for every city because this is where the future leaders of society are going; and I pray for every nation because this is the final destination, to preach the gospel to all creation, back to Jerusalem, and then the end will come.[3]

If we can plant simple churches on campus, we can plant simple churches in the workplace and in the city. If we can plant simple churches in the city, we can plant simple churches anywhere, anytime, in any nation. This is it. *God, raise up a student missionary force. In Your great wisdom, release Your sons and daughters into all the earth to take dominion for Your glory! Release revival and reformation now!*

Finally, I pray with all my heart that we would know our identity in Christ. Our identity is not in what we do for God, but it is in what He has already done for us. It is in our knowing that God loves us, no matter what we do or don't do. Our identity is not our destiny; our destiny flows out of our identity in Christ.

It's easy to pick up a book like this, get excited, get passionate and try to start a revolution. But a revolution doesn't start "out there;" it starts in our hearts. It starts when we know there is nothing we can do to add to God's work. It starts when we know that Jesus is more interested in knowing us, truly as a friend, than seeing us make something great happen on our campuses or in the world. You are not a human doing; you are a human being. You are, therefore you do—not the other way around. You are not living for acceptance; you are living from acceptance. You have already been and always will be accepted and loved by God.[4] You are not a campus revivalist; you are a beloved son and daughter of God, well pleasing to Him (see Matt. 3:17)!

No one can bring revival, no one can bring reformation and no one can save the world. Only God can. He loves me and I love Him. This alone is my success: to know His manifest presence and to make His manifest presence known to my generation. Let the Spirit and the Bride say, "Come, Lord Jesus, Come!" Amen.

Notes
1. Paul Hattaway, *Back to Jerusalem* (Milton Keynes, UK: Authentic Media, 2003), p. 5.
2. Steve Shadrach, *The Fuel and the Flame* (Milton Keynes, UK: Authentic Media, 2003), p. 18.
3. For more information on the student Back to Jerusalem Movement, see http://campuschurch.net/download/materials/studentB2JPamphlet.pdf.
4. I have more to say about God's love and acceptance. If you want to know how God has changed my identity from slavery to sonship—from being a campus revivalist to being a son, dearly loved by God—go to my blogsite (www.jaesonma.blogspot.com), go to the archives in July 2006 and click on the post "Transformation of My Heart." I pray that it will bless you.

RESOURCES FROM CAMPUS NETWORKS (CCN)

WWW.CAMPUSCHURCH.NET

Simple Church-Planting Resources
Whether you are a student, staff leader, faculty or local church member, our desire is to help support and resource you to multiply simple churches on your target campus(es). To learn more about starting simple-church-planting movements on your campus or in your city or nation, please contact us at www.campuschurch.net or via e-mail at info@campuschurch.net.

CCN Coaching, Mentoring and Equipping
The CCN vision statement is "Every Campus, Every City, Every Nation for Christ." Our mission is "To fulfill the Great Commandment and the Great Commission in this generation through initiating and cultivating church-planting movements on every campus around the world."

CCN helps coach strategy coordinators who have a vision not only for planting a few simple churches within specific student groups on their campus, but also of releasing a campus-wide church-planting movement (CPM) that will extend into the surrounding region and affect every level of society. These strategy coordinators will have a long-term calling and vision for a region, will raise their own support, and will need to understand the core elements necessary to release a CPM. For more information, contact us at coach@campuschurch.net.

Transforming Campuses
To learn more about how to transform campuses through connecting leaders, mobilizing prayer, planting simple churches and starting a 24/7 campus house of prayer, go to www.campustransformation.com.

Student Back to Jerusalem Momement
To be a part of the new student volunteer missionary movement to bring the gospel back to Jerusalem, and to learn about a five-week intensive training program called "Antioch Forerunner Foundation," go to www.campuschurch.net.